ERROR-FREE WRITING

A Lifetime Guide to Flawless Business Writing

ROBIN A. CORMIER
Vice President, Editorial Experts, Inc.

PRENTICE HALL
Englewood Cliffs, New Jersey 07632

Prentice-Hall International, Inc., *London*
Prentice-Hall of Australia Pty., Ltd., *Sydney*
Prentice-Hall Canada, Inc., *Toronto*
Prentice-Hall Hispanoamericana, S.A., *Mexico*
Prentice-Hall of India Private Ltd., *New Delhi*
Prentice-Hall of Japan, Inc., *Tokyo*
Prentice-Hall of Southeast Asia Pte., Ltd., *Singapore*
Editora Prentice-Hall do Brasil, Ltda., *Rio de Janeiro*

Library of Congress Cataloging-in-Publication Data

Cormier, Robin A.
   Error-free writing: a lifetime guide to flawless business writing
/Robin A. Cormier.
      p.   cm.
   Includes index.
   ISBN 0–13–303587–5. — ISBN 0–13–303595–6 (pbk.)
   1. Business writing.   I. Title.
HF5718.3.C67   1995
808'.066'65—dc20   94–47978
                                                    CIP

ISBN 0-13-303595-6 (P)
ISBN 0-13-303587-5 (C)

 PRENTICE HALL
Career and Personal Development
Englewood Cliffs, NJ 07632
Simon & Schuster, A Paramount Communications Company

PRINTED IN THE UNITED STATES OF AMERICA

Contents

Preface

Virtually everyone in the working world has some role in creating written products at one time or another, and some people produce documents every day. Whether the documents are books, reports, letters, brochures, price lists, newsletters, or even advertisements, it can be difficult to find and remove every last error. It is especially frustrating to spend hours, days, and even months creating an important document only to discover later—after it has been distributed—that it contains embarrassing mistakes.

Companies take many different approaches to document preparation. Some hire staffs of specialists—writers, editors, designers, desktop publishers, proofreaders; in other offices, one person does it all. No matter what the process, all companies and individuals who care about quality share a common goal: to produce error-free written products. And each time an error gets through, everyone wonders if there isn't a better way to work.

There *is* a better way, and this book can teach it to you quickly. You don't have to spend hours in a grammar class or invest a lot of money in special software to improve the quality of your documents—you will see immediate results from the method described here. And whether you read the book cover to cover or keep it on your desk to use as a reference whenever you have a question, you will be able to find and correct more errors than ever before.

Advice on errors in writing is plentiful. The countless books on grammar, style, and writing can tell you *what* an error is, but they don't tell you *how* to find it. The advantage of the four-step method described in this book is that you don't have to be a professional editor or proofreader to make it work for you.

The four-step method has been fine-tuned during the past 22 years by EEI (formerly Editorial Experts, Inc.), a company that specializes in error prevention. We at EEI have talked to hundreds of people in corporations, associations, and government agencies about the kinds of challenges they face when they produce printed products. "I wasn't hired to be a proofreader!" is a common complaint. Yet they know they are being held accountable for the quality of the documents they produce, and in many cases their bosses will accept nothing less than perfection.

EEI, located in Alexandria, Virginia, employs more than 300 publications professionals—editors, proofreaders, indexers, graphic artists, and desktop publishing specialists—all of whom had to pass stringent tests to join EEI's staff. In fact, only 7 out of every 100 applicants pass EEI's testing and screening, so it is not an overstatement to say that EEI's publications professionals are among the best in the business. But even the very best people still make mistakes. That's why EEI created the four-step method. This technique helps people find errors in every phase of the writing process: creating, revising, polishing, and perfecting. We take the realistic view that errors are a natural, unavoidable part of the document production process. No document is perfect after the first production cycle, and most are still not perfect after the second and third cycles.

By building in the "safety nets" that the four-step method provides, you can help improve the quality of your documents *immediately*. This book will teach you the kinds of errors to look for and the places they usually hide. You'll learn to

- write more clearly and concisely;

- find and correct grammatical errors in your own writing;

- spot even the most subtle typographical errors and inconsistencies; and

- perform the essential final quality control review that can make the difference between a quality document and one that reflects poorly on you and your company.

In addition, you will see some related benefits:

- The hysteria usually associated with producing a document on deadline will be greatly reduced.

- Your documents will be less costly to produce because you will eliminate many unnecessary rounds of revisions.

- You will be able to produce documents faster because you aren't performing so many extra steps.

- You and your coworkers will still be on speaking terms when the project is finished.

Best of all, with the four-step method, you'll be able to produce documents to be proud of instead of documents you have to make excuses for.

The Four-Step Method: An Introduction

Almost everyone in the business world who has ever created a printed product has discovered a glaring error when it was too late to fix it. Whether the document was a proposal to a big client, a memo to the boss, or even a résumé, its credibility was diminished by the error. Errors, whether typographical, grammatical, or some other kind, seem to take on lives of their own. Once discovered, they seem to jump off the page. They divert the reader's attention from the content of the document, and they make the writer look bad—even if the errors were not the writer's fault. No writer wants to be thought of as careless or, even worse, ignorant.

One of the biggest changes brought on by the invention of the personal computer is that people at all levels of the corporate ladder are now producing their own documents. Gone are the days when the boss would write reports and letters in longhand and the secretary would type and proofread them. Astute business people know that if they are to survive in today's competitive environment, being competent in their area of specialty is not enough. They know that they are also judged on the quality of their written products. They also know that poorly prepared documents can detract from their credibility, damage their company's reputation, and reflect poorly on their job performance. What frustrates many business people is that they don't know how to prevent errors from making it into print.

Unfortunately, there is no magic solution when it comes to error prevention; even spelling checkers let us down. However, there is a proven method, developed over the years by publishing professionals, for producing virtually error-free documents. The best thing about this method is that anyone can use it, and it can be applied to all types of printed products—reports, brochures, newsletters, manuals, memos, letters, and proposals. Armed with this method, along with a knowledge of the most frequent types of errors, you will be able to prepare documents to be proud of, not embarrassed by. This book will show you how.

THE FOUR STEPS OF ERROR PREVENTION

Here's the first secret of error prevention: It takes at least *four revision cycles* to achieve an acceptable final product. That's the bare minimum; for large or complex documents, it takes many more. First you write and rewrite your first draft (step 1), then you edit it to remove errors in grammar and punctuation (step 2), then you proofread it for typographical and format errors (step 3), and finally you perform a quality control check of the document as a whole (step 4).

Many people either are unaware of the importance of these steps or choose to skip a few in the interest of saving time. They may think, *"Four drafts?* That's ridiculous—we have to produce our reports *quickly."* The point they miss is that it almost always *takes longer* to produce a sloppy document by cutting corners than it takes to follow the four steps. By the time you throw together a draft, fix the obvious mistakes, finalize the document, find more errors, fix them, readjust the format, find even more errors that were introduced when you hastily fixed the last batch, fix them, reproduce the document and bind the copies, find a critical error, take apart the bound copies and insert the corrected pages, and bind the copies again, you could have followed the four-step method, produced a document to be proud of, and taken a day off. By making the four-step method your standard procedure, you will accomplish these goals:

- You will eliminate—or at least greatly reduce—the hysteria that is often associated with producing a document on deadline.

- You will save time by avoiding the extra work associated with finding major errors at the last minute.

- You will save money by eliminating hours of unnecessary "re-do" time from the document production process.

■ You will minimize frustration for everyone involved in the process.

In the chapters that follow, you will learn what kinds of errors to look for at each step, where errors are commonly found, why errors occur, and how to fix them most efficiently.

WHY DO ERRORS OCCUR IN THE FIRST PLACE?

You may be wondering, "If it takes four revision cycles to eliminate errors, doesn't that mean someone in the process isn't doing a good job?" The answer is, not necessarily. The tendency to place blame when errors are found can be counterproductive, and often the blame-placers have unrealistic expectations. The four-step method is based on reality: Errors are a natural part of the document preparation process. To pretend that they will not occur, or to assume that intelligent, highly skilled people don't make mistakes, will only lead to frustration.

THE IDEAL: FOUR STEPS, FOUR DIFFERENT PEOPLE

Here's the second secret of error prevention: The four-step method works best when a different person performs each step. It is an unfortunate fact that the more familiar you are with a document, the less likely you are to spot errors. Every time a "fresh pair of eyes" is introduced into the process, the odds of finding more errors greatly increase.

Of course, not every writer has the help of a professional editor or proofreader. More often than not, one person must do it all. Or help may be available, but not from people who have specialized error-detection skills. The four-step method can still work in less-than-ideal circumstances and should not be abandoned for lack of an editorial staff.

Rewriting, Editing, and Proofreading: The Differences Explained

"Will you proofread this document for me?" There's a tricky question. When your coworker asks for your help, what is he or she really asking you to do? Should you mark grammatical errors or just typographical errors? Should you worry about inconsistent capitalization or abbreviations? Should you rewrite phrases that sound awkward? If you mark too many changes, you risk wasting time and infuriating your coworker. If you don't mark everything you see, you risk letting an error remain in the final product.

In the field of publishing, the terms *rewriting, editing,* and *proofreading* have very specific definitions. In other fields, these terms are often used generically to mean "find errors and fix them." Here are some definitions that can help clarify what is being requested when someone asks you to review a document:

- *Rewriting* (or substantive editing) means making major content and structural changes to a document. It may include reordering chapters or sections, rewriting the text to change the tone, and making recommendations about the overall approach taken in the document.

- *Editing* (or copyediting) means correcting errors in grammar, spelling, punctuation, and format; rewording awkward sentences; and enforcing consistency (on style issues such as capitalization and hyphenation) within the document.

- *Proofreading* means checking for typographical and format errors only. It may mean comparing an old draft against new copy, or it may mean simply reading through every page of a clean copy for errors.

■ DON'T DO TOO MUCH TOO SOON

For the four-step method to work, everyone who works on the document has to understand the process and be aware of what should happen at each step. If, for example, the person who is charged with reviewing the document decides to rewrite it at the last minute, after seeing it and approving it several times before, every step in the process will have to be repeated. Likewise, if in the early stages a reviewer marks typographical errors without paying attention to content, most of that effort will be wasted if the content changes later.

One of the biggest mistakes people make in preparing documents is that they approach every draft as if it is the final copy. They make too many refinements too soon, and when changes in wording are required (as they usually are), the entire text must be rechecked. If you are preparing a document for someone to review, it is natural to want it to be as close to perfect as possible. However, if you tell the reviewers of the document to focus on *content only* at first, assuring them that grammatical and typographical errors will be picked up in the later steps, you will save both time and money in the long run. Here are three simple rules that will help you avoid repeating the steps in the process:

1. Don't worry about fixing grammatical errors and style inconsistencies until everyone is satisfied with the content of the document.

2. Don't worry about catching every typographical error until all the grammatical errors have been fixed.

3. Don't worry about perfecting the format until all the typographical errors have been fixed.

If you edit out every single grammatical error and style inconsistency before the document has been reviewed for content, you will only have to edit it again if the document is revised (which it is likely to be, since, after all, the purpose of a review is to identify any portions that should be changed). If you make format adjustments (such as fixing end-of-line hyphenation and adjusting spacing) before the document has been proofread for typographical errors, you may find yourself making those same adjustments again if the final corrections cause the text to reflow from line to line and page to page. With the four-step method, you focus on one *type* of error at a time.

Reference Books: The Essentials

Here are the four types of reference books that you should have on your office bookshelf (or the "electronic bookshelf" of your computer) at all times:

- *A dictionary.* Almost every office has one, but have you checked the copyright date in your dictionary lately? The dictionary you use should not be more than a few years old. Dictionaries are updated regularly to reflect changes in the language, and old dictionaries contain some usages that are now obsolete. Also, to ensure consistency, everyone in the office should use the same dictionary. (*Merriam-Webster's Collegiate Dictionary, 10th Edition,* and the *American Heritage Dictionary of the English Language, 3rd Edition,* are among the most popular.) Dictionaries are not all alike, and they sometimes contradict one another on the fine points of language.

- *A style manual.* Your company may have its own customized style manual, or you may use one of the industry standards. (Four commonly used guides are the *Chicago Manual of Style, Words Into Type,* the *Associated Press Style Book,* and the *New York Public Library Writer's Guide to Style and Usage.*) Style manuals provide answers about capitalization, punctuation, abbreviations, and a wide variety of other consistency issues. As with dictionaries, style manuals differ. The advice given in one may be the exact opposite of that in another, so it is important to choose one and stick with it.

- *A spelling and word-division guide.* Sometimes you just need to confirm the spelling of a word; you don't need the definition. Or you may just want to know the correct way to divide a word when it falls at the end of a line. A spelling and word-division guide is a handy pocket-sized book that is easier to flip through than a five-pound dictionary when all you need is a quick answer.

- *A thesaurus.* A thesaurus lists words and their synonyms (that is, words that have similar meanings but different connotations). This type of reference book may be just what you need when you are struggling to put an idea into words but cannot think of the appropriate expressions.

■ WHAT'S THE GOAL?

The four-step method is meant for documents that have to be as close to perfect as possible. Common sense dictates that not all written products fall into this category. For example, in most cases an in-house memo would not warrant the same level of error-detection effort as the company's annual report or a proposal to a potential customer. Before you start, make sure that everyone agrees on the level of quality desired.

Details Count!

The printed materials you give your customers help them form opinions about you and your company. It is always worth taking the time to ensure that your documents represent you well. If you are ever tempted to cut corners, remember this story:

> I started my software company 5 years ago as a second-year student at the Harvard Business School. Two days after my first advertisement appeared in a trade journal, I was asked by a *Fortune* 500 company to provide a price quote for 10 copies of my software. I was ecstatic!
>
> Using my computer, I put my company name at the top of the page and printed out my "literature" and price quote. When I called my prospect the next week to follow up, I was treated somewhat rudely. She wasn't even interested in the quality of my product. The fact that my literature was shoddy had caused her to be more concerned about my company than the product. Needless to say, I immediately had stationery, business cards, and brochures printed. (Dan Slavin, founder of International Testing Services, Inc., in Cambridge, MA)

Dan Slavin's company eventually sold more than 15,000 copies of its job-training software.

(Reprinted with permission, *Inc.* magazine, Dec. 1993. Copyright 1993 by Goldhirsh Group, Inc., 38 Commercial Wharf, Boston, MA 02110.)

To avoid misunderstandings, some corporations have established quality levels for their written products and define specific quality control procedures for each level. For example, going from lowest to highest, Level 1 might be in-house memos, Level 2 might be customer correspondence, and Level 3 might be anything that is distributed widely either inside or outside the company (reports, newsletters, promotional pieces, and the like). For Level 1 documents, the required quality control step might be simply running a computerized spelling-check before distributing the document. Level 3 documents, on the other hand, should always go through the entire four-step method. Organizations have different types of written products and different priorities; the more clearly these priorities are defined, the less time and money will be wasted.

■ MAKING THE FOUR STEPS YOUR STANDARD PROCEDURE

The most difficult aspect of using the four-step method is training yourself to focus on one thing at a time. You may wonder, "If I am working on Step 2, revising my writing, and I see a typographical error, do I just ignore it?" You should never ignore an error when you see it, but you should be sure to readjust your focus once you've marked it. Always reread the entire paragraph after you've marked the error, this time paying attention to the *meaning* of the sentences. Likewise, if you are working on Step 3, proofreading, and you come to a sentence that sounds awkward, go ahead and rewrite it, but then reread it and the surrounding sentences for typographical errors. Soon you will train your eyes and mind to stay focused, and you will become more efficient at performing each step.

In addition to teaching you the four-step method, this book also provides mini-refresher courses on the most common errors in language, word usage, grammar, spelling, and punctuation. Once you polish your skills in these areas and then put the four-step method into action, you will see an instant improvement in your written products.

■ THE BEAUTY OF PLAIN ENGLISH

How long would you have to look to find a published document that is poorly written? Chances are there are examples right in your file cabinet or on your bookshelf. Regulations, contracts, instruction manuals—we've all seen poorly written examples of such documents. You can probably recall wrestling with assembly instructions that didn't make sense or wading through contract clauses that were unintelligible. The unfortunate truth, though, is that these writers did not intend to confuse you. Most likely, they had every intention of conveying information—they just didn't have the skills to do it clearly.

THE PLAIN ENGLISH MOVEMENT

In 1978, President Carter issued Executive Order 12204, Improving Government Regulations. This order, which began what is now known as the Plain English Movement, required that government agencies simplify their publications and make them easier to read. Agencies such as the Environmental Protection Agency, the Department of Housing and Urban Development, the Department of the Army, and others took serious action—they developed new guidelines to ensure that their regulations and reports would be understandable. Many corporations, including several large insurance companies, followed the government's lead and made clear writing a top priority.

Plain English simply means language that is clear, concise, accurate, and appropriate for its intended audience. There is no reason why plain English cannot be used in every type of writing, even the most official. Plain English is only one of the many elements of good writing, but using it is one of the best steps writers can take toward greater clarity.

Plain English Saves Pipes

As the story goes, a New York City plumber once wrote to the Bureau of Standards to report the success he had in using hydrochloric acid to clean out clogged drainpipes. Responding in typical government fashion, the bureau wrote, "The efficacy of hydrochloric acid is undisputable, but the corrosive residue is incompatible with metallic permanence."

When the plumber wrote back to say how pleased he was that the bureau agreed with him, the bureau urgently responded, "We cannot assume responsibility for the production of toxic and noxious residue with hydrochloric acid and suggest you use an alternative procedure."

This second letter from the government made the plumber even happier with his discovery, so once again he wrote to say how glad he was that the bureau liked his idea. This time, in desperation, the bureau broke down and used plain language to warn the plumber: "Don't use hydrochloric acid. It eats the hell out of the pipes."

(*The Editorial Eye,* December 1979)

THE CHALLENGE OF CLEAR WRITING

Writing well is never easy. Most people—even professional writers—would agree that writing is a skill that does not come naturally. It requires great effort to combine creativity and attention to detail in a way that results in a product that people can read and understand without effort. Writing is a requirement of almost every occupation in the business world today, and written products take many forms: sales proposals, technical manuals, monthly reports, service records, letters to customers, and even electronic-mail messages. Whenever a writer puts pen to paper—or fingers to keyboard, as is more likely the case today—the potential exists for misunderstanding. Even professional writers face the same problems and fall into the same traps as businesspeople who write only occasionally.

EVERY WRITER'S RESPONSIBILITY

Every writer has a responsibility to his or her audience: to communicate as clearly as possible. Using convoluted sentence structure, unfamiliar terminology, and a poorly organized format wastes the reader's time. The tips on writing in this chapter will help you communicate clearly, and they may also help make the writing process a little less painful.

■ THE BASIC PRINCIPLES OF GOOD WRITING

Although there are just about as many writing styles as there are writers, all *good* writing has one thing in common: The reader doesn't have to struggle to understand it. Whether you are writing a proposal to a client, a newsletter article, or a memo to your boss, following these principles of good writing will help ensure that your message comes across clearly.

DEFINING AUDIENCE, PURPOSE, AND FOCUS

Before you begin writing, you should ask yourself three questions:

1. Who is the *audience:* Who are the people who will read your document?

2. What is the *purpose* of the document: What are you trying to accomplish by writing it?

3. What is the *focus* of the document: Which aspects of the subject do you want to cover?

For most writing assignments, these questions will be easy to answer. In some cases, however, you may have to think a little harder and do some research. If you skip this step, the writing process can be very frustrating, and you may end up with a document that doesn't achieve its purpose.

Determine exactly who will be reading what you write. Think carefully: Are you writing for experts in your field or for people who know little or nothing about your topic? If you start to write without knowing who you are talking to or why you are talking to them, you run the risk of including too much explanation, or worse, not enough.

If you aren't sure who you are writing for, ask. For example, if your boss asks you for a report on a particular project, ask a few questions before you begin writing. Does your boss want a detailed description of every aspect of the project or just a brief update? Will this report be sent to someone else, either inside or outside your organization? Which aspects of the project should be stressed, and which are not as important? Is the purpose to satisfy a reporting requirement or to pave the way to ask for more funding for a project?

The audience will affect how you write the summary and what you include. Here are some possible variations:

- If the summary is for your boss' use only, you'll want to give a succinct review of progress and problems; you won't need to include much background information since your boss is probably already familiar with the project.

- If your boss is using the summary as part of a status report to upper management, you'll want to focus on the milestones achieved rather than on the problems encountered. You'll want to include some background information as well.

- If the summary will be included in your performance review and will be read by others who aren't familiar with your work, you'll want to emphasize your personal contributions to the project.

- If the summary will become part of an article for the company newsletter, you'll want to include points of general interest and omit most of the technical details.

Your intended audience determines everything about the piece you are writing: content, tone, approach, organization, and format. You will waste a lot of time if you write first and ask questions later.

Have a clear purpose in mind; avoid the "boilerplate" trap. Are you trying to justify an approach, explain a concept, or initiate an action? What, specifically, do you hope to accomplish? Many writers have made the mistake of trying to save time by writing "boilerplate" or generic text that will suit many purposes. The usual effect of this type of writing is that the text isn't really a good fit for any of the intended uses, and the writer spends more time sculpting the words than it would have taken to write to a specific purpose in the first place.

Make your focus as narrow as possible. First, think about the purpose of the document. Include only the information needed to achieve that purpose. If you give lots of unrelated or unnecessary details, your readers may lose interest. Then think again about your audience. Decide which aspects of your topic will be the most important to them. What knowledge do you want them to gain, or what action do you want them to take, after reading your document? You may decide to change your focus slightly as you write, but choose one approach as a starting point.

BRINGING TOGETHER AUDIENCE, PURPOSE, AND FOCUS

Suppose you are asked to write a description of your company. What you will say depends entirely on audience, purpose, and focus. Imagine what you might include—and *not* include—in your discussion for the following audiences:

- Prospective clients

Purpose:	To encourage them to buy your product or service.
Focus:	The time- or money-saving features of your product or service; the benefits it offers them.

- Prospective employees

Purpose:	To convince them that they should come to work for your company.
Focus:	The challenges and opportunities for personal reward and growth; how their contributions will make a difference.

- Potential investors

Purpose:	To convince them that they should invest their money in your company.
Focus:	The actions your company is taking now to ensure future growth; the quality and talent of the manage-

ment and staff; a picture of where your company could be in 1 year or 5 years, given adequate support.

■ Your parents

Purpose:	To give them a better understanding of what you do every day; to impress them.
Focus:	Your accomplishments; your personal role in the grand scheme of things.

Although these various descriptions would have some common elements, each would be quite different. Writing a "boilerplate" description to suit all these purposes equally well would be an impossible task.

PLANNING AND ORGANIZATION

Figure out what you want to say before you say it. You don't have to do a formal outline complete with roman numerals and stair-step indentions, but you should chart your course before you start to write. Make a list of the topics you want to cover, and then put them in the proper order (for example, explanation of the problem, description of alternatives, recommendations). Then take the list a step further by adding subheadings. Some writers prefer to outline in a circular format (Figure 1), with the main point as the center circle and the subtopics branching from it.

Give the reader a map. Be generous with formatting elements such as subheadings, lists, and running heads—they will help guide the reader through your text. Make your document as skimmable as possible. Although you want your readers to read every word of your creation, they probably won't. Breaking up narrative text with subheads, lists, illustrations, and tables makes it easy for them to grasp the important messages.

Make it a smooth journey. Help the reader glide through your text by adding invisible directional signs such as topic sentences, transitions, and summaries. The topic sentence is the first sentence in the paragraph; it states the main point of the paragraph, and the sentences that follow provide explanation or background. Transitions are sentences that link one

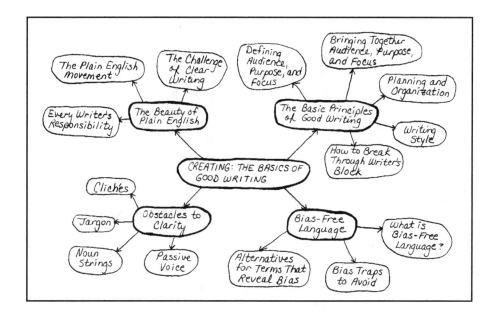

Figure 1. Some writers prefer to sketch out a circular outline rather than use the traditional kind. This example shows the outline of this chapter.

paragraph to the next so that the reader doesn't experience a sudden change of subject. When you begin a new paragraph, it is helpful to repeat a word or two from the last sentence of the previous paragraph so that the text flows smoothly. Summaries recap for the reader the information that has been covered. Depending on the length and complexity of the subject matter, summaries can be single sentences or entire paragraphs.

WRITING STYLE

Get to the point. Some writers think their work won't be impressive if it is too short. This problem was caused by our high school English teachers, who required us to write 1,000 words on topics about which we had nothing to say. Our main objective was length, not clarity. We tried to stretch the few words we came up with by adding "padding"—phrases that lengthened our

Head Levels

Formatting a document is an important part of clear writing. The format of the document's headings shows the reader how the text is organized. The position, type size, and appearance of the headings tell the reader whether the text that follows is a major section or a subsection. Even if a draft document will eventually be reformatted in a desktop publishing program, it is important to differentiate the heads consistently at the draft stage so that the correct hierarchy will be preserved in the final format. There are many different ways to format a document, but there are a few conventions that you should observe with any format:

Headings that are in all caps indicate a higher level in the hierarchy than those in upper- and lowercase.

Headings in bold are a higher level than those in italic.

Headings that are flush left are a higher level than those that are indented.

Here is an example of a commonly used heading structure:

THIS IS AN *A* HEAD (CENTERED, ALL CAPS)

THIS IS A *B* HEAD (FLUSH LEFT, ALL CAPS)

Xxxxx xxxxx.

This Is a *C* Head (Indented, Caps and Lowercase)

Xxxxx xxxxx.

This is a **D** *head* (indented, italic, run-in).   Xxxxx xxxxx.

Putting It All Together

Which comes first, the executive summary or the table of contents? Does the glossary come before the index? Questions like these frequently arise when a document is in the final stages of preparation.

The order of the elements of a document can vary; there is no one right way to assemble them. Also, not all documents have the same elements. One may have an introduction; another may have a preface; still another may have both. As with many other aspects of publication production, the key is consistency: Choose a format for the type of publications you produce and make it your standard. Here is a suggested order of contents for a report:

1. cover
2. title page
3. foreword
4. table of contents
5. preface
6. list of figures and tables
7. executive summary
8. introduction
9. main body of report
10. endnotes
11. bibliography
12. glossary
13. appendixes
14. index
15. back cover

documents without adding any useful information. Some writers have not corrected this bad habit and use these phrases automatically. Here are some examples of these phrases, along with more succinct alternatives:

Wordy	**Succinct**
in addition to the fact that	additionally
on a regular basis	regularly
at the present time	now
in a sufficient number	enough
a large number of	many
few in number	few
a majority of	most
in the majority of cases	usually
in this day and age	today
to the fullest possible extent	fully
bring to a conclusion	conclude
make an assumption that	assume that
it is recommended that consideration be given to	please consider
due to the fact that	because
of considerable magnitude	large
within the realm of possibility	possible
for the purpose of explaining	to explain
to be cognizant of	to know
in the not-too-distant future	soon
one and the same	the same
according to the law	legally
afford an opportunity	allow
exhibit a tendency to	tend to
revise downward	lower

Avoid smothered verbs. Smothered verbs are action words that are buried in a group of other words. Eliminating the other words usually creates a clearer, more forceful sentence. Smothering phrases often begin with a form of *be, give, have, make,* or *take.* The noun in the phrase often ends with *-ion* or *-ment.* Here are some examples of smothered verbs with their clearer alternatives:

Smothered	**Clearer**
be in agreement	agree
be in attendance	attend
be in possession of	have
be in receipt of	receive
give authorization to	authorize
give consideration to	consider
give a description of	describe
give encouragement to	encourage
give instruction to	instruct
have a belief	believe
have a need to	need
have a requirement	require
have a suspicion	suspect
make an adjustment	adjust
make an assumption	assume
make a choice	choose
make a comparison	compare
make a decision	decide
make a determination	determine
make provision for	provide
take action	act
take into consideration	consider
arrive at a conclusion	conclude
arrive at a solution	solve
effect an improvement	improve
extend an invitation	invite
hold a discussion	discuss
put in an appearance	appear
render assistance	help

Avoid lengthy introductions, sprawling narrative, and buried conclusions. A guideline that used to be given to writers was "Tell them what you are going to say, say it, then tell them what you said." The problem with this approach is that the repetition can be tiresome. A better approach is to include just enough background information to give the reader a starting point, and then jump right into the subject. When you've finished writing a document, go back and read it one more time to ensure that each word is essential.

Write like you talk, almost. So many writers in the business world try to adopt a stilted, official-sounding tone in their writing that simply isn't necessary. Write as if you are having a face-to-face conversation with your readers. In business writing, of course, you shouldn't go so far as to use slang or incomplete sentences, the way we sometimes do in informal speech, but neither should you use phrases that you would never utter in conversation. To determine whether your tone is appropriate, read your text aloud. If some passages make you sound like a robot, you'll need to make some revisions.

Wait a day or two if possible; then reread everything you've written. A sentence or paragraph may make perfect sense to you while you are writing, but when you step back and read it again after the document is complete, you may be surprised that you ever chose those particular words. Even the best writers cannot generate perfect text on the first try. The revision stage is a normal part of the writing process and may include many cycles. Don't be afraid to make changes, and don't become so wedded to a particular phrase or passage that you can't evaluate it objectively.

HOW TO BREAK THROUGH WRITER'S BLOCK

Writer's block is a term used to describe a condition that attacks all writers from time to time: It is when you have a writing task before you, usually with an approaching deadline, and you can't think of a single word to write. You panic, and even the few ideas you started with begin to slip away. An assignment that at first seemed simple now seems impossible.

Writer's block can be a sign of inadequate preparation (you tried to write before you knew what you wanted to say), or it can simply be a normal part of the writing process. And it can strike at any time—when you first begin a project, when you have written a first draft that you know needs revising, or when you have almost completed a document and need only one more paragraph to tie everything together.

Even professional writers occasionally find themselves paralyzed in front of their computers. There is no magic solution, but different approaches work for different situations. For example, sometimes a little procrastination helps get the creative juices flowing; other times it just makes matters worse. If you can figure out why you are stuck, it will be easier to get moving again. Here are some tips that can help you shake the block loose:

- Give in to your desire to procrastinate, but just for a little while. Get a cup of coffee, empty the pencil sharpener, file away the pile of papers on your desk. Sometimes these mindless tasks can give you a chance to collect your thoughts without the pressure of the empty computer screen glowing in your face.

- Focus on one small part of the project rather than the whole thing. Set small, specific goals for yourself. Instead of saying, "I'm going to spend all morning writing this report," tell yourself "I'm going to write one part of one section before lunch." Then when you finish one small part of the job, select another small section to concentrate on.

- Reread something you've written before that you are particularly proud of. Reading even an unrelated piece of writing can help you "find your voice." You may simply need a reminder that you indeed have the skills to put words together in a meaningful way.

- Write something; anything—a letter to a friend, a shopping list—anything to get your fingers moving across the keyboard. Then don't take a break; jump right into your document when you are warmed up.

- Write the easy parts first. Don't attempt to write the document from beginning to end; feel free to skip around. If you are stuck on the introduction, save it for last. If you know more about one area you want to discuss than the others, write about it first. Your word processing software will always let you move paragraphs around when you get further along.

- Don't try to edit yourself as you write. Stopping to come up with the perfect word before moving on to the next one will inhibit your creative flow. It is perfectly allowable, even preferable, to write sentences that you know will need smoothing out later just to get your ideas in place. You may decide to delete entire chunks later, but at least you will have a starting point. Some writers put in placeholders such as XXXXX when they have an idea that isn't fully formed but want to move on and return to it later.

- If you get off to a good start but then get stuck in the middle, reread what you've already written. It is possible to write yourself into a corner. You may have to abandon a particular approach if you are getting nowhere after several attempts.

- Do more research. It could be that you simply don't have enough information to write knowledgeably about the subject at hand. Take inventory of your background material and try to identify gaps.

- Write a more detailed outline. Maybe you haven't given enough thought to where you are going. You may have all the information you need, but it won't come spilling out of your brain because you haven't mapped out your document thoroughly enough. Once you have a good outline, writing will seem more like simply filling in the blanks and less like trying to create a beautiful sculpture from a hunk of clay.

- Reconsider your basic premise. You may be stuck because you are trying to convince your reader about a particular point or idea before you've convinced yourself. Think about the purpose of your document, and be sure that what you are trying to say helps achieve that purpose.

- Talk to a coworker about the ideas you are trying to express. Getting another person's opinion may help point out a weak spot that has caused you to get stuck. You may not agree with the advice you get, but hearing another point of view may help clarify your thinking. Also, sometimes it is easier to explain ideas aloud than to put them in writing. If you are simply struggling to put your thoughts into words and aren't really ready for any actual feedback, an "imaginary friend" works just as well as a coworker.

■ OBSTACLES TO CLARITY

The purpose of any written piece is to communicate thoughts or information. A document does not accomplish this goal if its message cannot be understood by its readers. Some writers have good intentions but have developed bad habits that keep them from conveying their thoughts clearly. Here are some common pitfalls to watch for and avoid.

CLICHÉS

Clichés are like cooking spices—a light sprinkling can enhance something that would otherwise be bland; too much can be sickening. Clichés are familiar phrases and expressions that have gotten a bad name because they have been overused by writers who were too lazy to think up new, original ways to express their thoughts. These same expressions, when used sparingly, can add humor to a piece of writing or can help a writer make a point succinctly and clearly. Certain phrases can "hit the nail on the head"—to use a common cliché—in a way that spares the reader several additional sentences of explanation. The problem is that some writers tend to use clichés as a crutch—they rely on clichés too heavily at the expense of meaning, and clarity suffers.

Many clichés originally came from proverbs and literature. For example, the phrase "be-all and end-all" came from Shakespeare's *Macbeth*. Some clichés are so common that you will be surprised to learn that they are thought of as clichés—"the bottom line," for example. A few clichés have been mangled over the years and used incorrectly so many times that the wrong version is almost as common as the original version. For instance, how many times have you heard someone say "I could care less" when what they really mean is "I *couldn't* care less"? Also, a "vicious circle" is frequently referred to incorrectly as a "vicious *cycle*."

One way to spot clichés is to look for phrases that cannot be taken literally. When you tell your boss you are going to "crank out the report" by tomorrow, you aren't actually going to turn a crank to generate the document. When your boss says that "heads will roll" if that report isn't on his desk by noon, you hope he only means it figuratively.

Clichés are more acceptable in some forms of writing than in others. In journalistic style, clichés are used freely. Pick up any newspaper and see how many clichés you can spot: The senator's wife "is the power behind the throne"; the ambassador "attempted to pour oil on troubled waters"; the football team "fought an uphill battle" to the championship. Corporate memos are another common source of clichés: The manager tells her staff to "pull out all the stops" to meet sales quotas; the CEO announces that there will be layoffs "if push comes to shove"; the computer specialist reports that the new software upgrade is "nothing to write home about"; the sales manager urges the sales force to get out and "rub elbows" with prospective customers. Advertising copy and promotional writing also rely heavily on clichés: The company's service is "second to none"; buying the product will give the customer "the best of all possible worlds"; the competitor's product "doesn't hold a candle" to ours.

300 common clichés to watch for. The list that follows is just "the tip of the iceberg"—there are many more. The "long and short of it" is this: It is not necessary to "avoid these phrases like the plague"; just be aware that they have attained cliché status in modern English usage and should be used sparingly, if at all.

1. ace in the hole
2. acid test
3. across the board
4. actions speak louder than words
5. add insult to injury
6. all in a day's work
7. all things being equal
8. arm's length
9. as luck would have it
10. at long last
11. at my fingertips
12. avoid like the plague
13. back to square one
14. back to the drawing board
15. balance of power
16. be that as it may
17. be-all and end-all
18. bear the brunt
19. beat around the bush
20. behind the eight-ball
21. benefit of the doubt
22. best of all possible worlds
23. better safe than sorry
24. between a rock and a hard place
25. blessing in disguise
26. blind leading the blind
27. blow hot and cold
28. bone of contention
29. bottom line
30. breeding ground
31. brink of disaster
32. by and large
33. by the same token
34. by word of mouth
35. call a halt
36. call on the carpet
37. call to action
38. calm before the storm
39. can't see the forest for the trees
40. change of heart
41. clean slate
42. clear the air
43. clear the decks
44. close call
45. cold feet
46. come full circle
47. come hell or high water
48. come up for air
49. conventional wisdom
50. couldn't care less
51. cream of the crop
52. cry wolf

53. cut and dried
54. damn with faint praise
55. days are numbered
56. deep six
57. die is cast
58. do an about-face
59. don't rock the boat
60. dot the i's and cross the t's
61. down and out
62. down in the dumps
63. draw a blank
64. draw the line
65. drop in the bucket
66. dropped the ball
67. eagle eye
68. easier said than done
69. easy come, easy go
70. eleventh hour
71. embarrassment of riches
72. explore every avenue
73. face the music
74. fact of the matter
75. fair and square
76. fair shake
77. fall by the wayside
78. fall on deaf ears
79. false alarm
80. far be it from me
81. far cry
82. feast or famine
83. feather in his cap
84. feel the pinch
85. fill the bill
86. finishing touch
87. first and foremost
88. fits and starts
89. flash in the pan
90. fly in the face of
91. food for thought
92. for what it's worth
93. force to be reckoned with
94. foregone conclusion
95. forewarned is forearmed
96. from A to Z
97. from bad to worse
98. from cradle to grave
99. from the frying pan into the fire
100. from the word go
101. from time immemorial
102. full head of steam
103. get a handle on
104. get a leg up on
105. get a second wind
106. get down to brass tacks
107. get in on the ground floor
108. get it down pat
109. get your act together
110. give short shrift
111. go against the grain
112. go by the board
113. go for broke
114. goes without saying
115. grasp at straws
116. grind to a halt
117. grist for the mill
118. half the battle
119. half-baked idea
120. handwriting on the wall
121. hang by a thread
122. hard and fast rule
123. have a field day
124. have an ax to grind

125. head and shoulders above
126. heads will roll
127. heart-to-heart talk
128. high and dry
129. hit below the belt
130. hit pay dirt
131. hold a candle to
132. hold the fort
133. hook, line, and sinker
134. hope against hope
135. horse of a different color
136. in a nutshell
137. in hot water
138. in one ear and out the other
139. in the heat of battle
140. jaundiced eye
141. keep the ball rolling
142. keep your fingers crossed
143. keep your head above water
144. know the ropes
145. knuckle under
146. labor of love
147. last but not least
148. last resort
149. last-ditch effort
150. lay down the law
151. leave no stone unturned
152. left holding the bag
153. left in the lurch
154. leg to stand on
155. lie low
156. light at the end of the tunnel
157. lock, stock, and barrel
158. long and short of it
159. loud and clear
160. low man on the totem pole

161. make a clean breast of it
162. make no bones about it
163. make the grade
164. moment of truth
165. more power to you
166. move heaven and earth
167. movers and shakers
168. muddy the waters
169. name of the game
170. neither here nor there
171. nip in the bud
172. nose to the grindstone
173. not my cup of tea
174. not what it's cracked up to be
175. nothing to write home about
176. off the cuff
177. off the deep end
178. off the wall
179. on the ball
180. on the level
181. on the up-and-up
182. once in a blue moon
183. one fell swoop
184. open and aboveboard
185. out of the woods
186. out on a limb
187. pain in the neck
188. par for the course
189. part and parcel
190. pay the piper
191. pay through the nose
192. pie in the sky
193. piece of cake
194. play it by ear
195. point of no return
196. pour oil on troubled waters

197. pull out all the stops
198. pull the rug out from under
199. push comes to shove
200. put a good face on it
201. put on the back burner
202. rack my brain
203. raise the roof
204. rake over the coals
205. read someone like a book
206. read the riot act
207. red-carpet treatment
208. rest on one's laurels
209. ride roughshod over
210. rising tide
211. run circles around
212. run of the mill
213. run off at the mouth
214. run the gauntlet
215. safe and sound
216. scratch the surface
217. seat of the pants
218. second to none
219. see eye to eye
220. see the light
221. sell like hotcakes
222. shed light on
223. short and sweet
224. short end of the stick
225. shot in the arm
226. sign of the times
227. signed, sealed, and delivered
228. sink or swim
229. sitting duck
230. sitting pretty
231. six of one, half dozen of the other
232. skating on thin ice
233. sky's the limit
234. snow job
235. sooner or later
236. sour grapes
237. split hairs
238. spur of the moment
239. square peg in a round hole
240. start from scratch
241. steal his thunder
242. steer clear of
243. stem the tide
244. stew in his own juice
245. stick in the mud
246. stick to your guns
247. sticky wicket
248. stonewall it
249. straight from the shoulder
250. stretch the truth
251. strike while the iron is hot
252. string along
253. take a raincheck
254. take by storm
255. take it or leave it
256. take it with a grain of salt
257. take the wind out of his sails
258. taken to the cleaners
259. takes the cake
260. tell tales out of school
261. third degree
262. thorn in the side
263. throw caution to the winds
264. tighten your belt
265. tip of my tongue
266. tip of the iceberg
267. to all intents and purposes
268. too many irons in the fire

269. toot your own horn
270. tough nut to crack
271. tough row to hoe
272. treat with kid gloves
273. turn over a new leaf
274. turn the tables
275. under a cloud
276. unvarnished truth
277. up for grabs
278. up in arms
279. up to par
280. uphill battle
281. vicious circle
282. walk on water
283. walking on eggshells
284. water over the dam
285. water under the bridge
286. wave of the future
287. wear two hats
288. wet behind the ears
289. when all is said and done
290. whole new ball of wax
291. whys and wherefores
292. wild-goose chase
293. win hands down
294. wing it
295. wishful thinking
296. without further ado
297. wit's end
298. word to the wise
299. worth its weight in gold
300. wouldn't touch it with a 10-foot pole

JARGON

Jargon is any expression that is not familiar to the reader. Jargon can be a single word or a phrase, or it can be an expression of familiar words used in an unfamiliar way. Contracts, for example, often contain collections of perfectly common words that make no sense when strung together. Also, computer-related documents such as user manuals often contain baffling terminology.

There is no official list of jargon terms and phrases; technical terms that are perfectly acceptable in one context may be considered jargon in another, depending on the audience's familiarity with the subject. If you are writing to an audience of computer experts, it is probably acceptable to use phrases like "digital convergence" or "multimedia multiparty teleconferencing." If you are writing to a more general audience, you'll leave them scratching their heads if you don't tell them what these expressions mean.

Some writers use jargon without realizing it; they are so familiar with a particular term that it doesn't occur to them that their readers won't know what it means. Others use jargon in an attempt to impress; they feel that tossing around technical terms makes them sound more knowledgeable.

The key to eliminating jargon is to write from the reader's point of view: If you must use a term your readers *may* not recognize, define it. If there are more common alternatives for potentially confusing terms, use them instead.

Noun Strings

Nouns are words that name a person, place, or thing. Words that are used as nouns sometimes can also be used as adjectives—words that describe nouns. For example, in this sentence the word *computer* is a noun:

> *My assistant borrowed my* **computer.**

But in this sentence the same word is used as an adjective:

> *My assistant borrowed my* **computer** *manual.*

The word *computer* modifies, or tells us more about, the word *manual.*

Writers create noun strings when they use several nouns in a row as modifiers, as in this sentence:

> *My assistant borrowed the* **invoice payment system software modification** *manual.*

There are five modifiers before the noun *manual.* When too many modifiers are piled on top of one another before the noun, it can be difficult to tell what modifies what. The noun string shown above can be avoided by rearranging the sentence:

> *My assistant borrowed the* **software modification manual** *for the* **invoice payment system.**

Eliminating noun strings usually creates slightly longer sentences, but the additional words help the reader grasp the meaning more quickly. When it comes to sentences, shorter is usually better, but not when the meaning of the sentence is blurred. Longer can be better if the sentence is easier to understand.

Passive Voice

Voice is a term that describes the type of verb (action word) that is used in a sentence. A verb is in the *active voice* when the subject of the sentence performs the action of the verb:

*The sales manager **hired** the new account executive.*

A verb is in the *passive voice* when its action is performed on the subject. A form of the verb *to be* (in the next example, *was*) is usually added as a helping verb:

*The new account executive **was hired** by the sales manager.*

Passive voice, also called passive construction, is an obstacle to clear writing for two reasons: It creates unnecessarily wordy sentences, and it can dilute the impact of the writer's statement. Sentences with active verbs make the writer seem confident; sentences with passive verbs sound evasive and often give less information:

Passive: *The decision **was made** to eliminate employee bonuses.*
            (Who made the decision?)

Active: *The president **decided** to eliminate employee bonuses.*

Sometimes writers use the passive voice deliberately (as is often the case with sentences like the passive example above). Other times the passive construction is necessary; for example, you may use it when you want to emphasize the person or thing receiving the action rather than the actor. Sometimes the passive voice is appropriate when the person who took a particular action is unknown:

*The accident occurred because the machinery **had not been serviced.***

Sometimes the actor of the sentence is unimportant, as in this example:

*Batteries **are not included.***

The focus of the sentence is the batteries. The actor is the company that chose not to include them with the product.

When you *do* use the passive voice, be careful not to switch from one voice to the other in the middle of the sentence:

Weak: *She **returned** my phone call, but an apology **was not offered.***
Better: *She **returned** my phone call, but she **did not offer** an apology.*

Overuse of the passive voice is such a common writing problem that some writers step too far in the other direction—they try to eliminate the passive voice entirely, which can cause just as many problems. Here is the most important point to remember about the passive voice: Avoid it whenever possible, but don't eliminate it automatically without examining the meaning of the sentence.

■ BIAS-FREE LANGUAGE

WHAT IS BIAS-FREE LANGUAGE?

Using bias-free language means not using terms that suggest offensive stereotypes. Biased language contains words or phrases that can be offensive because they imply stereotypes that apply to sex, ethnic origin, age, disability, sexual orientation, socioeconomic background, or a wide variety of other categories. Because society's values are constantly changing, terms that were perfectly acceptable for years are now taboo.

Bias-free language can be difficult to achieve because writers who use biased terms usually do so unintentionally. A writer who uses the biased term *businessman* instead of the neutral term *business executive* probably does not mean to imply that women do not belong in the workplace, but that is how such usages can be interpreted. Your writing can reflect your attitudes and values, even when you are writing about a neutral topic. Worse yet, careless word choices can cause your readers to draw conclusions about your prejudices, even though those conclusions might not be accurate. The best way to keep your writing free of bias is to reread everything you've written with an eye toward outdated or potentially offensive terms and phrases.

Here are some tips for avoiding sexism, racism, ageism, cultural insensitivity, and other usages that can divert the reader's attention from the message you are trying to convey or, worse, turn the reader against you.

BIAS TRAPS TO AVOID

Gender-specific suffixes for occupations. There are few—if any—occupations that do not include members of both sexes, so gender-specific suffixes such as *-ess, -trix,* and *-ette* are now virtually obsolete.

Wrong: *Perhaps one of the **stewardesses** can find a place for your coat.*

Correct: *Perhaps one of the **flight attendants** can find a place for your coat.*

Occupational names that end with *-man* should be changed to a neutral term:

Wrong: *This problem can be solved only with the help of a computer* ***repairman.***

Correct: *This problem can be solved only with the help of a computer* ***technician.***

The list of bias-free alternatives that appears at the end of this section gives preferred choices for terms with gender-specific suffixes.

Unnecessary modifiers. A modifier is a word that tells us more about the word that comes after it. Terms that indicate sex, race, or some other characteristic are sometimes included as modifiers even though the additional information they provide is irrelevant, as is likely the case in these sentences:

*The guest of honor was a **black** Air Force general.*

*During the surgery, the doctor was assisted by a **male** nurse who specialized in the procedure.*

*Judge Mary Jones, **a 55-year-old grandmother,** sentenced the defendant to 12 months of community service.*

We can tell if modifiers are necessary only by examining the context in which they appear. Sometimes the information they add is important; often it is not. One good clue that a modifier is unnecessary is if other similar terms are not similarly modified, as in this sentence:

*The panel included a journalist, a politician, and a **female** lawyer.*

Here we are told the sex of one of the panelists but not of the other two. Unless the modifier adds specific information that is essential to the meaning of the sentence, it should be deleted.

***The generic* he.** Using the pronoun *he* to refer to all members of the human race was once common. Today, however, this usage is socially unacceptable. Many people believe that this usage unnecessarily excludes women and perpetuates the belief that the male of the species dominates the female. The problem is that avoiding *he* leaves us at a loss for a third person singular pronoun when we are writing generically rather than referring to a specific person:

*Everyone should stand up for **his** rights.*

To avoid this problem, writers often use *his or her:*

*Everyone should stand up for **his or her** rights.*

Using *his or her* repeatedly in a long passage can be cumbersome and can create some unnecessarily awkward sentences. For this reason, many writers use *their:*

*Everyone should stand up for **their** rights.*

Technically, using *their* is cheating, because *everyone* is singular and *their* is plural. However, this usage has become so common that some authorities on language no longer consider it an error. In casual speech this usage probably won't cause anyone to wince, but you should avoid it in business writing.

The best way around the *his or her* vs. *their* problem is to rewrite the sentence. For example, suppose this sentence appeared in a company memo:

*__Anyone__ who wants **his** paycheck on Wednesday should turn in **his** timesheet by Friday.*

Unless all of this company's employees are men, this sentence needs repair. The challenge is to purge the sexism (*his* paycheck, *his* timesheet) without creating new errors. Changing *his* to *their* in both cases will not work because *their* is a plural pronoun, and *anyone* requires a singular pronoun. Here are some solutions to this problem:

- Make the entire sentence plural:

  *__Employees__ who want **their** paychecks on Wednesday should turn in **their** timesheets by Friday.*

- Use second person *(you):*

  *If **you** want **your** paycheck on Wednesday, turn in **your** timesheet by Friday.*

- Use an article instead of a pronoun (*a* instead of *his*):

  *__Anyone__ who wants **a** paycheck on Wednesday should turn in **a** timesheet by Friday.*

- If nothing else will work, change to the passive voice:

  *__Paychecks will be distributed__ on Wednesday **to those who** turn in timesheets by Friday.*

Some writers choose to alternate pronoun genders throughout a document (that is, using *his* in one sentence and *her* at the next occurrence) when referring to people in general or when the sex of the person doesn't matter or is unknown. This practice is not a good choice because it can be confusing to the reader: It may seem that the *he* references apply only to men and the *she* references apply only to women. Also, this method requires the writer to expend much mental energy ensuring that the usages are absolutely equal. This energy can be better spent finding other alternatives.

Outdated expressions. Using terms and phrases that are no longer considered appropriate is the quickest way to offend your readers. Eliminating sexist language is often easier than eliminating the appearance of racial, ethnic, and social bias because changes in terminology occur more frequently in those areas and can be more difficult to keep up with. In just the past few decades, *Negro* and *colored* were replaced by *black,* and more recently by *African American,* as the preferred term for referring to people of African descent. *Asian* has replaced *Oriental,* and *Native American* has replaced *Indian.* The expression *sexual orientation* has replaced *sexual preference,* and *disabled* has replaced *handicapped.* Unfortunately, there is no way to be absolutely certain that your writing is free of offensive terms. Even within certain groups, there is disagreement about the preferred form of reference. The safest approach is to avoid such terms unless they are absolutely necessary, substitute neutral alternatives whenever possible, and keep up with current usage as reflected in respected publications.

The Bias Test

If you are not sure whether a particular term could be offensive, apply this test:

1. If you substituted an opposite term for the one in question (such as "man" for "woman" or "white" for "black"), would you still include the word, or would it seem unnecessary?

2. If you substituted a word that described yourself, would you be offended if the sentence referred to you in that manner?

ALTERNATIVES FOR TERMS THAT REVEAL BIAS

Here are some words and terms that are commonly thought of as biased, along with preferred alternatives:

Avoid	Use
anchorman	anchor; newscaster
barmaid	bartender
businessman	business executive
chairman	chair
congressman	member of Congress; representative
elderly	senior citizen; senior
fireman	firefighter
gentlemen's agreement	unwritten agreement
handicapped	people with disabilities
handyman	maintenance worker
Indian	Native American; American Indian
mailman	mail carrier
man-hours	staff hours; work hours
mankind	humanity; people
manmade	synthetic
meter maid	meter reader; parking monitor
middleman	go-between; liaison; intermediary
Negro	African American; black
Oriental	Asian
policeman	police officer
repairman	technician
right-hand man	assistant
salesman	sales clerk; sales associate; representative
serviceman	service member; member of the armed forces
spokesman	speaker or spokesperson; representative
statesman	leader; diplomat
stewardess	flight attendant
unmanned	crewless

Avoid	Use
watchman	security guard
weatherman	weather forecaster; meteorologist
workman's compensation	worker's compensation

▪ THE RIGHT WORD: THE 25 MOST FREQUENTLY CONFUSED WORD PAIRS

Everyone has trouble with words now and then. When you consider the fact that there are more than 600,000 words in the English language, it is easy to see why mistakes happen. Words can be troublesome for many reasons:

- Some words sound alike but are spelled differently and have different meanings (such as **compliment** and **complement**).

- Some words sound similar and are related although they have slightly different meanings (such as **assure** and **ensure**).

- Some words have similar meanings but have important differences and therefore should not be used interchangeably (such as **common** and **mutual**).

We all have our own "red flag" words—words that send up a red flag in our minds because we know we sometimes get them wrong. We should be sure to look up these words in a dictionary before using them.

Another approach is simply to avoid troublesome words. Sometimes this method works fine—most people can write for years without ever using the word *comprise*. However, if you don't want to limit your power of communication by limiting your word choices, learn the 25 most commonly confused word pairs listed below.

1. *accept/except*

   To **accept** something is to receive it willingly, to recognize it as true, or to approve of it:

   *Do you think the boss will **accept** your explanation?*

   *Jane was **accepted** by the university.*

Except means to leave out or exclude:

*Employees who do not work full time will be **excepted** from the program.*

2. *accessible/assessable*

Accessible means easily approached, reached, or attained:

*The file is not **accessible** on this computer.*

Assessable means capable of being evaluated:

*The fire damage will not be **assessable** until the building is cleaned out.*

3. *adverse/averse*

Adverse means harmful, unfavorable, or acting against one's interests:

*The plan had some unforeseen **adverse** effects.*

Averse means opposed to, reluctant, or having a feeling of distaste:

*I am not **averse** to your idea.*

(*Adverse* is frequently used incorrectly in this sense.)

4. *affect/effect*

To **affect** something or someone is to bring about a change:

*A price increase will **affect** the bottom line.*

Although less commonly used this way, **affect** can also mean to simulate or imitate; an **affectation** is an artificial behavior designed to impress others:

*She **affects** flashy jewelry to get attention.*

An **effect** is a result:

*What is the **effect** of the price increase on profits?*

Used as a plural noun, **effects** are personal belongings:

*Terminated employees should be supervised when they pack their personal **effects**.*

When **effect** is used as a verb, it means to bring about:

*The new policies are intended to **effect** a change in morale.*

5. *among/between*

Among means in the midst of; surrounded by:

*I am more relaxed when I am **among** friends.*

Between means in comparison of, or the time or space that separates:

*I have to choose **between** a high salary and interesting work.*

Use **among** with three or more; use **between** when there are only two:

*The profits will be divided **among** the three partners.*

*The profits will be divided **between** the president and the vice president.*

Between can be used with more than two elements, however, to emphasize a close relationship:

***Between** the mortgage, my car payment, and the grocery bill, there isn't much money left over for entertainment.*

6. *appraise/apprise*

To **appraise** is to evaluate, or to estimate the value of:

*Your supervisor will **appraise** your performance twice a year.*

*Have the ring **appraised** before you sell it.*

To **apprise** is to inform:

*Keep me **apprised** of your progress while I'm out of town.*

7. *assure/ensure*

Some dictionaries list these words as synonyms, but there is a difference in the way they are used. **Assure** means to inform (someone else) confidently or to remove doubt:

*He **assured** his client that he would deliver the product on time.*

Ensure means to guarantee and is usually followed by the word "that":

*To **ensure** that the package arrived on time, I delivered it myself.*

8. *bimonthly/semimonthly*

A **bimonthly** meeting occurs every other month; a **semimonthly** meeting occurs twice a month. (Note that there is no hyphen after the prefixes.) **Bimonthly** has been used incorrectly for so long, however, that it has come to mean the same as **semimonthly.** Most dictionaries now give two definitions for **bimonthly:** occurring every 2 months and occurring twice a month. To ensure that your meaning is clear, avoid both words and use **every other month** or **twice a month,** as appropriate.

9. *censor/censure*

To **censor** something is to review it and remove the parts that are believed to be objectionable:

*His status report included a **censored** version of the irate client's comments.*

To **censure** is to find fault with or to express blame or disapproval:

*A good manager knows not to **censure** a staff member in front of others.*

10. *common/mutual*

Common, in this sense, means belonging equally to all:

*Outselling our competitors is our **common** goal.*

Mutual has a slightly different definition—it means possessed together; interchanged; reciprocal:

*It is in our **mutual** interest to reach an agreement.*

11. *compliment/complement*

These sound-alikes are frequently reversed. To **compliment** someone means to express praise or admiration. **Complement** means to complete, perfect, or make up a whole.

*I will **compliment** my friend by mentioning that her shoes **complement** her outfit.*

12. *compose/comprise*

    To **compose** is to create or form something by putting together elements:

    > *The proposal team is **composed** of staff members from three different divisions.*

    To **comprise** is to consist of or to be made up of:

    > *The proposal team **comprises** the company's top marketing specialists.*

    It is never correct to say "the team **is comprised of...**," although this error is common. Remember that the whole **comprises** the parts.

13. *consecutive/successive*

    Consecutive means following one after the other without interruption. **Successive** means following one another in order but not necessarily without interruption:

    > *The years 1980, 1981, and 1982 are **consecutive**; the years 1980, 1985, and 1990 are **successive**.*

14. *continual/continuous*

    Because the difference in their meanings is subtle, these two words are confused **continually**. **Continual** means recurring often, usually in rapid succession:

    > *His **continual** absences are causing his work to suffer.*

    Continuous means occurring without stopping:

    > *The clock will tick **continuously** until its battery wears out.*

15. *discreet/discrete*

    Discreet means having good judgment in terms of conduct:

    > *Everyone knew about their office romance because they were not **discreet**.*

    Discrete means separate and distinct or individual:

    > *The committee meeting and the conference were two **discrete** events.*

16. *distinct/distinctive*

Many people do not realize that there is a **distinct** difference between the meanings of these two words. **Distinct** means individual, discrete, or clearly perceivable:

> *We noticed the **distinct** smell of smoke in the hallway.*

Distinctive means distinguishing:

> *His voice was easy to recognize because of his **distinctive** accent.*

17. *eminent/imminent*

Eminent means distinguished in reputation; prominent:

> *The book was written by an **eminent** scientist.*

Imminent means impending, about to occur, or threatening:

> *The financial statements indicated that the company was in **imminent** danger of bankruptcy.*

18. *exceedingly/excessively*

Exceedingly means extremely or extraordinarily:

> *The president of the company was **exceedingly** happy with this month's sales totals.*

Excessively means exceeding a reasonable degree or amount:

> *The applicant was not selected because he talked **excessively** during the interview.*

19. *fewer/less*

The difference between **fewer** and **less** has to do with what is being referred to. If you can count the items as individual units, use **fewer:**

> *She completed the job in **fewer** hours than we had projected.*

If you are referring to a quantity of something, expressed as a singular noun, use **less:**

> *She completed the job in **less** time than we had projected.*

There is one exception—when you are talking about money, use **less,** even though dollars can be counted as individual units:

*He will not accept **less** than $30 an hour.*

Although the sign in the express checkout lane at your grocery store may say "10 items or **less,**" it should say "10 items or **fewer.**"

20. *forward/foreword*

Forward means at, near, or belonging toward the front. A **foreword** is an introduction to a book or report. The **foreword** is usually written by someone other than the book's author, often an expert in the field of the book's subject. This part of the front matter is frequently mislabeled **forward,** probably because people think that its name describes what happens when you read it: You move **forward** to the main text. Remember that the prefix *fore-* means "before" and that the **foreword** comes before the rest of the book:

*Look **forward** in the book to the **foreword** that appears on page ix.*

21. *impediment/obstacle*

An **impediment** is a hindrance; something that slows progress toward a goal:

*The old computer is slower than the others; it is an **impediment** to our goal of producing the report on time.*

An **obstacle** is something or someone that completely stands in the way of progress:

*The broken computer is an **obstacle** to meeting the deadline; the report will be late.*

An **obstacle** prevents you from reaching your goal; an **impediment** just makes it harder to achieve.

22. *imply/infer*

To **imply** is to express indirectly or hint:

*She **implied** that we would win the contract if we decreased our price.*

To **infer** is to conclude or deduce:

*I **inferred** from her comment that we might win the contract if we decreased our price.*

23. *indexes/indices*

Some dictionaries list **indices** as an alternate plural of **indexes,** but technically these two terms have different meanings. An **index** is an alphabetical listing of the subjects in a publication with corresponding page numbers. It can also be a number that indicates a mathematical relationship. When **index** is used in a scientific or technical sense, the correct plural is **indices:**

*The report listed the cost-of-living **indices** for the past 5 years.*

Otherwise, use **indexes:**

*The book contains both author and subject **indexes**.*

24. *precede/proceed*

Because these words sound similar when spoken, they are often confused when written. To **precede** is to come before in time, place, or rank:

*According to the program, the speaker **precedes** the awards ceremony.*

To **proceed** is to advance or continue:

*Do not **proceed** until you receive instructions in writing.*

25. *principal/principle*

A **principal** is the head of a school, or anything or anyone foremost in importance:

*He is the **principal** investigator in this case.*

A **principle** is a basic truth, standard, rule, or ethical code:

*They are arguing over a matter of **principle**.*

The memory aid we learned in school is probably still the best way to keep these two words straight: "Your princi*pal* is your *pal.* A princip*le* is a ru*le*."

Everyday Confusables

Reader's Digest has a regular column called "All in a Day's Work" that gives amusing stories about situations that occur in the working world. The following anecdote, which appeared in September 1993, features a frequently confused word pair:

> Out on the road, I stopped in a small town for office supplies. There was a sign in one shop window that read "Stationary Store." "You sell stationery, don't you?" I asked the clerk. "Indeed we do," she replied. I pointed to the sign and told her they needed to spell it with an *E*, since the one with an *A* doesn't mean writing paper. "Oh," she said, looking perturbed. "What does that one mean?"
>
> "Unmoving, immobile, in one place," I explained.
>
> "Well, honey," she said, satisfied, "we've been at this location for 17 years."
>
> (Reprinted with permission from the Sept. 1993 *Reader's Digest.* Copyright 1993 by The Reader's Digest Assn., Inc. Contributed by Carol Andrus.)

■ WHEN WRONG BECOMES RIGHT: HOW THE ENGLISH LANGUAGE CHANGES

You and your office mate have an ongoing argument. He maintains that the word *data* is plural, as in the sentence "The data *do* not support your conclusion." You say that *data* is singular and that the sentence should be "The data *does* not support your conclusion." You even pull from your bookshelf three software manuals that support your case. Your office mate drags out *Webster's Third New International Dictionary, Unabridged,* which says that *data* is the plural of *datum.* You retaliate with the *American Heritage Dictionary of the English Language, 3rd Edition,* which says that *data* can be used with either a singular or plural verb. Who is right?

To settle questions like this one, the publishers of dictionaries put together panels of language experts and put debatable points up for a vote.

In the case of *data,* for example, 60 percent of the *American Heritage* usage panel voted that it was acceptable to use *data* with a singular verb, as in the sentence "Once the *data is* in, we can begin to analyze *it.*"

Data is an example of a word that is in transition. What was once considered unacceptable usage of the word *data* is now approved of by some, but not all, language authorities. Most people realize that English usage changes noticeably from one century to the next, but few realize that it also changes, although less dramatically, from one decade to the next. Good usage means following the rules that dictate common practice, not following obsolete rules simply because we memorized them in elementary school, and not disregarding rules prematurely because a particular usage is more convenient or "sounds better."

In his classic book *Miss Thistlebottom's Hobgoblins: The Careful Writer's Guide to the Taboos, Bugbears and Outmoded Rules of English Usage,* Theodore Bernstein lets us off the hook on some of the ironclad rules that were dictated to us by rigid schoolmarms like his Miss Thistlebottom. Bernstein's book, written in 1971, was one of the first to summarize the changing trends in usage. It isn't that we now have permission to break the rules; it's that the rules are no longer rules. The language evolves in this way when a rule no longer leads to clearer writing. For example, you have undoubtedly heard an English teacher say "Never end a sentence with a preposition." However, avoiding this construction usually means writing an unnecessarily long, convoluted sentence to get around the problem.

THREE RULES THAT CAN NOW BE BROKEN

Here are some examples of rules that are no longer considered hard-and-fast requirements, even though many of us were taught to observe them.

Outdated Rule #1: Never end a sentence with a preposition. Prepositions—words such as *at, about, for, of,* and *to*—are linking words that show a relationship between one element of a sentence and another. The rule used to be that prepositions should always come before their objects and not after. However, when the position of the preposition is determined by the desired emphasis of the sentence, instead of by a rigid rule, the result is greater clarity. In the examples below, the sentences that end with a preposition sound much less stilted:

Awkward: ***About** what is he calling?*

Better: *What is he calling **about**?*

Awkward: *Is there something **with** which I can help you?*

Better: *Is there something I can help you **with**?*

Awkward: ***To** whom did you speak?*

Better: *Whom did you speak **to**?*

Outdated Rule #2: Never split an infinitive. Infinitives are verbs that are preceded by the word *to*, as in *to write*. A split infinitive occurs when a word that modifies the verb is placed between the *to* and the verb, as in "*to **carefully** write* directions." Sometimes split infinitives can be eliminated with no loss of clarity:

Split infinitive: *I am going **to carefully write** the directions so you don't get lost.*

Better: *I am going **to write** the directions **carefully** so you don't get lost.*

However, sometimes rewriting to avoid a split infinitive introduces an awkward construction:

Awkward: *I am going **to write** the directions from my house to the wedding to the reception **carefully** so you don't get lost.*

Better: *I am going **to carefully write** the directions from my house to the wedding to the reception so you don't get lost.*

In cases like this, it is better to break the old rule and split the infinitive than to introduce confusion.

Outdated Rule #3: Never begin a sentence with a conjunction. Conjunctions—words such as *and, but, or, nor, if, because, since, however, yet,* and so on—connect two parts of a sentence. It was once against the rules to begin a sentence with a conjunction because doing so turned an otherwise complete sentence into a fragment (an incomplete sentence). Avoiding this construction can produce undesirably long sentences (when the conjunction is used to link two sentences together rather than start a new sentence) or choppy prose (when the conjunction is eliminated altogether and the flow of the paragraph is lost):

Awkward: *Applicants do not need a perfect score on all tests to qualify for an interview,* **but** *if the applicants do not pass at least three of the four tests, they will not be hired.*

(This sentence is too long.)

Awkward: *Applicants do not need a perfect score on all tests to qualify for an interview. If the applicants do not pass at least three of the four tests, they will not be hired.*

(Eliminating the *but* weakens the connection between the two sentences.)

Better: *Applicants do not need a perfect score on all tests to qualify for an interview.* **But** *if the applicants do not pass at least three of the four tests, they will not be hired.*

KEEPING UP WITH LANGUAGE CHANGES

Our language continues to evolve, and there will undoubtedly be many more changes in the coming years. How can you keep up? The best approach is to choose a well-known style and usage guide—your company may have adopted one as its standard—and use it consistently. Be sure that you are using the most current version—most style guides are revised at least every 10 years. If you don't want to take a chance on discarding a rule prematurely, be sure to rely on the advice of the experts rather than on your own intuition. No matter how many language changes the future brings, "because it sounds better" will never be an acceptable defense for incorrect usage.

How to Number Pages

There are two ways to number pages: consecutively throughout the document, or by section. The advantage to section numbering is that if changes are made to only one section of the document, only that section has to be reprinted. The advantage to consecutive numbering is that it is slightly easier for the reader to find a particular page. For example, the reader will know that if the document is 200 pages long, page 150 is about three-quarters of the way through. In a section-numbered document, page 4-20 could be anywhere.

In either case, front matter (table of contents, preface, introduction, and so on) is numbered with lowercase Roman numerals. The title page counts as *i*, although the number does not actually appear on the page. If the document will be printed double-sided, the back of the title page is *ii*. If the pages of the document will be single-sided, the page that falls right after the title page (usually the first page of the table of contents) is *ii*.

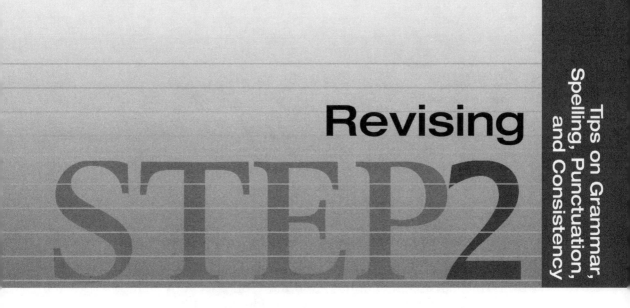

Revising

◼ REVISING: BECOMING YOUR OWN EDITOR

Once you have a draft that you are reasonably satisfied with—the organization makes sense, all the important points are covered, the writing style is appropriate—your next step is to shift your focus and take a closer look at what you have written.

During the writing process, you looked at "the big picture"—you kept in mind the needs of your audience, your purpose, and the focus of the piece. After you completed your first draft, you read it again from the reader's point of view: You made sure your language wasn't too stilted and your sentences weren't too rambling. You made sure that everything you said made sense. You removed the clichés and jargon, broke up the noun strings, and reversed the passive voice. You replaced any potentially offensive words or phrases with bias-free alternatives. Now you are ready to review your second draft.

Some writers have trouble revising because they become too attached to their own words. They are reluctant to look for problems because finding them will only lead to more work, so they review their material quickly, with one eye closed. Other writers are never satisfied with what they have written and will continue to revise and revise and revise again until someone finally yanks the document out of their hands. Obviously, you should aim for somewhere in between: Nobody ever writes a perfect document on the first try, but you do have to let go eventually.

When you reviewed your first draft, you were looking at whole pages and paragraphs. Now it is time to focus on individual words and sentences. The goal of reviewing the second draft is to find and correct errors in grammar, punctuation, and consistency. The rules and guidelines in this chapter will help you recognize problems and find solutions.

FINDING ERRORS IN YOUR OWN WRITING

Editing your own writing is difficult primarily because you are too familiar with your document. You may even have some sections memorized. When you reread your words, they seem to flow smoothly because they are so familiar—but they may not be grammatically correct. At the editing stage, you have to force yourself to read each word objectively. You have to consider each sentence as a separate unit and dissect it carefully.

Editing your own writing becomes easier the more you do it. With practice, you will become better at spotting problems and will be able to focus on several areas at a time. Here are some tips for focusing on the details and spotting the inevitable flaws:

- Don't try to edit your draft immediately after you finish it. Step away from it for awhile—ideally for an entire day or more. You'll be able to be more objective if you approach the material after a break.

- Perform the editing step in a place where you won't be interrupted. Don't attempt to revise a few pages, work on something else, and then revise a few more. Continuity is essential.

- Mark but don't fix problems that will take more than a few seconds to correct. Then go back and revise the places you've marked. If you stop at each problem area to recast a sentence or look up a grammar rule, you'll lose your train of thought, and you may miss errors.

- Make several passes through the document and look for a different kind of problem with each pass. It is impossible to remain alert to every possible kind of error in one reading. You may want to focus on punctuation errors on the first review, grammatical errors on the second review, and consistency errors on the third review. If you are unsure of your ability to spot problems, break the review cycles down even further: Look for comma problems in one pass, semicolon problems in the next pass, apostrophe problems in the next pass, and so on. You can even use the "search" feature of your word processing software to find each type of punctuation so that you can be sure to examine each one.

- Read a paper copy of your document; don't edit only on the computer screen. Although your computer can be a useful tool, it can also interfere with your ability to see your mistakes. Scrolling through text can be fatiguing to the eyes, especially if you can't see an entire line or page at once. You will be amazed at the things you missed on the screen when you see them in black and white.

- Keep a style sheet. A style sheet is an alphabetical list of terms used in the document. As you review the material, use the style sheet to keep track of the decisions you make and the items you check along the way. Is the correct name of the company you are writing to *The Acme Company, Acme and Company,* or *ACME Inc.?* Find out and add it to your style sheet. Does *IMP* stand for *International Monitoring Platform* or *Interplanetary Monitoring Platform?* Is *drawing board* one word or two? Should *fire resistant* be hyphenated when it is used in front of a noun, as in *fire-resistant material?* Don't trust your memory, especially when you are working on a long document. You'll spend a lot of time flipping pages back and forth or looking up the same style points again and again if you don't keep a style sheet.

- Don't rush. If you attempt to edit and revise your writing 10 minutes before the draft is due, you won't be giving yourself a fair chance to spot errors. It is human nature that the closer you are to the deadline, the better your document looks. Set aside enough time to perform a thorough, critical review.

To review your own writing (or anyone else's, for that matter), you have to know what you are looking for. The next sections will refresh your memory on the fine points of grammar and punctuation, give you some tips on how to become a better speller, and show you how to purge your document of stylistic inconsistencies.

Grammar-Checking Software—What It Can and Can't Do

Some people thought grammar-checking software would be the answer to a prayer: no more embarrassing errors, and no more having to memorize countless hard-to-remember rules. But unfortunately, most of these programs haven't lived up to their promises. Although they find some errors, they miss some, too. And they flag some things as errors that are actually correct. Some programs ask questions rather than provide answers: "Is this a dangling modifier?" Frustrated users can be heard muttering, "If I knew *that*, I wouldn't need this software!"

Grammar checkers use artificial intelligence techniques to analyze documents by applying preprogrammed rules. They have internal dictionaries and thesauruses that enable them to detect spelling errors and point out problems like missing punctuation (the lack of a closing quotation mark), temporal impossibilities ("Yesterday I will go to the store"), ambiguities (a pronoun that can refer to more than one antecedent), excessive use of passive voice or jargon, subject-verb disagreements, and unusual capitalization and special characters. Most grammar checkers will also perform a readability analysis to determine the reading grade level of what you've written. For example, if the program determines that the material is a level 10, that means that the readers will have to have at least a 10th grade education to understand it. Some programs will print out a summary that gives various statistics such as the average number of words per sentence, the number of prepositions, and so on.

Many programs give a more thorough explanation of the problem in the sentence or word being analyzed. Some checkers even have tutorials that explain the rules of grammar and style associated with each problem. Some programs have controls that allow you to enter the suggested corrections automatically or add and suppress individual grammar rules. For example, if you are writing a technical report, you might want to suppress the option that detects passive voice because it is likely that many of your sentences will be in the passive voice. Some checkers even allow you to fine-tune the program further by specifying the type of document you are creating (technical, business, and so on), and the checker will tailor its recommendations accordingly.

However, grammar checkers cannot understand what they are editing or make judgments, and so they often flag perfectly acceptable usage as wrong or, worse, ignore ridiculous sentences that happen to be grammatically correct ("Salamanders like to fly"). Some users have decided that the problems outweigh the benefits of using these programs. As artificial intelligence techniques improve in the years to come, so will grammar checkers; every time a new version of a grammar checker is released, it is a little better than the one before it. For now, there is still no replacement for careful scrutiny by a thinking human being.

■ GRAMMAR: CHOOSING YOUR WORDS CAREFULLY

Some writers who don't want to bother learning points of grammar say to themselves, "I know my audience, and I'm sure they don't know grammar any better than I do." There is a problem with that line of thinking: Although your readers may not frown at subject-verb disagreement or cringe when they see a misplaced modifier, they will still get the general impression that your document lacks *something*. When that happens, your credibility suffers. For example, you wouldn't want a potential client to read your report or proposal and say, "I can't put my finger on it, but I just don't feel comfortable trusting them with this project. The other company's document seemed much more polished and professional."

This book does not attempt to cover every element of grammar; the rules that follow are only the basics. But these rules will help you avoid the most common traps that writers stumble into and will help you spot grammatical errors in your own writing.

AGREEMENT ERRORS

Subject-verb agreement. The rule about subject-verb agreement is simple—when the subject is singular, the verb in the sentence must be singular as well:

> *The project **manager meets** with me once a week.*

The word *manager* is singular, so the singular verb *meets* is used. When your subject is plural—in this example, if you are talking about more than one person—the verb must be plural as well:

> *The project **managers meet** with me once a week.*

Most writers have no trouble with subject-verb agreement in simple sentences like these—it is unlikely that an educated professional would unknowingly say "The project *managers meets* with me once a week." However, subject-verb agreement gets tricky with more complex sentences, especially when the subject and the verb aren't right next to each other:

> Wrong: *Her **experience** with several different programming languages **make** her well qualified for the job.*

This sentence is incorrect because the subject—*experience*—is singular and the verb—*make*—is plural. The reason writers sometimes make this type of mistake is that they want to make the verb agree with the noun nearest to it, which in this example is *languages*. The word *languages* is plural, but although it is next to the verb, it is not the subject of the sentence.

Correct: *Her **experience** with several different programming languages **makes** her well qualified for the job.*

The trick to avoiding subject-verb disagreements is learning to find the subject of a sentence. In the above example, it isn't the *programming languages* that make her qualified for the job; it is her *experience* with them.

Here are some other common agreement errors:

Wrong: *A **total** of 35 votes **were** required to change the bylaws.*

Correct: *A **total** of 35 votes **was** required to change the bylaws.*

The subject of this sentence is *total* (which is singular), not *votes,* so the verb should be singular. Here is a similar example:

Wrong: *Only **one** out of every nine employees **contribute** to the fund.*

Correct: *Only **one** out of every nine employees **contributes** to the fund.*

The subject of this sentence is *one*, not *employees*. It sometimes helps to remove the phrase that separates the subject from the verb and read the sentence without it:

Only one...contributes to the fund.

Looking at the subject and verb together makes their relationship much clearer.

Although the wrong versions of these sentences may "sound better," they are incorrect. Unfortunately, we cannot always trust our ears when it comes to grammar.

Collective nouns. Figuring out subject-verb agreement gets even more complicated in sentences that contain collective nouns—that is, words that describe groups of people or things, such as *team, audience, majority, committee, couple, family,* and so on. In sentences that contain collective nouns, it can be difficult to decide whether the subject of the sentence is singular or plural. Consider the following example:

*The committee **has/have** reached a decision.*

Is *committee* a singular subject, because it is a single unit, or is it plural, because it is a collection of individuals? You have to examine the meaning of the sentence to decide which verb form to use. If the sentence describes something the group is doing *as a whole,* use a singular verb:

> *The **committee has** reached a decision.*

If the sentence describes *individual actions* of the members of the group, use a plural verb:

> *The **committee are** preparing their speeches.*

Each individual member of the committee is preparing his or her own speech, so a plural verb is the correct choice here. This construction sounds awkward, however, and can be smoothed out by changing the subject of the sentence:

> *The committee **members** are preparing their speeches.*

Adding the word *members* removes the ambiguity about whether the subject is singular or plural.

MODIFIERS: MISPLACED, DANGLING, AND SQUINTING

Modifiers are words or phrases that add information about other words. In well-written sentences, it is easy to tell which words modify which.

> *The report contains some **startling findings.***

In this sentence, *startling* is an adjective that describes, or modifies, the *findings.*

There are three kinds of modifier errors: misplaced modifiers, dangling modifiers, and squinting modifiers. All three types cause confusion for the reader. These kinds of errors can be difficult for writers to spot because they know exactly what they are trying to say; however, the reader may not.

Misplaced modifiers. Confusion can result when a modifier isn't close enough in the sentence to the word it modifies. Sometimes the result of this type of error is humorous, as in this sentence:

> Wrong: *She borrowed a computer from a coworker **with insufficient memory.***

In this sentence, a phrase, rather than a single word, is the modifier. Unfortunately, it is misplaced. The phrase *with insufficient memory* is presumably meant to modify *computer,* but the way the sentence is written, it sounds like the *coworker* had insufficient memory. There are a couple of possible fixes for this sentence:

Correct: *The computer **that she borrowed from a coworker** had insufficient memory.*

or

Correct: *She borrowed a **computer** from a coworker, but **it had insufficient memory.***

Dangling modifiers. Dangling modifiers are those that don't relate directly to any of the words in the sentence. A dangling modifier is a sign that the writer skipped a step by trying to combine two ideas into one sentence without linking them properly, as in this sentence:

Wrong: *While in the meeting, my car pool left.*

The phrase *while in the meeting* can't modify *car pool;* the car pool wasn't in the meeting. There are a couple of potential fixes for this sentence, depending on the writer's intent:

Correct: ***While in the meeting, I saw** my car pool leave.*

or

Correct: ***While I was in the meeting,** my car pool left.*

Squinting modifiers. A squinting modifier causes confusion because it can modify more than one word in the sentence, and the writer's intention may not be clear.

Wrong: *The technician fixed the copier **wearing a red bow tie.***

In this sentence, the phrase *wearing a red bow tie* can modify *technician* or *copier,* and the fix is a simple one:

Correct: *The technician who fixed the copier **was wearing a red bow tie.***

or

Correct: ***Wearing a red bow tie,** the technician fixed the copier.*

It is fairly obvious that the writer intended that the phrase refer to the technician (for one thing, copiers don't wear ties), but sometimes the meaning is not as obvious:

*The new clerk's method of working **quickly** impressed his boss.*

In this sentence, *quickly* is the modifier. Did the clerk's *method of working* impress the boss *quickly,* or was it his *method of working quickly* that impressed the boss? Sometimes these fine distinctions can be essential to understanding the meaning of the sentence. To double-check for correct positioning of modifiers, look at your sentences from the reader's point of view and make sure the intended meaning is clear.

MIXING PERSON

Another common source of confusion in writing has to do with *person.* When writing in *first person,* the writer speaks from his or her own point of view and uses *I:*

I *would like to request a transfer.*

When writing in *second person,* the writer speaks directly to the reader and sometimes uses *you:*

You *may request a transfer.*

Sometimes in second person, the writer speaks directly to the reader but the *you* is understood:

*To request a transfer, [**you**] fill out an application.*

When writing in *third person,* the writer speaks about something or someone using *he, she, it,* or *they* without using *I* or *you:*

He *requested a transfer.*

Writers *mix person* when they change from one point of view to another (within a sentence, paragraph, or document), such as when they shift from talking *about* someone to talking *to* someone, as in this sentence:

Wrong: *If **anyone** wants to request a transfer, **you** should fill out an application by Friday.*

Unintentionally mixing person is easy to do when you write about your company:

Wrong: *To give **our** clients better service, **ABC Company** has extended **its** business hours.*

Correct: *To give **its** clients better service, **ABC Company** has extended **its** business hours.*

or

Correct: *To give **our** clients better service, **we** at **ABC Company** have extended **our** business hours.*

Although it was once considered inappropriate to use anything but third person in business writing, that is no longer the case. In fact, using first or second person can make the writing more persuasive and can engage the reader better than the sometimes dull and stilted third person. The important point to remember is that you should choose one point of view and use it consistently throughout the document.

PROBLEMS WITH PRONOUNS

Who/Whom. The distinction between *who* and *whom* has haunted writers for years. There is an easy way to figure out which one to use: Temporarily substitute more familiar pronouns to see which one is required. For example, if you think of *he* as the equivalent of *who* and *him* as the equivalent of *whom*, the correct choice is usually clear. Consider the following sentence:

*He is the one **who/whom** will be promoted soon.*

First, look at only the part of the sentence that contains the *who/whom:*

*...**who/whom** will be promoted soon.*

Then substitute *he* and *him* in place of *who/whom:*

*...**he** will be promoted soon.*
*...**him** will be promoted soon.*

Obviously *he* is the correct choice, so then convert the *he* to *who:*

*He is the one **who** will be promoted soon.*

Here is another example:

*John Smith is the designer **who/whom** we chose for the project.*

In this sentence, the phrase must be inverted temporarily for the substitution trick to work:

*...we chose **who/whom**...*

Then substitute *he* and *him:*

*...we chose **he**...*
*...we chose **him**...*

Him fits here, so *whom* is the correct pronoun:

*John Smith is the designer **whom** we chose for the project.*

This trick also works with *whoever* and *whomever.*

*I will call **whoever/whomever** you choose for the project.*

Separate the part of the sentence that contains the pronoun in question:

*...you choose **whoever/whomever**...*

Substitute *he* and *him:*

*...you choose **he**...*
*...you choose **him**...*

Him is correct, so replace it with *whomever:*

*I will call **whomever** you choose for the project.*

Its/It's. The difference between these two words is hard to remember simply because they are used incorrectly so frequently, as in this sentence:

Wrong: ***It's** usefulness is debatable.*

The reason so many people make this mistake is that they associate apostrophes with possession. Usually possessives require apostrophes:

***Mike's** office is down the hall.*

Unlike other possessives, however, the possessive form *its* does not need an apostrophe. The apostrophe should be used only when the word is a contraction of the words *it is*. That is not what is intended here:

Wrong: *It is usefulness is debatable.*

In this sentence, *its* is intended to be a possessive, not a contraction:

Correct: *Its usefulness is debatable.*

In sentences in which *it is* can be substituted for *it's,* the apostrophe should be used:

Its/It's time to start the meeting.
It is time to start the meeting.
Correct: *It's time to start the meeting.*

Whenever you are unsure about whether to use an apostrophe, substitute *it is* and see if the sentence makes sense. If so, use the apostrophe. If not, don't.

Whose/Who's. Speaking of possessives and contractions, *whose* and *who's* are another frequently confused pair. They sound alike, but their uses are different.

Wrong: *Who's signature do we need on the contract?*

Like *its, whose* is a possessive pronoun. Like *it's, who's* is a contraction. To test whether the word in question is a contraction, substitute *who is* for *who's:*

Who is signature do we need on the contract?

This sentence does not make sense, so the contraction is not correct. The possessive pronoun *whose* is the correct choice:

Correct: *Whose signature do we need on the contract?*

Here is an example of a sentence in which the contraction is correct:

Whose/Who's going to sign the contract?

Replace the *whose/who's* with *who is:*

Who is going to sign the contract?

This sentence is correct, so *who's* is the right choice:

Correct: ***Who's** going to sign the contract?*

That/Which. To understand the difference between the relative pronouns *that* and *which,* you first have to understand the difference between restrictive and nonrestrictive clauses. A restrictive clause is one that is essential to the meaning of the sentence:

*I will give you the contract **that Pat signed yesterday.***

The phrase *that Pat signed yesterday* is essential to the meaning of the sentence because it tells us which contract is being given.

A nonrestrictive clause adds information to the sentence but does not change its basic meaning:

*I will give you the contract, **which Pat signed yesterday.***

This sentence implies that there is only one contract and gives the additional though nonessential information that Pat signed this contract yesterday. In the restrictive example above—the one that contains *that* instead of *which*—there may be many contracts, but the writer is referring specifically to the one Pat signed yesterday.

Sometimes it is not possible to tell what the writer means when *which* is used incorrectly, as in this sentence:

Wrong: *The president wants to discuss the sales figures **which** have decreased.*

The writer needs to either add a comma after *figures,* making the phrase nonrestrictive, or change the *which* to *that,* making the phrase restrictive. Does the president want to discuss the sales figures, which, by the way, have decreased, or does the president want to discuss *only* the sales figures that have decreased and not the others?

Remember this hint: If you see a *which* without a comma before it, you may be looking at a relative pronoun error.

Ambiguous antecedents. An antecedent is a word that is referred to by a pronoun in the sentence:

*Proofread the **memo** before you send **it.***

In this sentence, the pronoun *it* refers to the antecedent *memo.*

Pronouns and their antecedents can cause confusion when there is more than one word in the sentence that the pronoun can refer to, as in this sentence:

*If the computer prints an extra page, throw **it** away.*

The pronoun is *it,* but is the antecedent *computer* or *page?* In this sentence we can safely assume that the writer wants us to throw away the extra page and not the computer. Usually the pronoun refers to the word nearest to it, but you can eliminate the chance for confusion by repeating the word itself rather than using any pronoun at all:

*If the computer prints an extra **page,** throw the **page** away.*

Sometimes the meaning is not this clear when there is more than one possible antecedent:

***Managers** who don't give performance reviews to their **employees** must realize that **they** won't get salary increases this year.*

The pronoun is *they,* but which word is the antecedent? Is it the *employees* who won't get salary increases, or the *managers?*

SPELLING

You probably know at least one person who is an excellent speller. And it is likely that you know many more people who are poor spellers. Good spellers have one common characteristic—they all have good *visual* memory. When they think of a word, they can actually "see" the correct combination of letters in their mind's eye. The rest of us have to use a dictionary or memorize rules—and the exceptions to those rules—to avoid making embarrassing mistakes.

When you consider that there are hundreds of thousands of words in the English language, it is a wonder we spell as well as we do. Think of the spelling traps we face: There are silent letters, letters that are pronounced exactly the same as others, and letters that are pronounced different ways at different times. There are combinations of letters that produce sounds that don't resemble the sounds of any of the individual letters. There are words borrowed from foreign languages that don't follow any of the rules of English. And finally, there are words that can be spelled more than one way.

As a child, when you were struggling to learn the spelling of a particular word, your teacher would tell you to "sound it out." You would break the word into syllables and spell each syllable the way it sounded. Obviously, this technique didn't always lead to the correct spelling of the word, but it was a good start. Usually you could come up with enough of the correct letters to be able to look up the word in the dictionary.

Spelling-checker software has greatly reduced the number of times we have to consult the dictionary, and it has enabled bad spellers to produce better—although not perfect—documents. You can't rely on the spelling checker exclusively, and you won't always have a computer handy, so the rules we learned in school are still important.

The 25 Most Commonly Misspelled Words in Business Writing

1. accommodate	14. judgment
2. acknowledgment	15. liaison
3. argument	16. license
4. commitment	17. occasion
5. consensus	18. occurrence
6. deductible	19. perseverance
7. dependent	20. prerogative
8. embarrass	21. privilege
9. existence	22. proceed
10. foreword	23. separate
11. harass	24. supersede
12. inadvertent	25. withhold
13. indispensable	

TEN TIPS THAT CAN MAKE YOU A BETTER SPELLER

Even though they aren't always apparent, there are some patterns in the way words are spelled. Learning these patterns is the first step toward better spelling. Even though there are exceptions to virtually every rule, understanding the basic concepts will help you with most of the spelling challenges you encounter. Here are 10 of the most common questions about spelling patterns, along with easy-to-remember guidelines:

1. *How do I know when to use **ie** or **ei**?*

   The most commonly known spelling rule is still a good reminder: *i* before *e*, except after *c*, or when it sounds like *a*, as in *neighbor* and *weigh*. If the sound is *ee*, as in *brief*, use *ie*. If the sound is *ay*, as in *freight*, use *ei*. The combination *ie* occurs twice as often as *ei*.

2. *If I add a prefix to a word, and the last letter of the prefix is the same as the first letter of the base word, do I remove one of the doubled letters?*

   No; you can usually add a prefix without changing the spelling of the base word.

   > dis + **s**atisfy = dissatisfy
   >
   > il + **l**ogical = illogical
   >
   > over + **r**un = overrun
   >
   > un + **n**atural = unnatural

3. *When I add a suffix to a word that ends in **e**, do I delete the **e**?*

   It depends—leave the *e* if the suffix starts with a consonant:

   > achieve + **m**ent = achieve**m**ent

   Drop the *e* if the suffix begins with a vowel:

   > type + **i**st = ty**p**ist

   However, if either *c, e, g,* or *o* comes right before the final *e,* the *e* stays in when you add the suffix:

   > noti**c**e + able = noti**c**eable
   >
   > agre**e** + ing = agre**e**ing
   >
   > chan**g**e + able = chan**g**eable
   >
   > h**o**e + ing = h**o**eing

4. *How do I know when to add a **k** when I add a suffix to a word that ends in **c**?*

   Add a *k* when the *c* is "hard"; that is, when it sounds like a *k:*

   > pani**c** + ing = pani**ck**ing
   >
   > picni**c** + ed = picni**ck**ed

5. *How do I know when to double the final consonant of a word when I add a suffix?*

If the word has two syllables, and it is pronounced with the emphasis on the second syllable, double the final consonant:

ad**mit** + ance = admittance

oc**cur** + ence = occurrence

If the word is pronounced with the emphasis on the first syllable, don't double the consonant:

order + ing = ordering

credit + ed = credited

If the word has only a single syllable and a vowel comes before the final consonant, double the final consonant:

run + er = runner

hit + ing = hitting

6. *How can I remember whether a word ends in **-cede, -ceed,** or **-sede?***

By far the most common spelling of this suffix sound is *-cede.* Only three words end in *-ceed:*

exceed

proceed

succeed

Only one word ends in *-sede:*

supersede

The others end in *-cede.*

7. *How do I know whether the adverb form of a word should end in **-ly** or **-ally?***

Most base words take *-ly:*

complete + ly = completely

quick + ly = quickly

Some base words already end in *-al,* so *-ly* is simply added:

fundamental + ly = fundamentally

monumental + ly = monumentally

If the base word ends in *-ic,* then *-ally* is added:

basic + ally = basically

magic + ally = magically

athletic + ally = athletically

(An exception to this rule is the word *publicly.*)

8. *How can I tell whether a word should end in* **-ance** *or* **-ence?**

If the base word ends in a vowel followed by *r,* and when the word is pronounced, the emphasis is on the last syllable, use *-ence.* Otherwise use *-ance.*

con**fer**	conference
oc**cur**	occurrence

9. *What is the rule for making plurals out of words that end in* **y?**

Change the *y* to an *i* and add *es:*

city	cities
story	stories

If a vowel precedes the *y,* do not change the *y* to *i:*

monkey	monkeys
tray	trays

10. *How do I make a plural out of a compound term—where does the* **s** *go?*

Add the *s* to the most important word in the term:

joint **chiefs** of staff (*not* joint chief of **staffs**)

attorneys general (*not* attorney **generals**)

When the words in the term are of equal significance, add the *s* to the last word in the term:

go-be**tweens**

run-ons

How to Make the Most of Your Word Processor's Spelling Checker

As you've probably discovered by now, your word processor's spelling checker isn't foolproof—errors can escape its notice, even when it is used faithfully. It doesn't recognize as errors actual words that are used in the wrong context (such as *in* instead of *it*), and it doesn't recognize many proper names and technical terms. Most spelling checkers recognize about 100,000 words, but that is only about one-sixth the number of words in the English language. Some spelling checkers recognize the individual letters of the alphabet as legitimate words, so if you typed the phrase "n error" instead of "an error," the mistake would not be caught. Although the spelling checker will never be able to guarantee error-free text, there are some ways to make it more effective:

- Customize the spelling checker's electronic dictionary. Add words that you use frequently, such as names of people in your organization or specialized terms that are unique to your field. Then the checker won't flag them as unrecognizable every time they are used.

  If you have a tendency to mistype certain words in a way that forms other actual words (for example, if you always type *form* when you are trying to type *from*), delete these words from the spelling checker's dictionary so that you are forced to double-check them. The spelling checker will then stop on even correct uses of *form* if you delete it from the dictionary, but at least you will have the chance to verify that they aren't errors. You also may want to delete words that could only be typos in the kind of material you write or produce (for example, *pubic* instead of *public*).

- Don't use the "automatic correction" or "auto-replace" feature. Some word processing software allows you to designate some words as automatic corrections—the spelling checker changes them automatically without flagging them for your confirmation. This feature saves only a few seconds and can introduce errors that you may overlook.

- Run the spelling checker twice if you are checking text that contains a lot of proper names or other words that you ask it to skip over. It is easy to hit the "skip" key reflexively when you are skipping a lot of correctly spelled but unrecognized words and accidentally pass over an actual error.

- Be sure you are checking your entire file rather than just a small part of it. Most word processing software gives you the option of checking the whole file, one section, one page, or even one word. If you make the wrong selection inadvertently, a large portion of your text will remain unchecked.

- If you make *any* changes to the text after you run the spelling checker, run it again. Don't assume that because you changed only a few words, everything is fine. It only takes one keystroke to introduce an error.

- Remember to save the corrected file after you run the spelling checker. This step is easy to skip. We've all experienced the frustration of purging a document of its errors only to see them reappear because we forgot to save the file. Also, save the file before you run the spelling checker as well. That way, if you change something unintentionally, you can abandon the file without losing the work you did before you ran the spelling checker.

■ PUNCTUATION: THE KEY TO CLARITY

Punctuation, when used correctly, can turn a long chain of words into an understandable, meaningful sentence. Punctuation allows us to "hear" the writer's words by adding pauses and emphasis in the appropriate places. However, decisions about punctuation should not be arbitrary. Some people punctuate with their ears; they say, "I read the sentence aloud, and whenever I take a breath, I stick in a comma." This approach rarely results in correctly punctuated sentences; learning a few simple rules is your best bet.

A quick survey of the most popular style and usage guides will confirm that there is a trend toward less punctuation rather than more. Most authorities offer similar advice: If the punctuation is optional and the meaning of the sentence is clear without it, leave it out. One reason may be economy: When there are fewer punctuation marks, more text fits on each page. Fewer total pages means lower printing costs.

COMMAS

Commas are easy to understand. There are really only three kinds of mistakes you can make with commas: You can use too many, you can use too few, or you can put them in the wrong places. Here are some guidelines to help you ensure that your commas don't go astray.

The $2 Million Comma

An unidentified congressional clerk was instructed to write "All foreign fruit plants are free from duty." Instead, he wrote "All foreign fruit, plants are free from duty." It cost the U.S. Government $2 million before a new session of Congress could rectify the error.

(*The Book of Lists*, Wallechinsky, Wallace, and Wallace, 1977)

The serial comma. When you have a list of items in a sentence, they are separated by commas. The serial comma is the one that comes before the last item in the series.

With the serial comma:	*I am bringing my computer, my briefcase, and my umbrella.*
Without the serial comma:	*I am bringing my computer, my briefcase and my umbrella.*

There is no universal rule about whether or not to use the serial comma; it is an editorial style decision. It is not wrong to omit the serial comma, as long as you do so consistently. Journalistic style usually forbids the serial comma because leaving it out saves space (every little bit of space counts in newspapers and magazines). Most other styles, however, require the serial comma because it leaves no chance of misunderstanding. Consider the following example:

Traveling with Tom, Fred and Ann will save time.

Without the serial comma, the meaning of this sentence could be misinterpreted. It sounds like Fred and Ann will save time by traveling with Tom, but see the difference a serial comma makes:

Traveling with Tom, Fred, and Ann will save time.

Now the sentence says that anyone who travels with this group of three—Tom, Fred, and Ann—will save time. If that is the meaning the writer intended, the serial comma is essential for clarity.

Unless you are given style guidelines that say otherwise, it is always best to use the serial comma.

Introductory words and phrases. Another type of comma that is sometimes optional is the one that comes after an introductory word or phrase.

With the introductory comma:	*For this meeting, we don't have an agenda.*
Without the introductory comma:	*For this meeting we don't have an agenda.*

For short introductory phrases, the comma can be omitted without making the sentence difficult to read. However, when the introductory phrase is long, the comma helps the reader follow the meaning:

With the introductory comma:	*For the meeting that will take place in my office next week, we don't have an agenda.*
Without the introductory comma:	*For the meeting that will take place in my office next week we don't have an agenda.*

The second sentence is harder to follow because there is no comma to signal the end of the long introductory phrase. Sometimes you have to read a sentence twice to figure out where the introductory phrase ends and the rest of the sentence begins:

While we were eating the president came over to our table.

At first glance you thought they were eating the president, didn't you? In cases like this, it is best to use the introductory comma even when the phrase is short. Without the introductory comma, the reader is tripped up and sent back to the beginning of the sentence.

Appositives. An appositive, or appositional phrase, is a phrase or word that defines or further describes phrases or words that come before it in the sentence:

> *The mail room, **the heart of the company,** is the busiest part of the building.*

In this sentence, the phrase *the heart of the company* further describes the mail room.

When an appositive is restrictive—that is, when it adds essential information—it is not set off with commas:

Restrictive: *The large conference room **next to the president's office** has a breathtaking view of the city.*

Since the appositive *next to the president's office* is not set off with commas, we can assume that there is more than one conference room, but only the one near the president's office has the breathtaking view of the city.

If the appositive is nonrestrictive rather than restrictive—meaning that it merely adds nonessential information—it should be set off with commas:

Nonrestrictive: *The large conference room, **next to the president's office,** has a breathtaking view of the city.*

In this sentence, the appositive simply gives the additional information that the conference room being mentioned happens to be next to the president's office. The phrase could be removed without changing the meaning:

> *The large conference room has a breathtaking view of the city.*

In the previous example about the mail room, you can tell that the appositive is nonrestrictive because it too can be removed:

With the appositive: *The mail room, **the heart of the company,** is the busiest part of the building.*

Without the appositive: *The mail room is the busiest part of the building.*

Remember—nonrestrictive appositives (nonessential information) are set off with commas; restrictive appositives (essential information) are not.

Transitions and interrupters. These are words that interrupt the flow of the sentence. They are set off with commas:

> *Miskeying an access code can,* **in fact,** *cause the network to shut down.*
>
> *Our original plan,* **I think,** *is still the best approach.*
>
> *The three main volumes of the report,* **not to mention the appendix,** *are almost too heavy to lift.*

Some style manuals say it is acceptable to omit the commas when interrupters are short phrases:

> *You* **too** *can earn this much money.*
>
> *Total annual revenue* **therefore** *exceeded our expectations.*

Series of adjectives. When several adjectives modify the same word or phrase, they are separated by commas:

> *He still wears that* **torn, stained, moth-eaten** *jacket.*

Note that there is never a comma between the last adjective in the series and the word it modifies. (In the example above, there is no comma between *moth-eaten* and *jacket.*)

However, when one adjective modifies another, which in turn modifies either another adjective or a word or phrase, no commas are used:

> *Hand me the* **bright red vinyl** *notebook.*

A simple test to tell whether or not commas are needed is to mentally add the word *and* between each adjective:

> Correct: *He still wears that torn* **and** *stained* **and** *moth-eaten jacket.*
>
> Wrong: *Hand me the bright* **and** *red* **and** *vinyl notebook.*

Adding *ands* to the first sentence shows that all of the adjectives modify *jacket* equally. In the second sentence, however, it is clear that each adjective modifies the word next to it: *Bright* describes the shade of red, *red* tells what color the vinyl is, and *vinyl* describes the notebook.

Compound sentences. A compound sentence is one sentence that is made up of two independent clauses (phrases that have a subject and verb and could stand as complete sentences) that are connected with a conjunction *(and, but, so, or, nor, for, yet)*. The two independent clauses in the compound sentence are separated with a comma before the conjunction:

> *The printer promised to deliver the job by Tuesday,* **but** *I know he will take longer.*

> *You can stay and finish the job tonight,* **or** *you can come in early tomorrow morning.*

Some style guides say that it is allowable to leave out the comma when the sentence is short:

> *Sue paid for the gas* **and** *I drove.*

One of the most common comma errors is inserting a comma in a sentence that has a *compound verb* but is not a compound sentence. This type of error is called a *comma splice:*

> Wrong: *The persistent applicant delivered his résumé in person, and called the next day.*

The words *delivered* and *called* make up the compound verb. The phrase *called the next day* is not a complete sentence, so no comma is necessary. If the second part of the sentence had a subject, this example would be a compound sentence, and a comma would be necessary:

> Correct: *The persistent applicant delivered his résumé in person, and* **he** *called the next day.*

Dates and places. When listing a city and state, put a comma before and after the state (except when the state is the last word in the sentence):

> *The annual conference will be held in Blacksburg,* **Virginia,** *this year.*

The same goes for dates—put a comma before and after the year when it does not fall at the end of the sentence:

> *The conference will start on March 15,* **1996,** *and run for 3 days.*

It is not necessary to use a comma when only the month and year are given:

The conference is scheduled for January 1996.

How *Not* to Use a Comma

Don't separate a compound verb with a comma the way you would separate two independent clauses (that is, clauses that could be complete sentences):

Wrong:	She made all the arrangements for the company holiday party, and collected everyone's money.
Correct:	She made all the arrangements for the company holiday party, and she collected everyone's money.

Forget what you may have learned about using commas to show pauses in speech. Don't separate a subject and verb with a comma just because the subject is a long phrase:

Wrong:	Encouraging all employees to sign up for the new health insurance plan, is the purpose of the memo.
Correct:	Encouraging all employees to sign up for the new health insurance plan is the purpose of the memo.

Don't forget the second comma when setting off appositives or interrupters:

Wrong:	The caller, a man from California wouldn't leave his name.
Correct:	The caller, a man from California, wouldn't leave his name.

Wrong:	The meeting will take place on June 29, 1996 in Orlando, Florida at the Hyatt Regency.
Correct:	The meeting will take place on June 29, 1996, in Orlando, Florida, at the Hyatt Regency.

APOSTROPHES

Misplaced apostrophes are easy to spot. You see them everywhere: on signs, on billboards, on menus, in newspapers, and in magazines. Humorist Dave Barry once said that people seem to think apostrophes are used "to signal the reader that an *s* is coming."

The rules for using apostrophes are really quite simple. Apostrophes are used in three ways: with possessives, with contractions, and with plurals of letters and numbers.

Possessives. A possessive is formed by adding an apostrophe and *s* to a word to show ownership:

*I borrowed my **roommate's** car so I wouldn't be late for work.*

There is one exception: the word *its*. This word shows ownership, but it does not take an apostrophe; otherwise, it would be confused with the contraction *it's,* which stands for *it is.*

Possession:	*The old desk collapsed under **its** own weight.*
Contraction:	***It's** not safe to sit at that old desk.*

Where does the apostrophe go? If the word is singular, the apostrophe comes before the *s*. If the word is plural, the apostrophe comes after the *s:*

*Without my **roommates'** rent money, I won't be able to pay my mortgage.*

(The writer has more than one roommate.)

*His résumé says he has **4 years'** experience with computer-based training.*

Remember that apostrophes are not used to form plurals that don't indicate possession:

Wrong:	*Wanted: two **roommate's** to share a three-bedroom townhouse.*
Correct:	*Wanted: two **roommates** to share a three-bedroom townhouse.*

When adding an *s* to a person's last name, do not add an apostrophe unless possession is indicated:

Plural:	*We live next to the **Johnsons**.*
Plural possession:	*Our house is next to the **Johnsons'** house.*
Singular possession:	*I was able to call Smith, but **Johnson's** phone number was unlisted.*

If the word has a plural form that doesn't end in *s*, the apostrophe goes before the *s:*

Singular (one child):   *I got a call from my **child's** school.*

Plural (more than one child):   *I got a call from my **children's** school.*

If the word already ends in *s,* add the apostrophe but not the extra *s:*

*I'm using my **boss'** office while she is on vacation.*
*I borrowed **Chris'** notes from the meeting.*

Pronouns have their own possessive forms, so they don't take apostrophes:

Wrong: *Our product is superior to **their's**.*
Correct: *Our product is superior to **theirs**.*

Wrong: *The samples are **your's** to keep.*
Correct: *The samples are **yours** to keep.*

When something belongs to two or more people equally, the apostrophe and *s* belong with the last name in the series:

***Steve and Karen's** office is bigger than mine.*
(Steve and Karen share an office.)

When each person possesses his or her own, the apostrophe and *s* go after each name:

***Steve's** and **Karen's** offices are bigger than mine.*
(Steve and Karen each have an office.)

Sometimes modifiers look like possessives when they are really plurals. Plural modifiers do not take apostrophes:

*Look it up in the **users** manual.*
*The **officers** meeting is always at 10:00 on Mondays.*

Contractions. A contraction is the combination of two words:

isn't (is not)
don't (do not)
who's (who is)

The two words are bumped together, and the apostrophe takes the place of one or several missing letters. Sometimes writers accidentally put the apostrophe between the two words that are being joined rather than in place of the missing letter or letters:

Wrong: *have'nt*

Correct: *haven't* (combines *have* and *not;* the apostrophe takes the place of the *o*)

Abbreviated years are also considered contractions:

We calculated the costs using '95 prices.

Plurals of letters and numbers. Even though plurals don't normally take apostrophes, here is an exception: When you add an *s* to a single letter or number, it is necessary to use an apostrophe so that it won't be misread. For example, making the letter *i* plural would look like the word *is* without an apostrophe.

*The auditor makes sure we dot our **i**'s and cross our **t**'s.*

*His handwriting is almost illegible; his **l**'s look like **1**'s, and his **n**'s look like **m**'s.*

This rule does not apply, however, when you are referring to a particular decade:

*It was a shock to discover that some of my coworkers were born in the **1960s**.*

Apostrophes are not used to form plurals of acronyms or abbreviations that are made up of capital letters not separated by periods:

*My daughter is taking the **SATs** next weekend.*

However, if periods are used in the abbreviation, an apostrophe is used to prevent misreading:

*Sandy is one of three **Ph.D.**'s in our department.*

QUOTATION MARKS

Quotation marks are used to enclose words or phrases that are repeating something that was spoken or written. They are also used to set off words or phrases that must stand out from the rest of the text.

When to use quotation marks. Next to the comma, the quotation mark is the most overused type of punctuation. Writers who don't know the rules seem to say to themselves, "When in doubt, put it in quotation marks!" Here are the five correct uses of quotation marks:

- With direct quotations:

  "I told you so," I said to her.

  If you are using a direct quotation but are only repeating part of a person's sentence, be sure to place the opening quotation marks at the point where the actual quotation begins:

  *Jim promised us that the product would be delivered **"in perfect working order."***

  (Jim's actual words were "By the time you get the product, it will be *in perfect working order."*)

  To indicate a quotation within a quotation, use double (regular) quotation marks on the main quotation and single quotation marks on the internal quotation:

  The letter said, "Please send me a copy of your article, 'How to Cheat on Your Taxes and Get Away with It.'"

- With titles of magazine articles, short stories, presentations, papers, essays, speeches, songs, chapters within books, and separately titled sections of other publications:

  The book's first chapter, "Assembling Your Computer," is the most helpful.

- To call attention to words that may be unfamiliar to the reader:

  To "boot up" the computer, you must insert this disk.

- To indicate a word or phrase that is written elsewhere:

  The shipping crate was marked "This side up."

- To set off nicknames:

Terry "Hulk" Hogan was selected as the spokesperson for the product.

Where to put the punctuation. Commas and periods almost always go inside the quotation marks, whether the word or phrase in quotes is at the end of the sentence or in the middle:

> *Ralph calls himself our **"commander in chief,"** even though we do not report to him.*
>
> *Even though we do not report to Ralph, he says he is our **"commander in chief."***

Colons and semicolons go outside the quotation marks:

> *Ralph is not our **"commander in chief "**: He does not sign our time cards, set our work hours, or conduct our performance reviews.*
>
> *Ralph is not our **"commander in chief "**; we do not report to him.*

The position of question marks and exclamation points depends on whether they go with only the quoted matter or with the entire sentence.

Part of quote:	*I said to Ralph, "When did you become our **supervisor?"***
Goes with entire sentence:	*Why does Ralph say that he is our **"commander in chief "**?*

The same rule applies to exclamation points:

Part of quote:	*I yelled at Ralph, "You are not my **supervisor!"***
Goes with entire sentence:	*I will not allow Ralph to be my **"commander in chief "**!*

If the quotation takes one type of punctuation but falls at the end of a sentence that would take a different type of punctuation, do not use both. Let the punctuation within the quotation also serve as the end-of-sentence punctuation:

Wrong:	*I knew he was going to ask, "What happened to our profit margin?".*

Correct: *I knew he was going to ask "What happened to our profit margin?"*

When quotation marks are not to be used. There are several types of text that should not be set off in quotation marks.

- *Indirect quotations.* When you are paraphrasing what someone else said rather than repeating the words exactly, don't use quotation marks:

  *She said **that the package arrived this morning.***

  (Her exact words were "The box was delivered at 9:00 a.m.")

- *Block quotations.* Quotation marks are not used with block quotations; that is, long passages of quoted material that are indented from one or both margins and are often set in a smaller typeface, as shown below:

  > Punctuation is a device used to clarify the meaning of written or printed language. Well-planned word order requires a minimum of punctuation. The trend toward less punctuation calls for skillful paraphrasing to avoid ambiguity and to ensure exact interpretation. The *Manual* can only offer general rules of text treatment. A rigid design or pattern of punctuation cannot be laid down, except in broad terms. The adopted style, however, must be consistent and be based on sentence structure. (*U.S. Government Printing Office Style Manual,* March 1984)

  Block quotations are used when long passages of material (more than a sentence or two) are extracted from an already-published document. The indention indicates that the passage is a direct quote, so quotation marks are not necessary. As with any quotation, you should be sure to use the material exactly as it was printed and make clear what the source is.

- *Certain titles.* Titles of books, newspapers, magazines, pamphlets, plays, movies, and works of music and art are usually italicized rather than set off in quotation marks.

How to Handle Errors in Quoted Material

Most people know that when they use someone else's words in writing, those words should be used verbatim and set off in quotation marks. But what if the original words or sentences contained errors—do the errors have to be repeated as well? It depends on whether the words you are quoting were written or spoken:

- Quotations that are taken from a written source should be repeated exactly as they were written originally. However, you may correct spelling or punctuation errors. If you choose to repeat these errors, you may insert the word *sic* (from Latin, meaning "this is the way it was") in brackets after the error to emphasize that the error was the original writer's and not your own.

- Quotations that repeat words that were spoken rather than written can be changed somewhat. No changes in meaning should be made, but it is acceptable to correct any grammatical errors made by the speaker.

HYPHENS

Hyphens are used two different ways: to divide and to connect. They are used to divide words at the ends of lines of text so that the text doesn't violate or fall too far short of the margin. (The rules for end-of-line hyphenation are covered in the next chapter.) They are also used to connect compound nouns and adjectives. (Appendix B gives an alphabetical list of compounds.)

Hyphens with compound words. Compounds are words that are made up of two or more individual words joined by hyphens. Compound words can be nouns or adjectives. Compounds can be tricky: It isn't always easy to tell whether the correct choice is two words without a hyphen, two words hyphenated, or two words bumped together as one without a space or hyphen between them. Sometimes words that are actually unit modifiers do not take hyphens because the meaning is clear without them.

Hard, Soft, and Nonbreaking Hyphens

"Hard" and "soft" hyphens? Since when do the elements of punctuation have texture?

Hyphens weren't described in this way until the advent of word processing software. Programmers had to develop a way for the software to know the difference between hyphens that should appear only at the ends of lines and hyphens that are needed as a permanent part of the word.

The term "hard hyphen" is used to refer to hyphens that are typed in at the ends of lines rather than generated automatically. If a writer types in hyphens rather than letting the software put them in, the hyphens will remain even if the text reflows when further changes are made. The result is a common typographical error:

Before:	Errors can occur when the *automatic-hyphenation* feature is used.
After rewrap:	Errors can sometimes occur even when the *automatic- hyphenation* feature is used.

A "soft" hyphen, on the other hand, is one that disappears when the hyphenated word no longer appears at the end of a line. Soft hyphens are placed automatically by the software's internal hyphenation dictionary.

Still another type is the "nonbreaking" hyphen. These hyphens can be inserted with special codes. They ensure that when a compound word falls at the end of a line, the software breaks the word at the hyphen rather than in the middle of the first word in the compound:

Wrong:	Errors can sometimes occur when the *auto-matic-hyphenation* feature is used.
Correct:	Errors can sometimes occur when the *automatic-hyphenation* feature is used.

Compound nouns are formed by combining words with hyphens to make another word with its own specific meaning:

My **father-in-law** *retired after 40 years with the company.*

Jeff is such a **know-it-all** *that nobody takes him seriously, even when he is right.*

The newspaper's **editor-in-chief** *must approve the proposed design.*

The best way to determine if words should be joined by hyphens is to check a current dictionary.

Compound adjectives are words that are joined to describe the noun that follows them. They are also called unit modifiers because the words in the compound function as a unit rather than individually:

> *A **$20-an-hour** pay rate is an unreasonable expectation for a beginner in this field.*
>
> *John is taking a **4-week** trip to Colorado.*
>
> *The client's request goes beyond the **agreed-upon** scope of work in the contract.*

Never use a hyphen after words that end in *-ly:*

Wrong: *The experiment must be conducted under **carefully-controlled** conditions.*

Correct: *The experiment must be conducted under **carefully controlled** conditions.*

Be sure to use a hyphen when a modifier could apply to more than one word in the sentence:

> *Bill is an **old-car** enthusiast.*
>
> *Julie is a **small-business** owner.*

Without the hyphen, it wouldn't be clear whether Bill is a car enthusiast who happens to be old, or whether he likes old cars. Likewise, without the hyphen, it wouldn't be clear whether it is Julie or her business that is small.

The need for a hyphen is determined by the phrase's position in the sentence, not by the phrase itself. If the phrase comes after the word it describes, no hyphens are necessary:

> *Kathy received a **well-deserved** bonus.*
>
> but
>
> *Kathy's bonus was **well deserved.***

In the first sentence, *well-deserved* is a unit modifier because it comes before *bonus,* the noun it modifies. In the second sentence, however, the phrase is no longer a unit modifier and does not need a hyphen.

The term *suspended compound adjective* is used to describe a compound adjective that has an element in common with another adjective in the sentence. It is acceptable to use the common element only once and end the prefixes that come before it with a hyphen:

> *In addition to being there the day of the conference, we can provide* **pre-** *and* **post-conference** *services as well.*

This rule applies even when the first part of the compound is an actual word rather than just a prefix:

> *The plan addresses both the* **short-** *and* **long-term** *effects of the merger.*

If a compound word does not need a hyphen when used alone, it should not be hyphenated just because a suspended compound is used in the same sentence:

> Wrong: *Both* **near-** *and* **far-sighted** *patients can wear these contact lenses.*
>
> Correct: *Both* **near-** *and* **farsighted** *patients can wear these contact lenses.*

Hyphens with numbers. Hyphens are used to connect numbers used in text to make it clear that the numbers should be read as a unit. For example, when fractions are spelled out in text, a hyphen connects the numbers:

> *This year's sales totals are* **two-thirds** *higher than last year's.*

Even when fractions are not spelled out, a hyphen helps make them easier to read when they are set with full-sized numbers and a slash:

> *The recipe calls for* **2-1/2** *cups of flour.*

When stacked fractions (smaller numbers) are used, the hyphen is not necessary:

> *The recipe calls for* **2 $^1/_2$** *cups of flour.*

COLONS

Colons are used to set off or introduce information. They tell the reader to pause and expect further explanation. A colon can be used instead of a period to help one sentence lead into the next:

> **The new offices are beautiful:** *The carpeting is plush, the view is exquisite, and the lobby is full of fresh flowers.*
>
> **Kevin has three children:** *Tiffany, Tyler, and Truman.*

Em Dashes and En Dashes

The distinction between hyphens and dashes was once important mainly to typesetters. There was no em dash key on a typewriter, so writers who worked on typewriters had to improvise by typing two hyphens to make an em dash and typing one hyphen to make an en dash. Now writers have a full range of special characters at their disposal when they use word processing and desktop publishing software, but many still key dashes as if they were using a typewriter.

Em dashes and en dashes were given names that indicate their length: The em dash is as long as the letter *m* is wide, and the slightly shorter en dash is as long as the letter *n* is wide. The actual size varies from typeface to typeface. The hyphen is shorter than both types of dashes and should not be used in their places. Using real em dashes and en dashes instead of hyphens gives a document a more professional look.

An em dash is used to separate an interrupting clause from the rest of a sentence:

> He came to my office—*without calling in advance*—and demanded to see me immediately.

It is also used to separate a word or words from a phrase that summarizes or explains those words:

> Paid holidays, subsidized health insurance, and free parking— *these are the only benefits I require.*

An en dash is the equivalent of the word *to*. It is used to separate letters and numbers, especially when a range or time span is given:

> The gift shop in the lobby is open *Monday–Saturday, 10:00 a.m.– 6:00 p.m.*

> The test will cover chapter 12, sections *A–F,* so read pages *212–275.*

(In formal writing, the words *to* and *through* should be used instead of en dashes.)

There should be no spaces before or after em dashes and en dashes.

Wrong: The test will cover chapter 12, sections *A – F,* so read pages *212 – 275.*

Correct: The test will cover chapter 12, sections *A–F,* so read pages *212–275.*

If the clause that comes after the colon is a complete sentence, the first word of the clause is capitalized:

Carol was frantic when I saw her this morning: **She** *had less than an hour to run home and pack, go to the office, stop at the bank, and get to the airport.*

If the phrase introduced by the colon is not a complete sentence, the first word should not be capitalized:

Carol has three stops to make on her way to the airport: **her** *house, her office, and the bank.*

Colons can also be used to introduce a list of items or a direct quotation:

My presentation will cover three topics: **project organization, staffing, and milestones.**

I remember her exact words: **"Do not call me unless there is a problem."**

Colons are only used after complete sentences. Do not use a colon to introduce a list that falls in the middle of a sentence:

Wrong: **The movers have been instructed not to touch personal items such as:** *lamps, picture frames, vases, posters, and plants.*

Correct: **The movers have been instructed not to touch the following personal items:** *lamps, picture frames, vases, posters, and plants.*

SEMICOLONS

Semicolons are connectors; they take the place of words like *and, but,* and *or* (the semicolon in this sentence takes the place of the word *for*). Semicolons connect related phrases and sentences, but they don't *introduce* the way colons do. They are more like links, whereas colons are more like arrows that point to the words to come.

Semicolons emphasize the relationship of two complete sentences by bringing them together into one:

Dennis still doesn't know if he will need surgery; the tests were inconclusive.

Tom missed the deadline; however, the work he finally submitted was perfect.

Using a comma instead of a semicolon in sentences like the ones above is a common error:

Wrong: *This newsletter design contains some basic flaws,* **for example,** *the columns are too wide.*

Correct: *This newsletter design contains some basic flaws;* **for example,** *the columns are too wide.*

Do not use a semicolon to connect two clauses when one of them is not a complete sentence:

Wrong: *The union's demands are simple;* **shorter workdays and higher hourly wages.**

Correct: *The union's demands are simple;* **they want shorter workdays and higher hourly wages.**

The semicolon is also used to separate elements in a series when one of the elements contains its own series of elements separated by commas. Without the semicolons, it is difficult to see where the elements in the main series begin and end:

Wrong: *Research assistants will photocopy meeting handouts,* **track down books, reports, and magazine articles,** *and take phone messages.*

Correct: *Research assistants will photocopy meeting handouts;* **track down books, reports, and magazine articles;** *and take phone messages.*

PARENTHESES

Parentheses are used to enclose information that is incidental or is less important than the rest of the sentence.

The steady decrease in interest rates over the past decade **(as shown in Figure 3)** *has prompted many people to refinance their mortgages.*

The parenthetical phrase could be removed from the sentence above without changing the meaning. Do not enclose in parentheses any information that is essential to the point of the sentence:

Wrong: *I called because I was concerned* (**not because I wanted to spread gossip**).

Correct: *I called because I was concerned*, **not because I wanted to spread gossip.**

If the parenthetical phrase falls at the end of a sentence, the final punctuation goes outside the closing parenthesis:

We will have the party in the courtyard (**as we did last year**).

Do you want to have the party in the courtyard (**as we did last year**)?

If the parentheses surround a complete sentence, the period goes inside the closing parenthesis:

I told the caterer that we would like to have the party in the courtyard. (**We had it there last year.**)

If a parenthetical phrase falls within another phrase that is already in parentheses, use brackets to set off the internal phrase:

The results of the experiment (which are supported by an earlier study **[Brown and Jackson, 1992]**) *indicate the need for further research.*

Never put a comma or semicolon before an opening parenthesis:

Wrong: *We would like to buy item 31-A, ($29.95), item 42-C, ($112.95), and item 112-F, ($149.95).*

Correct: *We would like to buy item 31-A ($29.95), item 42-C ($112.95), and item 112-F ($149.95).*

◼ CONSISTENCY

Consistency simply means doing things the same way throughout a document. Inconsistencies are just as much errors as grammar mistakes and typos are: They show a lack of attention to detail. Not every inconsistency can be resolved by invoking a rule; sometimes there is more than one "right" way, in which case a style decision has to be made. Here are some of the areas in which there are style variations that can become inconsistencies if guidelines are not followed faithfully.

Smoothing Out the Rough Spots

If you don't want to spend a lot of time wrestling with consistency issues when revising a document, you should make as many style decisions as possible before you begin to write. This point is particularly important when many writers are contributing to a single document.

The easiest way to achieve consistency while keeping arguments to a minimum is to follow one style guide faithfully. Style guides differ on their advice about style points such as capitalization, abbreviations, number style, and so on, so it is important to choose one and stick with it.

Many organizations have "house" style guides that contain answers to the kinds of questions that come up about their particular specialty field or subject matter. These customized style guides reflect the preferences of the organization's management and can be very effective in reducing the number of revision rounds a document needs before it conforms to "company style."

A variety of specialized style guides are also available from associations and trade publishers:

NEWSPAPER

Associated Press Style and Libel Manual, The Associated Press, 1993 (345 pages)

The New York Times Manual of Style and Usage, Times Books, 1976 (231 pages)

ACADEMIC

The Chicago Manual of Style, 14th edition, University of Chicago Press, 1993 (936 pages)

The MLA Style Manual, Modern Language Association, 1985 (272 pages)

SOCIAL SCIENCES

Publication Manual of the American Psychological Association, 4th edition, American Psychological Association, 1994 (368 pages)

LIFE SCIENCES

Scientific Style and Format: The CBE Manual for Authors, Editors, and Publishers, Council of Biology Editors, 1994 (784 pages)

CHEMISTRY

The ACS Style Guide: A Manual for Authors and Editors, American Chemical Society, 1986 (264 pages)

> ## Smoothing Out the Rough Spots *(cont'd)*
>
> #### MEDICINE
> *American Medical Association Manual of Style,* Williams and Wilkins, 1989 (377 pages)
>
> #### FEDERAL GOVERNMENT
> *U.S. Government Printing Office Style Manual,* U.S. Government Printing Office, 1984 (488 pages)
>
> #### GENERAL
> *The New York Public Library Writer's Guide to Style and Usage,* HarperCollins Publishers, 1994 (838 pages)
>
> *Prentice Hall Style Manual: A Complete Guide with Model Formats for Every Business Writing Occasion,* Prentice Hall, 1992 (525 pages)

CAPITALIZATION

Although there are many rules for capitalization, there are some gray areas as well. In general, capital letters should be used lightly—when in doubt, lowercase the word. Capitalization should not be used arbitrarily to emphasize words that the writer feels are important, just for the sake of calling attention to them:

Wrong: *Be sure to come in and see our **New Product Line** sometime this month.*

Correct: *Be sure to come in and see our **new product line** sometime this month.*

Here are some guidelines for the correct use of capitalization.

Sentences within sentences. Capitalize the first word of a direct quotation when it forms a complete sentence within the whole sentence:

*The security officer said, "**You** will have to leave your briefcase at the desk."*

Complete sentences that follow colons. When a sentence uses a colon to introduce another complete sentence, the first word of the second sentence is capitalized:

*His message was clear: **If** he didn't receive better service, he would switch to our competitor.*

However, when a sentence with a colon introduces a phrase that is not a complete sentence, the first word is not capitalized:

*We knew what he would do: **switch** to our competitor.*

Proper names. Capitalize all proper names, such as personal names, geographical names, names of religions, names of the days and months, names of holidays, names of organizations, and trademarks and trade names.

Sometimes companies adopt an unconventional capitalization style for their organization name or product names. (Software companies are particularly fond of this practice, presumably because the capitalization produces a visual cue that will make the name more memorable.) Be careful to use the correct mix of capitalization when referring to these types of names:

*I got an answer to my question by logging onto **CompuServe** and selecting the **dBASE** forum.*

In document titles. Capitalize the first and last words and all verbs, nouns, and adjectives in a title. Traditionally, the *to* in infinitives, prepositions (*for, by, in,* and so on), conjunctions (*and, but, or,* and so on), and articles (*a, an, the*) are not capitalized unless they are five or more letters long or are the first or last words in the title.

*The paper I will present at the conference is entitled "Building **a** Foundation **for** International Trade."*

*You may want to read her article, "How **to** Prosper **in the** Year 2000 **by** Planning **for the** Future."*

In job titles. Capitalize job titles only when they are used directly before or after a person's name:

***Program Manager** Sally Smith will give the first presentation.*

*Nicky Jones, **Director of Administration,** will conduct the employee orientation program.*

Lowercase titles when they appear without a person's name:

*The **program manager** will give the first presentation.*

*Our **director of administration** will conduct the employee orientation program.*

One exception to this rule is the word *President,* which is always capitalized when referring to the President of the United States, whether or not a name is given.

> *When my grandfather turned 100, he received a birthday card from the* **President.**

but

> *If I don't get my money back soon, I'm going to write to the* **president** *of the company.*

In titles of offices and departments. Capitalize the names of offices and departments when they are being referred to specifically but not when those same terms are used generically:

> *To pick up an application, go to* **Human Resources** *on the fourth floor.*

but

> *Every* **human resources** *department should have reference books on personnel law.*

Abbreviations

Like capitalization, abbreviations should be used sparingly. Before you use an abbreviation, ask yourself if there is a good reason not to use the spelled-out version of the word. Sometimes, of course, the answer is yes. If you are using a term repeatedly in your document, abbreviating it can ease reading

---

Advice About Acronyms

The word *acronym* is often used to mean any abbreviation that is formed by capitalizing the first letter of each word in the expression. Technically, that is not entirely correct: Acronyms are abbreviations that form pronounceable words.

IRA (individual retirement account) and NASA (National Aeronautics and Space Administration) are acronyms; CPR (cardiopulmonary resuscitation) and ICBM (intercontinental ballistic missile) are not. Remember, if you can't pronounce it like a word but instead you say each individual letter, it isn't an acronym—it's an abbreviation.

and save space without confusing the reader. Technical documents often contain many abbreviations for this reason. However, if a term appears only once, it is not usually necessary to abbreviate it, unless the abbreviation is more common and recognizable than the spelled-out version (such as *a.m.* for *ante meridiem* and *ZIP* for *zone improvement plan*). (Appendix A gives a list of common abbreviations and their definitions.) The following guidelines will help you decide whether or not an abbreviation is appropriate.

Defining abbreviations. When you use abbreviations, it is important to define all but the most obvious ones when they are first mentioned. Remember that even though you may be familiar with an abbreviation, your readers may not be. Give the spelled-out version first; then put the abbreviation in parentheses. After that, use the abbreviation alone:

> *The system's most important feature is the **magnetic tape subsystem (MTS)**. The **MTS** ensures that there is always a backup file of the data.*

If the abbreviation is actually more recognizable to your readers, give the abbreviation first and put the spelled-out version of the term in parentheses:

> *The **CD-ROM (compact disk–read-only memory)** version of the document will be released soon.*

In long documents, it may be necessary to redefine abbreviations in every section or chapter, particularly if the reader is likely to skip around in the text or read only parts of the document.

When you use an abbreviation after you define it, be careful not to repeat the last word of the abbreviation:

Wrong: *I had to call the bank because I had forgotten the **PIN number** I use to transfer funds into my **IRA account.***

In this sentence, *PIN* stands for *personal identification number,* and *IRA* stands for *individual retirement account.* So, the sentence actually says "...I had forgotten the personal identification *number number* I use to transfer funds into my individual retirement *account account.*"

Correct: *I had to call the bank because I had forgotten the **PIN** I use to transfer funds into my **IRA.***

Plurals of abbreviations. When you are defining a plural abbreviation, be sure that both the spelled-out version and the abbreviation are plural:

Wrong: *All-terrain vehicles (**ATV**) are not allowed on this part of the beach.*

Correct: *All-terrain vehicles (**ATVs**) are not allowed on this part of the beach.*

Use an apostrophe to form a plural of an abbreviation *only* if the abbreviation is made up of lowercase letters or contains periods and could be misread:

*The personnel manager was told to recruit more **Ph.D.'s**.*

Otherwise, no apostrophe is used to form plurals:

*The football team scored three **TDs** in the final quarter of the game.*

Abbreviations with periods. Generally speaking, abbreviations that are all uppercase do not take periods after each letter, but abbreviations that are all lowercase usually do:

*I have a meeting with the **CEO** at 2:00 **p.m.***

If an abbreviation with periods falls at the end of the sentence (as in the sentence above), it is not necessary to add a second period to end the sentence.

Articles before abbreviations. When an abbreviation will be preceded by *a* or *an,* how do you know which one to use?

*The scanner comes with **a/an OCR** software package.*

Pronounce the abbreviation as if you are reading it aloud *(oh-see-arr).* If the abbreviation starts with a vowel sound, use *an:*

*The scanner comes with **an OCR** software package.*

If the abbreviation starts with a consonant sound, use *a:*

*The scanner comes with **a CBT** program.*

NUMBERS

Numbers raise one basic style question: When do you spell them out and when do you use numerals? There are about as many suggested ways of handling this problem as there are style guides in print. Here is simple method that covers most situations.

Use numerals—

- Whenever you are referring to time, regardless of the size of the number:

  *It can take **5 minutes** to print a single page if it contains complex graphics.*

- Whenever you are referring to money:

  *The government spent **$2 million** on a program that was subsequently canceled.*

- With numbers that appear with abbreviations:

  *Add **2 tsp.** vanilla and **4 oz.** milk.*

- For numbers that indicate the elements of a publication:

  *See **Chapter 2, Figure 4,** for an illustration of this technique.*

- In a sentence that contains a mix of numbers under 10 and larger numbers as well:

  *The office supply store delivered **5** cases of pens, **10** packages of laser paper, and **25** boxes of diskettes.*

Spell out—

- Numbers one through nine:

  *It is almost impossible for **five** analysts to write **one** report.*

- Large numbers that are rounded off:

  *There are more than **five million** potential customers in California alone.*

- Numbers that begin a sentence:

  ***Forty-nine** states have amended that law.*

- Numbers that appear right next to other numbers that are written as numerals:

*Her kindergarten class had **twenty** 5-year-olds and **two** 4-year-olds.*

- Ordinal numbers used in a sentence, except dates:

  *This is the **fifth** sick day he has taken this month.*
  but
  *He was out sick on the **5th** and the **12th** last month.*

LISTS: FORMATTING AND PUNCTUATION

There are so many ways to format information presented in a list that inconsistencies are common. It is allowable to use different list formats within the same document, as long as the same kinds of lists are formatted the same way. There are two basic types of lists: *run-in* lists and *displayed* lists.

Run-in lists. A run-in list is part of a sentence; it isn't broken out as a separate format element. Run-in lists are used to break up particularly long sentences or to emphasize a series of items or a chronology of events:

If you take an order that must be shipped the same day, you must (1) enter the stock numbers into the computer, (2) print out a packing slip, and (3) hand-carry the packing slip to the stock room.

Do not use a colon to introduce a list if the phrase that introduces it is not a complete sentence. Use a colon only after a complete sentence:

Wrong: ***The forms of identification that are required are:*** *(1) a driver's license, (2) a passport, and (3) a birth certificate.*

Correct: ***Three forms of identification are required:*** *(1) a driver's license, (2) a passport, and (3) a birth certificate.*

If the items in the list are short, they are separated by commas (as in the example above). If the items are long, or if one or more items contain internal commas, the items are separated by semicolons:

Qualified applicants must have (1) a master's degree or Ph.D. from an accredited college or university; (2) experience working with software such as word processing, spreadsheet, and desktop publishing packages; and (3) availability to travel at least 2 weeks every other month.

Displayed lists. Displayed lists contain at least two items. The items are set off from the text with numbers or bullets and are separated by a line space.

If the displayed list is introduced by an incomplete sentence, the items in the list should begin with a lowercase letter:

To qualify for a bonus, employees must

- *work full-time,*
- *receive a rating of above average or better on their performance reviews, and*
- *demonstrate a personal commitment to the company's goals.*

If the items in the list are punctuated as they would be in a single long sentence (in this example, separated with commas), the word *and* ends the next to the last item, as shown above. If they are not punctuated, the *and* is not added.

If the items in the list are introduced by a complete sentence, the bulleted items may be complete sentences themselves or may contain several sentences:

There are three simple ways to guarantee customer satisfaction:

- *Respond to customer requests immediately. Do not put a request on hold for more than 24 hours.*
- *Be sure shipments are complete. Double-check the contents of every package before it is mailed.*
- *Quote prices accurately. Let customers know that items on back-order for more than 2 months are subject to price increases.*

The first word of each sentence is capitalized, and each sentence of each bullet ends with a period.

If the introductory sentence is complete but the bulleted items are incomplete sentences, only the last bullet ends with a period.

Our biggest customers all have the same expectations:

- *quick response*
- *complete shipments*
- *accurate price quotes.*

Parallelism. One rule is common to all types of lists: The items in the list should be grammatically parallel. If one item is a complete sentence, they all should be. If one item is written in second person, the others should match:

Wrong: *Anyone who uses the staff kitchen must abide by the following rules:*

- *Wipe out microwave.*
- *No smoking.*
- *Dishes left in the sink overnight will be thrown away.*
- *Bags of ice in freezer not for general use.*

Correct: *Anyone who uses the staff kitchen must abide by the following rules:*

- *Wipe out the microwave after you use it.*
- *Do not smoke in the kitchen.*
- *Do not leave dishes in the sink.*
- *Do not take ice from the bags in the freezer.*

Do not use a list format if any of the elements in the list are more than a half page long. The benefit derived from using this format—clearer organization—will be lost if the reader can't keep track of how the elements relate to one another.

Polishing

STEP 3

■ PROOFREADING: THE HUNT FOR ERRORS

Virtually everyone in the working world has to proofread at one time or another. Whether you are checking over a friend's résumé, rereading your own memo to the boss, or scrutinizing a price list that will be printed in your company's catalog, your goal is to find errors so that your reader will not. We all know that some errors are more critical than others, but knowing that does not make them any easier to find. The following section gives tips on how to spot even the most subtle errors and offers advice that will make the proofreading process easier.

WHAT PROOFREADING IS AND WHAT IT IS NOT

Some people use the word *proofreading* to mean looking for errors. That definition is not really accurate, though; proofreading means looking for *certain types* of errors. Proofreaders do not look for every possible misuse of the English language; they focus on details. When you are proofreading, your job is to look at the words with a magnifying glass (figuratively, and sometimes literally).

An Attempt at Perfection

Even back in the 1800s, perfection was the goal of most publishers. Here is one innovative method of proofreading that, alas, did not prove to be successful:

> The Foulis' editions of classical works were much prized by scholars and collectors in the nineteenth century. The celebrated Glasgow publishers once attempted to issue a book which should be a perfect specimen of typographical accuracy. Every precaution was taken to secure the desired result. Six experienced proofreaders were employed, who devoted hours to the reading of each page; and after it was thought to be perfect, it was posted up in the hall of the university, with a notification that a reward of fifty pounds would be paid to any person who could discover an error. Each page was suffered to remain two weeks in the place where it had been posted, before the work was printed, and the printers thought that they had attained the object for which they had been striving. When the work was issued, it was discovered that several errors had been committed, one of which was in the first line of the first page.
>
> (William Keddie, *Anecdotes Literary and Scientific*; quoted in *Books* by Gerald Donaldson, 1981)

THE BEST TIME TO PROOFREAD YOUR DOCUMENT

One of the easiest ways to waste time when producing a document is by having it proofread too soon. Proofreading should not take place until the document has been edited, revised, and formatted. If the content of the document is still changing, it is too soon to proofread. If the format of the document has yet to be approved and may change, it is too soon to proofread. If someone in the review process has not yet read the document and is likely to rewrite portions, it is too soon to proofread. The proofreader should see the document in the form in which it will be read by its audience.

What Makes a Good Proofreader?

The truth is that not everyone can become a good proofreader. Some people can learn the techniques, practice the marks, and try their best, but they will never be able to find errors as well as some of their coworkers. However, the lack of strong proofreading skills should not be viewed as a fault. Usually people who are not good at proofreading excel in some other area—they may be very creative, for example. And often people who *are* good proofreaders have difficulty "seeing the big picture"—their attention to detail limits their long-range vision. Trying to make a professional-level proofreader out of someone who just does not have the aptitude is a waste of time. Trying to improve error-detection skills, however, is a reasonable goal for people at all levels of skill and experience.

Here are some of the traits that good proofreaders possess:

- A good command of the English language
- A broad vocabulary
- A natural curiosity about a wide variety of subjects
- A good eye for typography
- A streak of perfectionism
- Patience
- The ability to concentrate on a single task for long periods of time
- The ability to understand and follow instructions
- A good memory
- Tact and diplomacy
- A sense of proportion

SETTING THE STAGE: WHAT TO DO BEFORE YOU PUT PENCIL TO PAPER

If you think the first step in proofreading is to pick up a pencil, read on. There are several things that you should do before you make a single mark on a page.

Having the right tools can help you find errors that you might not catch otherwise. Also, your surroundings can have a great effect on your accuracy. Errors that remain in a document when it gets to the final stages are the subtle kinds of errors that everyone has missed along the way. The errors you are about to look for have probably made it past several pairs of eyes already, so you may be the last line of defense. You can make sure the odds are in your favor by taking a few simple steps before you begin.

First, a caveat: Obviously proofreading a one-page memo that will only go to two of your coworkers doesn't require the same amount of care as proofreading your company's annual report that will go to all of your customers and stockholders. Naturally you will adjust your level of effort to the level of accuracy required. Although the tips given here can improve your proofreading in any situation, they particularly apply to critical proofreading tasks—those documents for which every error must be caught.

SWITCH YOUR BRAIN INTO PROOFREADING MODE

Chances are that your job includes a wide variety of tasks, and proofreading documents is just one of the many things you do in the course of a typical day. You may not even proofread every day—for example, your only proofreading task may be checking your department's status report once a month. If this is the case, it is especially important to remind yourself what it is that you are trying to do before you begin proofreading.

Proofreading means examining every letter of every word on every page—and the spaces between them as well. This is not the stage at which you look for flaws in the overall organization of the document or rewrite sections to improve the flow of the text. Reviews for these types of problems should already have taken place before proofreading begins. If you try to look for these problems while also trying to find typographical errors, you will be certain to miss things.

Before you read any of the text, review in your mind the kinds of errors you are looking for. You may even want to make a list (typographical errors, misspellings, format inconsistencies, mathematical errors, and so on). That doesn't mean that if you see a larger problem along the way, you should ignore it. On the contrary; proofreaders often run across factual inaccuracies and errors in logic on their hunt for more detailed errors. If you find such errors, it may be a sign that the document is not yet ready for final proofreading and should go through another content review.

The Types of Proofreading

In the publishing world, there are several different types of proofreading. The type used depends on the way in which the document is being produced, the type of material to be proofread, and the level of accuracy desired.

Single proofreading (also called comparison proofreading, solo proofreading, or straight proofreading): The proofreader compares the dead copy (the old version) of a document against the live copy (the new version) and marks any deviations.

Editorial proofreading (also called noncomparison proofreading or dry reading): The proofreader reads through a single copy of a document and looks for errors. This type of proofreading is used when there is no dead copy—for example, when the editor has made his or her changes directly to the electronic file rather than marking up a printout.

Team proofreading (also called partner proofreading): Two proofreaders work together on the same document. One person holds the dead copy and reads it aloud while the other person follows along on the live copy and marks any deviations from the dead.

Double proofreading: This is the least common type of proofreading and is used only when an extremely high accuracy level is required. Two proofreaders proofread separate, identical copies of the same document. Their marks are merged onto one copy before the document is revised.

GATHER YOUR TOOLS

You may be surprised to learn that proofreading requires more than just a pair of eyes and a pencil. Although not all of the tools mentioned next are essential for every job, they will help you to focus on the task at hand and to work in an efficient manner.

Good lighting. Natural light is best. If a window is not available, or if the sun is not shining, a desk lamp is the next best thing. The worst light for proofreading is overhead artificial light—the kind found in most offices. Overhead lights simultaneously produce glare and cast shadows on the pages, so you have to strain your eyes to focus on the print. Eyestrain can greatly reduce your effectiveness, potentially leaving you with an error-ridden document *and* a headache.

Colored pencils and a pencil sharpener. Pencils are better than pens, provided that their colors are dark enough to see, because you will inevitably make marks that you will later want to erase. For example, you may spot what you think is an inconsistency, only to discover that what you marked was actually correct but an earlier instance, which you did not mark, is the incorrect version. Or, you may write a query to the author and then find the answer to your question later in the text. Making marks and then crossing them out will produce a very messy copy that will likely confuse and annoy the person who has to make the revisions. Use a pencil, and be sure it has a good eraser.

It is important to have a pencil sharpener within easy reach so that you do not have to keep interrupting your work to sharpen your pencils. The fewer interruptions you have, the better your proofreading will be.

Self-stick notes. These little adhesive notes are ideal for flagging pages that have errors or marking sections you want to refer back to as you proofread. You may want to use different-colored notes, such as Post-its, to code your marks. For example, you might use one color to flag pages that need correction, another color for pages that contain questions that still have to be resolved, and yet another color to mark pages that will have graphics added to them later in the production cycle.

Reference books. You will need a current dictionary to verify spelling and word usage and your company's in-house style guide, if you have one, to ensure consistency and conformity to the chosen style for the document. (Style issues should have been resolved in the previous revision round, as described in Step 2, but when you are proofreading, you should mark any inconsistencies that may have slipped through.) You may also want to gather any specialized reference works that are used in your particular field, such as a list of abbreviations.

A ruler. Proofreading with a ruler can make it easier to focus on one line of type at a time. You can slide the ruler down the page as you read so that your eye does not wander prematurely to the next line. (End-of-line errors are among the most common things missed by wandering eyes.) A ruler is also necessary to measure spacing, rules, and margins.

A type gauge. A type gauge helps you check the various typefaces used in a document to ensure that sizes are consistent and that they match the specified design. It is easy for the typesetter or desktop publisher to enter a wrong digit when selecting type size. The type may be only a fraction of a point size off, which would probably not be apparent at a glance. A type gauge is made of clear plastic and shows one capital letter in each of a wide range of type sizes. To check type, you place the gauge over the page and align any capital letter on the page with the one on the gauge that indicates the specified size. You then look to see that the height of the letter is the same as the one on the gauge for that size. Type gauges can also be used as rulers to measure type.

A calculator. If you are proofreading text that includes numerical data, a calculator is essential. In addition to proofreading the numbers in a table against the previous draft, it is also important to check totals. You will be amazed at how often you find columns and rows that do not add up correctly, even when the tables were produced with spreadsheet software.

A magnifying glass. There is no need to struggle with tiny type. Most office supply stores carry bar-shaped magnifying glasses that allow you to magnify one line of text at a time; you can slide the bar down the page as you go. Even for people with good vision, a magnifying glass can be particularly helpful for footnotes, references, and figure captions, all of which are typically set in type that is smaller than that in the rest of the document.

A clear plastic grid. A see-through grid can help you check alignment and indention when you are checking the formatting. You can lay the grid over the page and easily see the lines that do not conform to the page design for the document.

A light table. When you get to the final stages of production—that is, when you are checking to see that the errors you marked in earlier rounds were corrected properly—a light table can be a very handy tool. Once you have proofread the change, you can place the new, corrected page over the old page on the light table to ensure that nothing else was changed inadvertently. The light shining through allows you to quickly see where the new and old text no longer line up—a possible indication that a new error has crept in. (Professional proofreaders call this type of checking *slugging* the text.) You can also use this method to check that repeating elements such as headers and footers appear in the same place on every page. If your office does not have a light table, holding the pages up to a window works just as well.

Find a Quiet Place

Very few proofreaders have the luxury of working in complete silence with no interruptions, but that is the ideal environment for proofreading. When you have a significant amount of text to proofread, you should look for the next best thing within the realities of your work environment. That could mean simply closing your office door and putting up a "Do Not Disturb" sign. If you don't have your own office (let alone a door), you may have to find a conference room or an empty office in which to work. You cannot possibly proofread accurately if your concentration is continually broken by ringing phones, people with questions, or a chatty officemate. You might even have to save your proofreading task for a quiet time of day, such as when everyone else is at lunch or late in the day when most people have left. If none of these options will work for you, invest in a pair of earplugs.

Take Regular Breaks

Take note of the time when you start proofreading and plan to take a break about an hour later. Set an alarm if you concentrate so deeply that you tend to forget where you are. The break can be a quick one—even 2 or 3 minutes helps. Stand up and stretch, get a cup of coffee, return a few phone calls—anything to temporarily get your eyes off the pages and your mind away from the material you are proofreading. When you come back, your awareness will be sharper because you won't be as likely to become mesmerized by the stream of words and numbers you are looking at.

Even with breaks every hour, it is unwise to proofread for more than 8 hours straight. Even professional proofreaders report that their effectiveness starts to drop off after 6 or 7 hours.

Terms Used by Professional Proofreaders

author's alteration (AA)	a change made by the author (as opposed to an error made by the typesetter)
bad break	an incorrectly hyphenated word
bang	an exclamation point; also called a "screamer"
bump	an instruction to the typesetter to close up characters (do not separate with spaces or punctuation)
copy holder	in team proofreading, the person who reads the copy aloud while the other person marks the pages
dead copy	the original copy that the proofreader is checking the new (or live) copy against
dry reading	proofreading a single copy rather than comparing live copy against dead copy
hang	to set type so that it aligns with the indented line above it rather than extending back to the margin (as in a bulleted list)
inferior	a subscript character
kill	to delete unwanted text
knotholes	identical characters stacked up on consecutive lines
ladders	stacks of three or more end-of-line hyphens in a row
live copy	the new copy that the proofreader is comparing against the dead (original) copy
orphan	the last line of a paragraph left alone at the top of a page
out	a section of text that has been inadvertently omitted from the live copy ("The proofreader found several *outs* in this section.")

Terms Used by Professional Proofreaders *(cont'd)*

printer's error (PE)	an error made by the typesetter (as opposed to a change made by the author)
query	a proofreader's question to the author or the editor
repro	reproduction proof; the final pages that are proofread before printing
specs	type specifications, including type size and style, line length, and spacing
square up	align straight on a page
stet	a mark that means "let it stand" or "ignore the correction"
superior	a superscript character
widow	an undesirably short line at the end of a paragraph or column of text, or the first line of a paragraph left alone at the bottom of a page

ERROR-DETECTION TECHNIQUES FROM PROFESSIONAL PROOFREADERS

This section describes some of the methods that professional proofreaders use to enhance their error-detection abilities. Knowing *how* to proofread can be just as important as having a "sharp eye." Some of these methods vary depending on the circumstances (for example, if you are proofreading against a previous draft or just reading through the latest version of the document). Also, some are matters of personal preference. Try them all, then use the methods that work best for you.

THE FIRST LOOK

- Don't try to focus on everything at once. Make at least three separate passes through the document: the first to look for typographical errors

The "Love Is Blind" Theory

The saying "love is blind" applies to writing just as it applies to affairs of the heart. In the writing sense, it means that it is much more difficult to spot errors in your own writing than it is to spot them in someone else's. The reason is simple: You are intimately familiar with your own words. You understand what you've written, so when you are checking the text, you read much faster than when you are checking something you have never seen before. Your eyes may slide right over errors.

    This tendency is particularly dangerous when you have seen the material through many drafts. When you reach the point where you can practically recite certain passages from memory, the odds that you can find errors are greatly reduced. It is always best to have someone else—even someone who is unfamiliar with your subject matter—give your words a final look. If you are overly familiar with the document, serve as your own proofreader only as a last resort.

and missing words or lines; the second to look for text inconsistencies (for example, *four feet* in one place and *4 ft.* in another); and the third to look for format inconsistencies, errors in type specifications, and mechanical errors (such as wrong or missing pagination). No one— not even professional proofreaders with years of experience—can catch every type of error in just one pass through a document.

■ Put the copy you are marking next to the hand you write with. If you are right-handed, put the old version of the document on your left and the new version on your right.

■ Use a ruler to keep your place on the old copy. Slide it down the page as you go along.

■ Read one word at a time, and for unfamiliar terms read one character at a time. Don't assume you know what comes next.

■ Try to maintain a steady, even pace. Do not rush, but monitor the speed at which you are working.

■ If you are checking new copy that has been completely retyped, read only as many words as you can hold in your short-term memory before you move your eyes from the old copy to the new copy. Some people do best by reading only about seven or eight words at a time; others can retain several sentences. You will be able to retain more words at once if the text is simple than if it contains lots of technical terms and proper names. If you try to read too many words at a time, you risk skimming right past errors, particularly the subtle ones like missing words.

- Do not become distracted by the content of the material you are proofreading. If you find that you are so interested in what is being said that you are reading for overall comprehension rather than for typographical errors, read the material once to satisfy your curiosity and then begin proofreading it.

- If you are interrupted while you are proofreading, make a mark on the page at exactly the point at which you stopped.

- If you are having trouble following the text, read it aloud. Then repeat it aloud when you look at the live copy. Also read punctuation marks and other symbols.

- Do not read the text backward when doing a word-for-word proofreading. Some authorities have suggested this method because it forces you to slow down and look at the words individually. The problem with this technique is that you are not reading for meaning at all, so you would not be likely to catch actual words that appear in the wrong context, like *form* for *from.*

- Do not skip around in the document—proofread it from beginning to end. You will be much more likely to find errors and inconsistencies if you see the material in the proper order.

- When you find an error, take an extra close look at the text around it. Errors often appear in clusters.

- Look carefully at characters that are used in pairs, such as brackets, parentheses, and quotation marks. One mark of the pair without the other is a common error.

- Take an extra hard look at small words—*in, an, to, do,* and so on.

- Check the order of all numbered lists. It is easy to add or delete an item in the middle of the list and then forget to update the numbers that follow. The same applies to alphabetical elements; errors in alphabetization are extremely common.

- Do not trust your memory; keep a style sheet (Figure 2). Although style issues should have been resolved in the previous review cycle, you are bound to find at least one or two style deviations that slipped through. Keeping a list of the style discrepancies you find will make it easier to spot problems and enforce consistency. Also, do not drive yourself crazy (and waste valuable time) hunting for things that can be searched for automatically on the computer. If you think you saw *down sizing* somewhere but in other places it appears as *downsizing,* just make a note asking the person doing the revisions to do a global search.

STYLE SHEET

Abbreviations:

Brig. Gen. kW Insp. Gen.
Lt. Col. C. Cls. Supp. Rev. Stat.
ft³ R&D

Capitalization:

Cook County, the county
Figure 3
title IV a Representative
(U.S. Congress)

Numbers:

0.25 inch 20/20 vision
1984-85

Compounds:

long-range navigation
10-percent increase
high-speed engine

Figure 2. Writing down your style decisions as you make them is the best way to ensure consistency. This sample style sheet has general categories for types of style points; you may prefer to keep an alphabetical list instead.

- Do not mark changes that are not within the range of your authority. If you find a passage that you feel is poorly written or a fact that you believe is incorrect, ask the person who wrote the piece about it. State exactly what you think is wrong. No author will appreciate a query like "Should this awkward sentence be fixed?"

- Never mark a correction that you are not sure about. If you think you have found an error but are not sure about a particular rule, look it up. The worst thing you can do is introduce an error.

- To check formatting, hold the page upside down or sideways. This technique will help you see the actual shape of the words on the page rather than the individual letters, making it easier to spot formatting inconsistencies.

- Do not bother marking end-of-line hyphenation problems if there are many revisions still to be made. If you have found a number of other errors, it is likely that the text will reflow when those errors are fixed. Check hyphenation at the next stage, when you are proofreading revisions.

- Before you turn over the document to the person who will revise it, reread your own marks. Be sure they are legible and complete.

Dual Keyboarding

Dual keyboarding is a method that ensures virtually error-free text. This technique is used by publishers of material for which absolute accuracy is critical. Two different input operators key the same text. Then their two files are compared electronically and the differences are highlighted. The corrections are made by checking only the highlighted portions against the original, rather than proofreading the entire text. This method does not guarantee 100 percent accuracy—it is possible, though highly unlikely, that the two operators could make an identical error and it would not be flagged as a discrepancy.

End-of-Line Hyphenation

Sometimes words have to be divided at the ends of lines to ensure that the text doesn't look too "ragged." When right-justification is used (that is, when all of the lines of text end at the same point at the right margin but the spacing between words varies), hyphenation is used to ensure that there are no large gaps between words. Here are some general rules for correct end-of-line hyphenation:

- Hyphenate words between syllables *(intro-duction)*. Don't hyphenate long words after the very first syllable if there is room for another syllable on the line.

  The head of the committee gave me a flattering in-
  troduction.

- Never hyphenate one-syllable words, even long ones like *thought*.

- Divide words between double letters when possible *(syl-lable)* or between consonants *(con-sonants)* but not when doing so divides a syllable *(recal-led)*.

- If a word ends in *-ing*, hyphenate right before the *-ing* rather than where the syllables divide or between double consonants *(call-ing)*.

- Avoid hyphenating when the leftover syllable is only one or two letters long *(man-y, remind-ed)*.

- Don't hyphenate words at the end of more than two lines in a row. (Style manuals vary on this rule; some allow three hyphenated lines in a row but not four.)

- Check the dictionary when you are in doubt about hyphenation; don't trust your ear. Sometimes words that are spelled the same are hyphenated differently, depending on their meaning:

  The members of the committee asked him to pre-
  sent his findings to the group.

  but

  Every year at Christmas, the boss gives a pres-
  ent to every person in the department.

End-of-Line Hyphenation *(cont'd)*

Those who don't take the classes will not pro-
gress to the next level.

but
Those who are taking the classes are making prog-
ress and will reach the next level.

Not all dictionaries give the same advice on word division, so be sure to use the same dictionary consistently.

■ Don't leave hyphenation up to your word processing or desktop publishing software. Although these software packages are pro-grammed to break most words correctly, and they can be cus-tomized with your own style preferences, they are not foolproof. Always double-check word breaks when you use the automatic-hyphenation feature.

OLD AGAINST NEW: CHECKING CORRECTIONS

■ Before you start proofreading, find out if anything was rekeyed. Just because there was only one minor correction marked on a page doesn't mean that it is safe to look at just that word. It is very easy for the person making revisions to accidentally delete a sentence or even a paragraph. Ask the person making revisions to mark on the old copy any portions that were rekeyed. He or she may choose to mark those passages with a highlighter or flag them with Post-its.

■ Read several words on either side of a correction. Also, check the spac-ing before and after the word or words that were revised to see that no extra spaces were introduced and that no spaces were deleted.

■ Reread the entire paragraph if it contained multiple corrections.

■ Check the beginning and end of each page carefully if the last round of changes caused the text to reflow in a way that caused the pages to break differently.

■ Check all end-of-line hyphenation.

■ Watch for inadvertent format changes. "Slug" the text by folding the page from the old copy vertically and holding it against the new copy.

Compare each line to see that it ends at the same place on both versions.

■ MAKING YOUR MARK: HOW TO MARK TEXT SO THAT EVERYONE WILL UNDERSTAND YOUR CHANGES

In most companies, everyone has his or her own style for marking up a draft document. Some styles are more easily understood than others. Some people mark a paragraph for deletion by drawing a precise, civilized diagonal slash through it; others scribble across it until it is barely visible. The people who have to make the revisions become frustrated when they do what they think is intended, only to get the document back for another round of revisions because they guessed wrong.

One way to eliminate needless revision cycles is to adopt a standard set of marks and have everyone agree to use them. In the publishing world, professional editors and proofreaders have been using standard marks for years to communicate with authors and typesetters. The sections that follow discuss some of these standard proofreading marks. There are many more that are specific to typesetting, but these basics should be easy to learn and will cover virtually all of the errors that typically occur in business publications.

First, here are some tips about marking copy:

- Use a dark-colored pencil. Colored pencils are better than plain black because the changes are easier for the reviser to see. The pencils should be dark, though, so that in case the pages have to be photocopied, the marks will show up on the copies. Professional proofreaders often use two colors: red for indicating errors and blue for indicating queries to the author or editor.

- Make a check mark in the margin whenever you make a mark in the text. That way the revisions can be made more quickly—the reviser scans only the margins of each page rather than looking at every single line.

- Make your marks as legible as possible. If you take extra time to print neatly and carefully, it will save everyone time in the long run. If you have long passages (more than a sentence or two) to insert, type them and attach them on a separate sheet of paper.

INSERTING

Insert a character:

r
poofreading
∧

Insert a word: **proofreading**

Use standard marks so I will understand your changes.
∧

Insert a sentence or paragraph:

If you use standard proofreading marks, I will understand your changes and will be able to revise the document quickly. We must work efficiently to meet the Friday deadline.
∧
insert Ⓐ

The insert can be written in the margin if it is short (a single sentence), or typed on a separate piece of paper and labeled with the insert letter or number as shown here.

Insert a line space:

>

- Do not rewrite any of the text at this stage; mark only typographical errors.
- Make your marks in dark pencil so that they will show up when we photocopy the pages.

Insert a hyphen:

=
error free publications
∧

Insert an apostrophe:

Quality is not only desirable; its essential.

Insert a semicolon:

Quality is not only desirable it's essential.
∧
;

Insert a comma:

Enclosed are the final draft, the disk and your original.

Insert a colon:

Enclosed are three items the final draft, the disk, and your original.

Insert a period:

Enclosed are three items:

- the final draft,
- the disk, and
- your original

Insert double quotation marks:

Do not bother proofreading the document, my boss said.

Insert single quotation marks:

"All it needs is your John Hancock," I told him.

The Five Most Common Places to Find Errors

1. **In headings and titles**
2. **At the beginning or end of a page or paragraph**
3. **At the beginning or end of a line**
4. **Where typefaces change**
5. **Near other errors**

Delete a character and close up the space from which it was removed:

proofreading

Delete a character but do not close up spacing:

The document is error free.

Delete several characters or an entire word:

I work better in a noncompetitive environment.

Delete a paragraph:

The memo that the boss sent to us on Thursday states that we must have the final draft of this document on her desk by Monday. She will read it and give us her revisions by Wednesday. We must produce the final report and deliver it to the client by Friday.

Since the boss has only seen this document once before, I think it is likely that she will make many changes. We must be prepared to spend all day Thursday responding to her comments.

I will incorporate any changes you make to this draft; please mark them on the attached copy. If you use standard proofreading marks, I will understand your changes easily and will be able to revise the document quickly. We must work efficiently if we are going to meet the Friday deadline.

Delete a space and make one word:

desk top publishing

Equalize spacing between words:

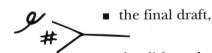 Justification ✔can ✔make ✔lines ✔look ✔too ✔"loose."

Use this mark when the words in a line are spaced out too much because of right-justification.

Delete a line space:

Enclosed are three items:

- the final draft,

- the disk, and

- your original.

REVISING

Replace a character:

pro*o*freading

Replace a word:

may

The technician ~~will~~ be here tomorrow to repair the copier.

Make a single letter lowercase:

The President has to sign this contract.

Make a series of letters lowercase:

CAPITALIZE only the first letter.

Capitalize a single letter:

capitalize only the first letter.

Capitalize a series of letters:

> Chapter 2. Proofreading

Transpose adjacent letters:

> prooﬁreading

Transpose adjacent words:

> Our company is a technical services support firm.

Spell out an abbreviation:

> Do not abbrev. any words.

Use a numeral rather than a spelled-out number:

> We will complete the project in three weeks.

Use a spelled-out number rather than a numeral:

> There are 3 people working on the project.

Correct word division:

> Software programs do not always make good deci-
> si ons about word division.

Superscript:

> References are indicated by superscript numbers.1

Subscript:

> The missing ingredient was H_2O.

FORMATTING

Move right:

> Chapter 2
> The Fine Art of Proofreading

Move left:

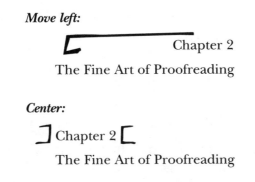

Chapter 2

The Fine Art of Proofreading

Center:

⌐ Chapter 2 ⌐

The Fine Art of Proofreading

Align vertically:

The White House

1600 Pennsylvania Avenue NW

Washington, DC 20500

Move text up to previous line:

I will incorporate any changes you make

to this draft; please mark them on the attached copy. If you use standard proofreading marks, I will understand your changes easily and will be able to revise the document quickly.

Begin a new line:

I will incorporate the changes to this draft. Please mark them on the attached copy. If you use standard proofreading marks, I will understand your changes easily and will be able to revise the document quickly.

Start a new paragraph:

The memo that the boss sent to us on Thursday states that we must have the final draft of this document on her desk by Monday. She will read it and give us her revisions by Wednesday. We must produce the final report and deliver it to the client by Friday. Since the boss has only seen this document once before, I think it is likely that she will make many changes. We must be prepared to spend all day Thursday responding to her comments.

No new paragraph:

 The memo that the boss sent to us on Thursday states that we must have the final draft of this document on her desk by Monday. She will read it and give us her revisions by Wednesday. We must produce the final report and deliver it to the client by Friday.

Replace double hyphens with an em dash:

Meeting the Friday deadline--even if we work overtime--looks impossible.

Replace double hyphens with an en dash:

Replace pages 31--36 with those attached.

Make italic:

 According to Webster's Collegiate Dictionary, that word is spelled correctly.

Make bold:

 Include a check or money order; do not send cash.

Wrong font:

 Font changes can appear mysteriously.

Special Instructions

Comment—do not type:

We need to verify these figures.

The Seattle office has doubled its volume since April. Also, the Houston office has shipped more than 10,000 units of the new product. Therefore, we expect an increase in revenue of more than $1 million in the coming year.

Ignore correction and leave as is:

stet

I work better in a noncompetitive environment.

Query to author:

Q:
Don't you mean an increase?

The Seattle office has doubled its volume since April. Also, the Houston office has shipped more than 10,000 units of the new product. Therefore, we expect a decrease in revenue of more than $1 million in the coming year.

What to Do When There Isn't Room to Make Marks

Sometimes when the material you are proofreading is single-spaced, it can be difficult to mark corrections legibly. When you do not have room to write in changes between the lines of text, you can mark them in the margin instead.

The memo that the boss sent to us on Monday states that *Thursday* we must have the final draft of this document on her desk by Monday. She will read it and give us her revisions by Wednesday. *e* We must produce the final report and deliver it to the client by this Friday.

Since the boss has only seen this document once before I think it is likely that she will make many changes. We must be pre-pared to spend all day thursday responding to her comments.

I will incorporate any changes you make to this draft; please mark them on the attached copy. If you use standard proofreading marks, I will understand your changes easily and will be able to revise the document quickly. We must work efficiently if we are going to meet the Friday deadline.

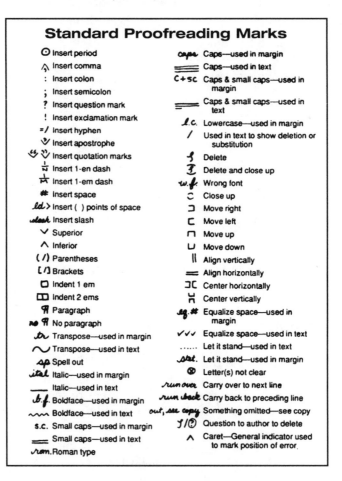

Standard Proofreading Marks

⊙ Insert period
⋀ Insert comma
: Insert colon
; Insert semicolon
? Insert question mark
! Insert exclamation mark
=/ Insert hyphen
ᐛ Insert apostrophe
ᐛ ᐛ Insert quotation marks
┴ Insert 1-en dash
⋈ Insert 1-em dash
Insert space
ld Insert ( ) points of space
slash Insert slash
∨ Superior
∧ Inferior
(/) Parentheses
[/] Brackets
▯ Indent 1 em
▭ Indent 2 ems
¶ Paragraph
no ¶ No paragraph
tr Transpose—used in margin
∽ Transpose—used in text
sp Spell out
ital Italic—used in margin
___ Italic—used in text
b.f. Boldface—used in margin
∿ Boldface—used in text
s.c. Small caps—used in margin
▬ Small caps—used in text
rom. Roman type

caps Caps—used in margin
══ Caps—used in text
C+sc Caps & small caps—used in margin
══ Caps & small caps—used in text
l.c. Lowercase—used in margin
/ Used in text to show deletion or substitution
ϑ Delete
ᗱ Delete and close up
w.f. Wrong font
⊂ Close up
⊐ Move right
⊏ Move left
⊓ Move up
⊔ Move down
‖ Align vertically
══ Align horizontally
⊐⊏ Center horizontally
ᗡ Center vertically
eq.# Equalize space—used in margin
✓✓✓ Equalize space—used in text
...... Let it stand—used in text
stet. Let it stand—used in margin
⊗ Letter(s) not clear
run over Carry over to next line
run back Carry back to preceding line
out, see copy Something omitted—see copy
ϑ/⊘ Question to author to delete
∧ Caret—General indicator used to mark position of error.

■ HOW FAST IS FAST ENOUGH?

Have you ever heard someone complain that it takes too long to get something proofread? How much time should you allow before it is fair to hold someone accountable for the quality of the document? Here are some rules of thumb.

Experienced, professional proofreaders work at a pace of approximately 10 double-spaced pages per hour. For estimating purposes, a page 8-1/2 inches by 11 inches with 1-inch margins and 12-point nonproportional double-spaced type, such as Courier, has 250 words. Few pages actually look like this, though, now that there are so many different formats and fonts available. To estimate proofreading time, the first step is to convert whatever type of text you have to this common denominator.

ESTIMATING PROOFREADING TIME: AN EXAMPLE

Let's say you have been given a 100-page document to proofread. It has been produced in a 2-column format, and 10-point type was used. There are some tables and graphics throughout, and each section starts on a new page.

First, count the number of tables and the number of graphics. The amount of time it takes to proof these elements varies according to their complexity, so it is necessary to assign an average amount of proofreading time per table and per graphic. (You could easily spend as much time doing an estimate as it would take to do the job if you try to assign an exact amount of time to each individual element.)

For example, if the graphics are fairly simple (pie charts and bar charts), you may want to allow 5 minutes per graphic. If they are more complex, such as detailed technical illustrations with lots of labels and annotations, you may want to allow 15 minutes each. If you are in doubt about your speed, the best bet is to proof two or three representative graphics and time yourself. You can then calculate an average time and apply this number to your estimate.

The time it takes to proof tabular material varies greatly, depending on the number of elements in each table. A small table of numbers with four columns across and four rows down should take about 5 minutes to proofread, including checking the totals. A large table with 10 columns across and 10 rows down takes about 15 minutes to proofread and check totals. The smaller the typeface and the more elements in the table, the longer it takes to proofread.

Let's say this 100-page document has 5 simple graphics and 10 simple tables, each of which takes up half a page. It also has 10 complex graphics and 5 complex tables, each of which takes up a full page. The time estimate can be calculated like this:

5 simple graphics × 5 minutes each = 25 minutes

10 complex graphics × 15 minutes each = 2 hours, 30 minutes

10 simple tables × 5 minutes each = 50 minutes

5 complex tables × 15 minutes each = 1 hour, 15 minutes

Total time to proofread tables and graphics: 5 hours

The next step is to estimate the time it will take to proofread the text. First we have to figure out exactly how much text there is. Simply counting the pages will not give an accurate estimate: We have to subtract pages to account for the graphics and tables, which we have already estimated; partial pages, such as the last page before the start of a new section; and blank pages, which are added for double-sided printing.

Scan through the text and count the number of full pages and the number of partial pages. Count each partial page as a half page, whether it has two lines of text or is three-quarters full. If a page is more than three-quarters full, count it as a full page. If a page has a half page of text and a half-page graphic, count it as a partial page. Do not include in the count the pages with full-page graphics, and do not include blank pages. Let's say our sample document breaks out like this:

7 blank pages

15 full-page graphics

18 partial pages of text

60 full pages of text

If we count the partial pages as half pages, they are the equivalent of 9 full pages; 9 + 60 = 69 full pages.

The next step is to convert the 69 pages into 250-word equivalents. Count the number of words on a full page. With the format given for this example—a 2-column format with 10-point type—there would be approximately 500 words on a page.

69 full pages × 500 words per page = 34,500 words

34,500 words ÷ 250 words = 138 double-spaced pages

That means that the text in this document is the equivalent of 138 double-spaced, 250-word pages. A professional proofreader would be able to review this material at 10 double-spaced pages per hour. To estimate your own proofreading time, use a rate that is reasonable for you. If you do not do very much proofreading, or if you are not confident about your skills, you'll want to estimate at a lower rate:

138 double-spaced pages ÷ 8 pages per hour = 17 hours, 15 minutes

Now add that amount of time to the total time you calculated to proofread the graphics and tables:

17 hours, 15 minutes (text) + 5 hours (graphics and tables) =

22 hours, 15 minutes to proofread the entire document

CALCULATING YOUR OWN RATE

The only accurate way to predict your own rate is to proofread a sample of text and time yourself. For the estimate to be valid, you'll have to work on a sample that will take at least an hour. Proofreading for 5 minutes and multiplying by 12 to get your hourly rate will produce an estimate that is artificially high. Speed varies over time, and productivity rates decrease because of many factors that don't emerge when testing with a small sample.

Once you have completed the sample, ask someone else to reproof it to find out how many errors you missed. Subtract one page per hour for every 4 errors you missed. In other words, if you proofread 10 pages in an hour but you missed 4 errors, adjust your rate to 9 pages per hour. If you missed 8 errors, adjust your rate to 8 pages per hour.

It is obvious from the example above that even a professional proofreader would need almost 3 full days of uninterrupted time to review this document thoroughly. Knowing how to calculate proofreading estimates can be helpful when someone asks you to review a document. Obviously there are times when 3 full days are not available to review a document like this, but everyone in the process must be aware of the compromises that are being made to meet deadlines.

FACTORS THAT MAY SPEED YOU UP OR SLOW YOU DOWN

Once you have carefully calculated a time estimate, you may need to add or subtract a "fudge factor"—a very nonscientific way to account for the fact that some types of text take longer than others.

The actual time may be less than the estimate you calculated if

- The text is very "clean"; that is, it contains very few errors (which will likely be the case if it has already been proofread once by someone else and revised).

- The space between lines (known as *leading*) is wider than standard, meaning fewer lines will fit on the page and each line will be easier to read.

- The material being proofread is familiar subject matter.

- The typeface used is proportionally spaced rather than monospaced.

The actual time may be more than what you calculated if

- You are proofreading against handwritten copy or typed copy with lots of editing and handwritten inserts. This type of material can be especially slow to proofread if the text has been reorganized and many sentences or paragraphs have been moved around.

- The text contains technical terminology, scientific notation or equations, foreign languages, many proper names, or any other unfamiliar words.

- You are proofreading against copy that is hard to handle, such as index cards or large computer printouts.

- You are proofreading a typeface with decreased legibility. Fancy or unusual type reduces speed by 7 to 10 words per minute; italic type reduces speed by 14 to 16 words per minute; and reversed type (white letters on a black background) and all-caps text reduce speed by up to 20 words per minute.

- The text contains many errors.

GRAB A PARTNER: TIPS ON TEAM PROOFREADING

Team proofreading (also called partner proofreading) is a method that professional proofreaders sometimes use, especially when they are checking number tables or long columns of data. Team proofreading is considered to be more accurate than single proofreading because two different pairs of eyes look at the copy. Also, the proofreaders do not have to shift their eyes back and forth between two copies, so their odds of catching errors are better. Team proofreading goes slightly faster than single proof-reading, but it is more expensive in terms of productivity because it takes up the time of two people rather than one.

Team proofreading works like this: The team consists of a copy hold-er and a copy marker. The copy holder reads aloud from the original copy—also called the "dead" copy—while the copy marker marks correc-tions on the new or "live" copy. Typically the more experienced proofread-er is the copy marker and the less experienced is the copy holder. If they have about the same amount of experience, the members of the team can take turns reading and marking to help them stay alert. Often the partners sit across the table from one another so the reader can see when the mark-er is writing a change and can stop reading for a moment.

Reading aloud for team proofreading isn't like reading a story to a child. The reader does not include the usual pauses and inflections; instead, he or she reads in a monotone voice. Each word, punctuation mark, and typographical element is spoken aloud during the reading. Proper names or unfamiliar terms are spelled out. Words that sound like other words but are spelled differently (such as *principle* and *principal*) are also spelled. Long words are pronounced one syllable at a time *(in-sig-nif-i-cant-ly)*. Numbers are pronounced one digit at a time (the number 235 would be read *two three five* instead of *two hundred thirty-five*).

Experienced team proofreaders use a sort of verbal shorthand to speed the proofreading process. Even saving a syllable or two every few words adds up to significant time savings when proofreading long passages. Here are some of the terms that team proofreaders abbreviate when speaking:

Term	**Abbreviation**
apostrophe	pos
bracket	brack
bullet	bull
initial capital letter	cap
all capital letters	caps or all up
centered	cen
close up	bump
colon	cole
comma	com
exclamation point	bang

Term	Abbreviation
hyphen	hyph
number	num or fig
paragraph	pare or graph
parenthesis	paren or pren
period	dot or point
question mark	ques
quotation marks	quo
semicolon	sem
subscript	sub
superscript	supe

Here is a passage of text and how it would sound when read aloud using this verbal shorthand:

The company's mission is stated on every product package: "We provide first-rate customer service while offering the best prices!" For every 100 customers we surveyed, 99 say they would recommend us to friends.[2] All ACME employees are dedicated to ensuring customer satisfaction.

(cap) *The company* (pos s) *mission is stated on every product package* (cole) (quo) (cap) *We provide first* (hyph) *rate customer service while offering the best prices* (bang) (quo) (cap) *For every* (fig one zero zero) *customers we surveyed* (com) (fig nine nine) *say they would recommend us to friends* (dot) (supe two) (cap) *All* (all up bump) *A C M E employees are dedicated to ensuring customer satisfaction* (dot)

■ HOW TO PROOFREAD GRAPHICS AND TABLES

Graphics and tables present a special challenge to proofreaders. Errors are more difficult to spot in graphics and tables than in text because there are so many variables and few rules with regard to format.

Graphics and tables should be looked at in three different ways: (1) to check for errors within the graphic or table, (2) to check for consistency among graphics and tables in the same document, and (3) to look at placement within the text, sizing, and relationship to the text that discusses the graphic or table.

GRAPHICS: GENERAL CONSIDERATIONS

Graphics come in many different types and formats, but there are some proofreading considerations common to all types.

■ Does the graphic convey the point the author is trying to make? Consider the example below (Figure 3):

So far in the 1990s, revenue has increased dramatically each year, from $4 million in 1990 to $8 million in 1994.

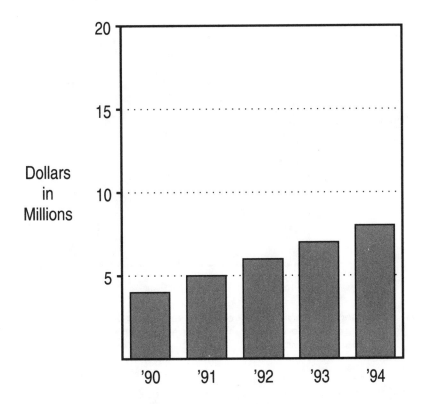

Figure 3. Because the vertical axis is too long for the data, this graph sends a message that contradicts the text.

According to the text, revenue doubled from 1990 to 1994, but the graph makes the increases look very small. Because the vertical axis (the line that shows dollars) is too long—that is, goes up to $20 million when the data points only go up to $8 million—it creates the illusion that the increases were slight rather than *dramatic,* as they are described in the text. See how changing the vertical axis produces a graph that gives an entirely different impression (Figure 4):

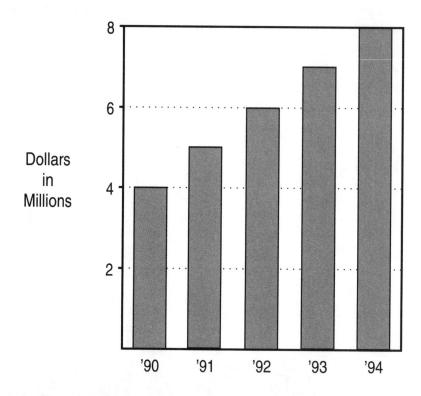

Figure 4. Changing the top of the vertical axis from $20 million to $8 million (the height of the tallest bar) creates a graph that makes it easier to see relative growth.

■ Can the graphic be easily understood by the reader, or is it trying to convey too much information (Figure 5)?

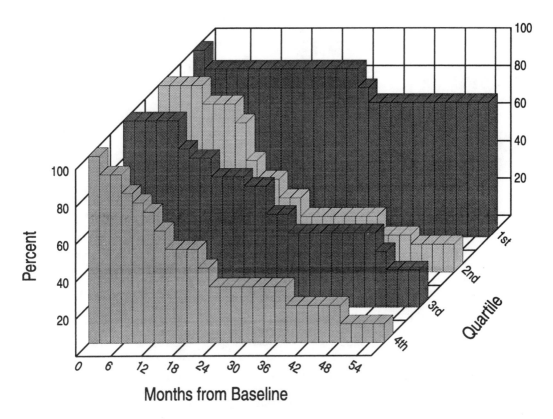

Figure 5. This graphic requires the reader to consider too many relationships at one time. The information in this graph would be easier to comprehend in two separate graphs.

If the reader can't understand the meaning of the graph at first glance and instead has to study it carefully to draw any conclusions from it, the graph may have too many elements.

■ Are any unintentional messages being conveyed by the graphics? Solid bars and heavy line weights can make some elements look more significant than the others on the graphic (Figure 6).

■ Are all the graphics in the document consistent with one another? That is, do they all contain the same typefaces, line weights, abbreviations,

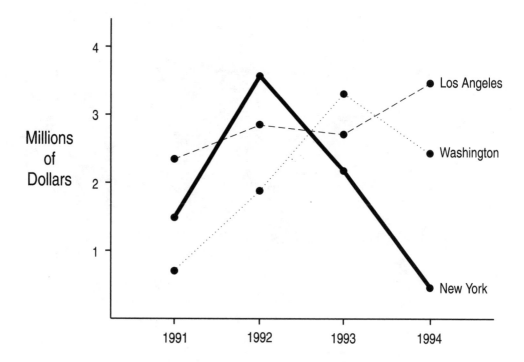

Figure 6. Because the line for the New York data is so heavy, it gives the incorrect impression that this information is more important than the data for the other cities.

and coding schemes? Are they sized to the same proportion? Often graphics are "borrowed" directly from other documents and no attempt is made to make them all look the same; a variety of styles can cause confusion for the readers and make the document look unprofessional.

- If two graphics appear together, are the same scales used on each axis? Consider Figure 7.

At a glance, this graph makes it look like Phase I and Phase II will take the same amount of time. At closer inspection, we see that the steps for Phase I are shown in weeks, and the steps for Phase II are shown in months. This detail is easy for readers to miss. The message of these two graphs would be much clearer if the same horizontal axis had been used on both parts.

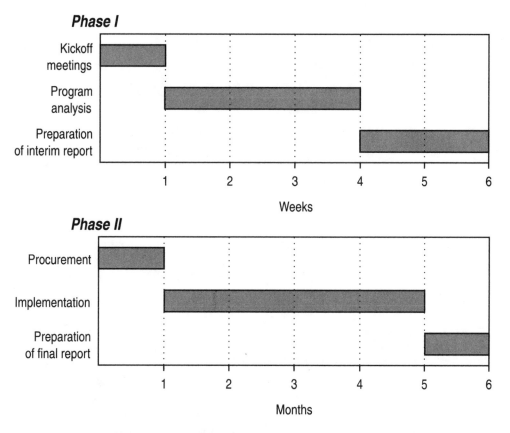

Figure 7. If graphs are shown side by side, be sure to use the same units of measurement (in this case, either weeks or months—not both).

- Is capitalization consistent on all graphics in the document? (Initial caps are usually much easier to read than all caps.)

- Are captions and titles placed consistently? If they are placed under the graphic, for example, is the amount of space between the graphic and the caption the same for every graphic in the document?

- Do all captions and titles appear in the same format? Here are some variations:

Figure 1. Revenue by Year

Figure 1. Revenue by year

Figure 1. *Revenue by Year*

figure 1—Revenue by Year

Figure 1: Revenue by Year

Figure 1
Revenue by Year

■ Are all figures numbered consistently? For long documents with many figures, it is better to number figures by chapter or section (for example, *Figure 3-2* for the second figure in Chapter 3) rather than consecutively throughout the document.

■ Are graphics referred to the same way throughout the document? Some documents distinguish between figures (graphics) and tables by having a separate numbering scheme for each. To get around the problem of having to decide whether an item is a figure or a table (it is not always obvious), you can call them all *exhibits* and have one numbering scheme throughout the document.

TYPES OF GRAPHICS

Business graphics: *line charts, bar charts, pie charts, organization charts, and flow charts.* These types of graphics are the most common because they are the easiest to create. It no longer takes an artist to display business data visually; most business software can generate line charts, bar charts, and pie charts with only a few keystrokes. Here are some things to look for when proofreading business graphics.

■ *Line charts.* This chart format is often used to show results over time or to show trends by comparing the progress of several different elements (as in Figure 8). Each line represents the connection of data points.

– Are the axis labels given, and are they correct?

– Are the divisions of each axis labeled? Do the axis labels look too cluttered because too many tick marks are labeled (as in Figure 9)?

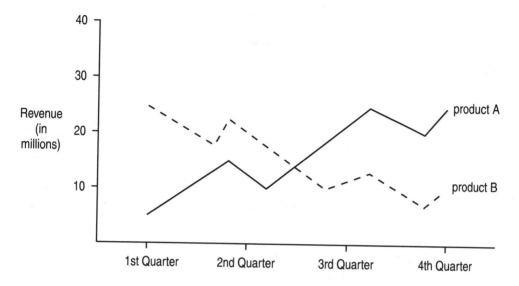

Figure 8. This line chart compares the revenue generated by two different products over the course of a year.

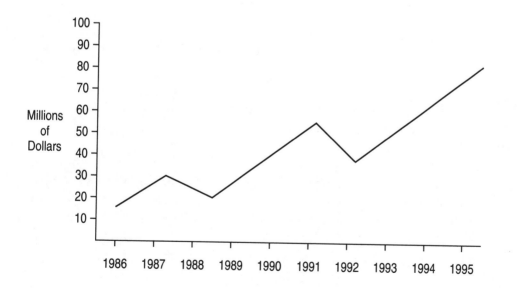

Figure 9. This graph has too many tick marks and labels for the information presented. It is not always necessary to label every tick mark.

Labeling only every few tick marks can produce a cleaner looking graph that is easier to follow (Figure 10):

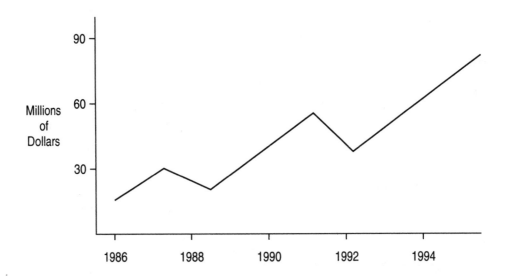

Figure 10. Here is the same graph as the one shown in Figure 9 but with fewer axis labels. This version is much easier to read.

- If different line patterns are used, is a key given to define them (Figure 11)?

- Are too many line patterns or too many lines included on the same graph (Figure 12)? The eye can discern only about four different patterns without struggling.

■ *Bar charts.* Bar charts are used to compare elements or amounts that vary. The bars can be either vertical or horizontal. Sometimes the bars on the chart are not actually bars but are graphic elements related to the subject (Figure 13 on page 132) that are used to show height.

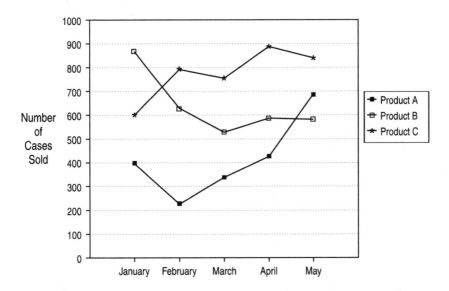

Figure 11.   Using a key or legend helps keep the information in the body of the chart uncluttered and easier to read. Simply defining the data lines in the text is not sufficient—the graphic should be able to stand by itself.

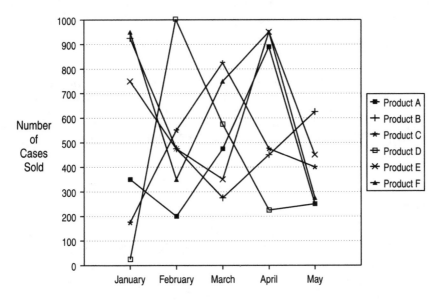

Figure 12.   Too many lines on one graph can confuse the reader. Look for other ways to present the information; in this example, separate charts for each product may be necessary.

Drug Use by City

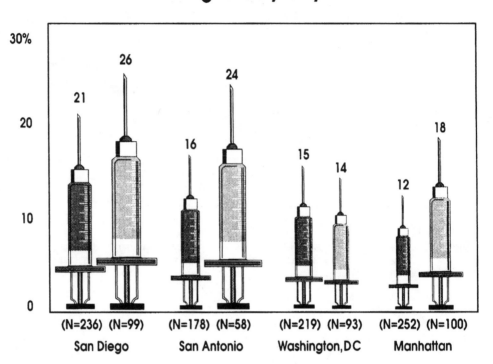

Figure 13. On this chart, hypodermic needles are used instead of plain bars. Using a graphic element that is related to the topic of the graph can add interest, but this type of chart can be deceiving because the reader's eye tends to compare the relative sizes of the syringes, not the end points that show the actual percentages.

Here are some things to check for when proofreading any type of bar chart:

– Are all bars (or graphic elements) the same width? (On the chart above, the syringes that represent the higher percentages are wider as well as taller, which could cause confusion.) Is the space between the bars consistent, and narrower than the bars themselves?

- Are all bars clearly labeled or coded? Will the reader be able to easily see what is being depicted?

- If a background grid is used to help the reader see the levels of the bars, is it clear without being obtrusive?

- If bars are segmented to show subelements, are the divisions clear and accurate?

■ *Pie charts.* The easiest way to illustrate the relative size of portions of a whole is with a pie chart. Pie charts make it easy for the reader to see the relationships between elements of a group, as in Figure 14:

Revenue by Branch Office

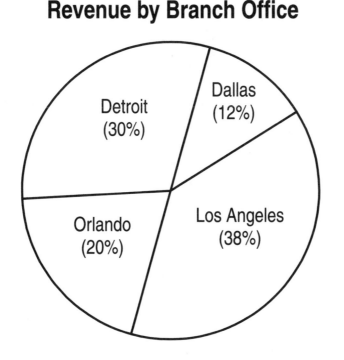

Figure 14. Pie charts are used to illustrate relationships. This chart shows the distribution of revenue by branch office.

Proofreading pie charts requires attention to the following elements:

– Is each slice of the pie either labeled or coded with a pattern or color? Is there a key that explains the coding scheme, and is it correct?

– If there is more than one pie chart in the document, is the same coding scheme used on every one?

– If the slices of the pie are labeled with percentages, do the percentages add up to 100? Are the slices the right size for their corresponding percentages?

– Are the slices of the pie large enough to be discernible? If the data indicate several very small percentages and one large one, a pie chart may not be the best type of graphic to use (Figure 15):

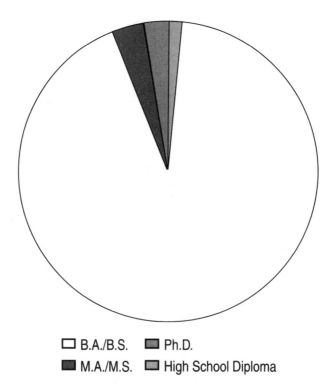

☐ B.A./B.S.   ■ Ph.D.
■ M.A./M.S.   ▨ High School Diploma

Figure 15. Because this pie chart consists of three very small slices and one huge one, it is an unattractive and hard-to-read format for presenting the data. A bar chart would work better in this case.

Small percentages can sometimes be combined into one category and shown as "other."

– Are there too many slices to show the information clearly? No more than six slices should be shown on one chart.

■ *Organization charts.* Almost every organization has one, and some organizations have many. Organization charts show the hierarchy of a company or team. The top box is usually the highest position, and the rest of the chart shows the reporting structure (Figure 16). Organization charts can show names of groups or divisions, names of individuals, or both. Although there are no strict rules regarding the format of organization charts, there are some conventions that can make them more understandable. Here are some things to check for:

– Are the sizes of the boxes consistent? The boxes on the chart do not all have to be the same size. Size is equated with importance, however, and the elements in large boxes will be interpreted as more important than the elements in small boxes.

– Are the levels of the boxes correct? Elements at the same level of importance should be exactly parallel at the tops of their boxes.

– Are the boxes linked together correctly? Direct reporting relationships are indicated by a solid line; indirect or secondary relationships are indicated by a dashed line.

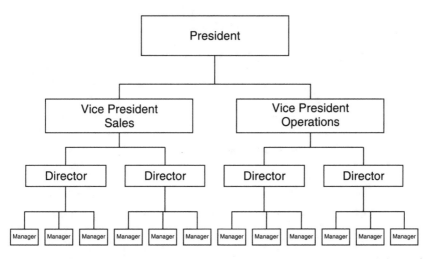

Figure 16. Companies use organization charts to show reporting relationships and offer a visual representation of a company's scope.

- *Flow charts.* Flow charts show the steps in a process. They are much more standardized than organization charts; all of the shapes and symbols used in flow charts have specific meanings. A good flow chart can summarize for the reader concepts that would take hundreds of words to explain in text. A poor flow chart can leave the reader lost in a maze of shapes and arrows, as in Figure 17:

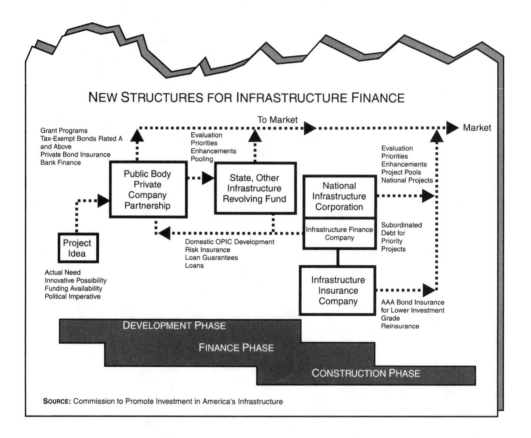

NEW STRUCTURES FOR INFRASTRUCTURE FINANCE

SOURCE: Commission to Promote Investment in America's Infrastructure

Figure 17. This poorly designed flow chart sends the reader in circles.

A careful review of flow charts includes checking the following items:

- Are the correct symbols used for the steps in the process? For example, one format uses circles for the first and last steps in the process, rectangles for the steps along the way, and diamonds to indicate points at which the process can go in one of two ways.

- Are arrows added to all of the lines that connect boxes so that the reader knows which way to go?
- Does the flow chart begin in the upper left corner, and is the beginning clearly labeled as such?
- Is the flow chart understandable, or does it have too many elements for the reader to sort out?
- Are abbreviations clear, or is there a key to define any elements that must be abbreviated to save space?

Reviewing and correcting these items will help ensure that the reader will grasp the process being depicted on the flow chart. A good flow chart can be understood immediately (Figure 18).

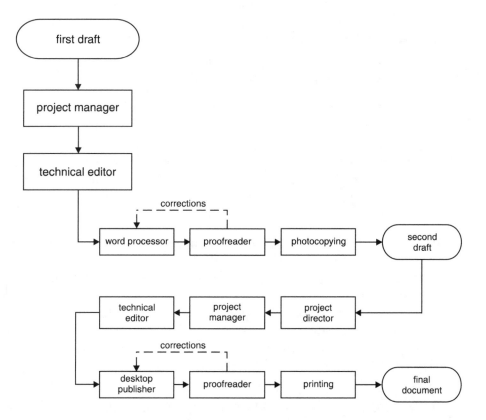

Figure 18. This flow chart shows a clear path from beginning to end and uses different symbols to differentiate the products (ovals) from the steps in the process (rectangles).

Technical illustrations. Unlike business graphics, most technical illustrations are created by graphic artists who use sophisticated illustrating software. With business graphics, there may not be an "original" to proofread against, because usually they are created directly from data. Technical illustrations, however, can be proofread against the artist's source material—an author's rough sketches, for example, or photos of a product or piece of equipment. You do not have to be a technical expert to spot errors in these types of graphics.

- If you are proofreading graphics against rough sketches, are they reasonably similar? Are all the elements of the sketch included in the final graphic, and are the elements in correct proportion to one another?

- Are the labels properly positioned, and are the names of the elements spelled correctly? (Verify the spelling of any technical terms you do not recognize.) If there are arrows from the labels to the element they are indicating, are the arrows pointing to the correct spot?

- If abbreviations are used in the labels to save space, are they spelled out in the text so that the readers will understand them?

- Is the graphic sized properly so that the readers will be able to see the appropriate level of detail?

Photos. Even photos require a proofreader's eye to ensure that they are positioned correctly and are understandable. You may not be familiar with the subject matter of the photo, but you will usually be able to find errors when they occur.

- Does the caption accurately reflect what is shown in the photo? For example, if a list of names is given, do they correspond with the people in the photo? Even if you do not know the people in the photo, you can check to be sure there are the same number of names as people and that men's names are given for the men and women's names are given for the women. Often errors occur because the photo captions were written by someone who did not yet have the actual photos in hand.

- Is the photo sized correctly? Do the important elements show clearly, and has the unimportant background been cropped out adequately? Can the reader tell what the important elements of the photo are?

- Is the photo positioned correctly? Sometimes photos that were processed from negatives are inserted backward. This problem isn't always obvious; you can spot it by looking at an element of the photo that has words on it and seeing if they appear to be printed backward.

Design elements. Some graphics are included in documents as decoration rather than to illustrate particular information. Though these graphics are unlikely to contain the same kinds of errors as you may find in the other types, they still should be checked for consistency and proper placement.

- *Icons* are small, simple illustrations that call attention to a particular type of text (Figure 19). They should be checked to see that they are placed consistently. For example, if they are placed in the margin, the amount of space between the icon and the text should be the same in all instances. All icons should be approximately the same size.

Notes to Teachers

Figure 19. Icons like this pen and apple are often used with headings that are repeated throughout a document, making them easier for the reader to spot.

- *Drop caps* are oversized capital letters that begin the first word of a chapter or section (Figure 20). They should be the same size in each chapter, and they should be dropped to the same level throughout the document. A common error that desktop publishers make is to insert the drop cap, size it, and position it, but then forget to take out the regular-sized letter that it is supposed to replace.

- Clip art is copyright-free generic graphics that can be purchased for use in all types of documents. Clip art can be scanned from a paper copy or imported directly from an electronic file and can be modified in any way the user desires. Check carefully to see that it is positioned

'm waiting for the other shoe to drop. It goes with the territory. She's marching to a different drummer. It really blew my mind. That's just the tip of the iceberg.

It's time we starting swearing off certain expressions before our minds rot. It isn't that these ways of putting things weren't originally useful, clever, or apt; it's just that they retain all the sparkle of six-day-old Perrier.

Figure 20. Although drop caps are not usually this fancy, they are often used as a design element at the beginning of a chapter or article. The drop cap is usually the same typeface as the text, only much larger.

correctly, that it is used appropriately, and that it is reasonably consistent with the style of the rest of the graphics in the document.

- *Screens* are shaded areas within a document. They can be used to highlight portions of the text, such as warnings or critical notes, or to separate out parts of the text, such as sidebars. Desktop publishing and word processing programs allow the user to set percentages for screens—the higher the percentage, the darker the screen. Screens should be checked to be sure that they are not too dark (screens greater than 40 percent will obscure text rather than highlight it) and that the degree of shading is consistent throughout the document.

- *Rules* are lines that separate text elements. The thicker the rule, the more definitive the break in text. Thick rules could be used to separate main sections from one another, and thin rules could be used to separate subsections. Rules should be checked to ensure that the thickness is used consistently and that the same types of rules stop and start at the same place on the line throughout the document. Rules should be used sparingly and only if they unobtrusively help the reader follow the organization of the text.

■ *Bullets* are symbols that are used to set off elements in a list. Bullets can be round, square, or just about any other shape a desktop publishing or word processing program can provide. Bullets should be checked for positioning—the same amount of space should be used before each bullet and after each bullet throughout the text. They should also be checked for consistency—the same types of bullets should be used for the same levels of text throughout the document. For example, a square bullet could be used for the main elements in the list and a star-shaped bullet could be used for the subsections. Care should be taken not to use too many types of bullets within a single document.

The Six Most Common Errors Found in Graphics

1. The numerical values indicated by the slices of a pie chart do not add up to the total mentioned.

2. Too many different or distracting fills or line patterns are used on the same chart.

3. Graphics are set up to be viewed in color on the computer screen but are meaningless when printed out in black and white.

4. No key or legend is given to explain the coding scheme used.

5. Too much information is crammed into one chart, making it impossible to quickly compare individual data elements.

6. The chart format obscures the data and causes the reader to draw incorrect conclusions.

TABLES

If a table is created properly, it can help the reader understand detailed information quickly. If the conventions of table creation are ignored, the table may be useless to the reader. Here are some things to check for—in addition to proofreading the table word for word and number for number—that can help make the difference between a useful table and one the reader will skip over in frustration.

- For tables that contain totaled columns or rows of numbers, are the totals correct? If totals are given in both directions (across the rows and down the columns), are they both correct?

- Are rules in the table used consistently? For example, if major sections of the table are separated by rules of a heavier line weight than the rules within sections, has this heavier line been used throughout the table (and in others like it)? Note that the trend is to use as few rules as possible in tables and to rely instead on spacing to differentiate table sections.

- Are capitalization and abbreviations consistent? If all column headings are set in caps and lowercase, are all row headings set the same way?

- Is alignment consistent within the table? Short elements are better centered; long elements are better flush left. Whether the headings and table elements are flush left or centered, each section of the table (headings and body) should be treated the same way. If centering is used, the elements should be centered from left to right *and* from top to bottom throughout. If centering is used but one or more columns contain numbers with decimal points, the numbers in these columns should be aligned on the decimal rather than centered.

- Is there enough spacing between table elements to make the table legible? There should be at least two letter-spaces between elements; more if there are no rules between the columns and rows. The spacing should be determined by the widest element in the column.

- Do all columns and rows have headings? Headings may be omitted if the content of the list is obvious. For example, a list of all states doesn't need a heading that says "States." However, if only certain states are included, the heading might be "States Surveyed."

- Are any elements of the headings incorrectly repeated in the body of the table? For example, if the column heading says "Price (in U.S. Dollars)," it is not necessary to have a dollar sign before every number in the column.

- Are all column headings bottom-aligned? When some column headings are stacked and others are not, they should all end on the same line:

Task	Budgeted Cost	Actual or Projected Cost

Column headings should not be more than three lines long. If column headings are rotated so that they run vertically to avoid having unnecessarily wide columns, they should all be left-justified.

- If a table is continued to another page, are the column heads repeated on the carried-over portion?

- Does the table contain any unnecessary words that make it look cluttered? Table elements do not need to be complete sentences. Also, it is not necessary to follow the same abbreviation conventions that are used in the text—using space efficiently is the primary consideration with tables.

- If there are footnotes or references within the table, are they indicated correctly? References within tables must use a different numbering scheme than those within the text to avoid confusion. Try to avoid using numerals for footnote references in a table that contains numerical data; it is safer to use superscript lowercase letters or traditional symbols (asterisks, daggers, double asterisks, double daggers, and so on). Footnotes and reference indicators within a table should run in order horizontally and then vertically (that is, across one row and then down to the next, rather than down one column and over to the next).

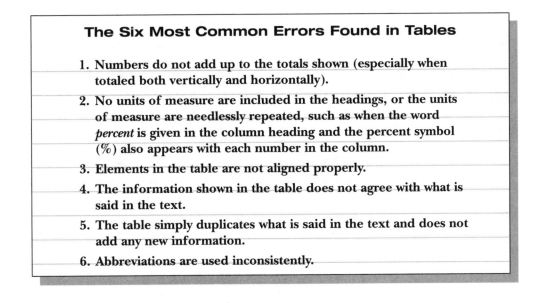

The Six Most Common Errors Found in Tables

1. Numbers do not add up to the totals shown (especially when totaled both vertically and horizontally).
2. No units of measure are included in the headings, or the units of measure are needlessly repeated, such as when the word *percent* is given in the column heading and the percent symbol (%) also appears with each number in the column.
3. Elements in the table are not aligned properly.
4. The information shown in the table does not agree with what is said in the text.
5. The table simply duplicates what is said in the text and does not add any new information.
6. Abbreviations are used inconsistently.

CHECKING GRAPHICS AND TABLES WITHIN THE TEXT

Placement. Graphics and tables should be placed in the text as soon as possible after their first mention in text. Full-page tables and graphics should fall on the very next page after they are mentioned. If changes are made to the text after the graphics are positioned and the graphics are not "tied" electronically to their references, the text may reflow in such a way that the graphics are no longer in the correct place. Placement of graphics and tables should be rechecked after every revision cycle.

Sizing. Because graphics are often created in one software program and then imported into another, their final size is not always determined when they are being designed. Consequently, some adjustments may have to be made when graphics and text come together.

The same is true for tables. They may be created with a word processing, database, or spreadsheet program, but often they are imported into a desktop publishing program, where they undergo formatting changes to make them consistent with the rest of the document. Even if the tables are imported directly without any rekeying, errors can still creep in. When you are asked to proofread a document, you should ignore instructions like "Don't worry about checking the graphics and tables— they were all imported directly."

Relation to the text. Once the figures are sized and positioned in the text, the next step is to ensure that they are in the correct place. Do not rely solely on the figure number to verify proper placement—figures can easily become misnumbered when they are imported. The safest way to check placement is to read the portion of the text that mentions the figure, examine the figure itself, and confirm that they agree. If the text says "The revenue generated by Product A far exceeded that of Product B in 1994 (see Figure 3)" and Figure 3 is a pie chart that shows percentages of customers by geographic region, you will have caught a placement error. If you had simply skimmed the figure numbers to ensure that they ran consecutively, you would have missed it.

Also, be sure that the figure title is an accurate reflection of the figure itself. Titles can be switched just as easily as figure numbers, so do not take it for granted that the title that appears is what the author intended—analyze its meaning in addition to making sure the words are spelled right.

Table Terminology

Headnote:	The definition of the elements of the table; for example, *Thousands of Dollars.* Appears at the top of the table or as part of the table title.
Stub:	The far left column; that is, the one that carries the headings for the rows.
Boxhead:	The top row or rows; that is, the ones that carry the labels for the columns.
Decked headings:	Column headings that have primary and secondary levels; that is, the top head in a deck spans more than one column and has subheads (the second level of the deck) beneath it.
Field:	The main body of the table, excluding the headings and footnotes.
Cells:	The individual elements or boxes within the main body of a table.

THE DANGERS OF DESKTOP PUBLISHING SOFTWARE: COMMON ERRORS TO LOOK FOR

Desktop publishing has been both a blessing and a curse to people who produce business publications. It has been a blessing because it has enabled the average person to do what in the past only typesetters could do—create documents using an almost infinite variety of formats and typefaces. Desktop publishing has been a curse because every feature that gave us more new options also gave us new ways to make mistakes. Proofreaders—both professional and occasional—should be aware of the timesaving features that desktop publishing provides and the pitfalls those features can create if used incorrectly.

The best thing about desktop publishing is that so many routine type-setting functions can be done automatically. Desktop publishing software allows you to set up the format for a document all at once by using an electronic specification sheet. These specification sheets have different names in different programs (*style sheets, master pages,* and *templates,* to name a few), but they all work basically the same way. You can set the specifications, insert codes into your word-processed text file, and then import the file directly into the format you selected. Then it becomes easy to make global changes to the document. For example, if you want all the second-level heads in the document to be 10-point Times Roman, but later you decide that 9-point type would look better, you only have to change the original specification; then all the heads in the document that are coded as second-level heads will change automatically.

The most common complaint about desktop publishing is that errors seem to creep in mysteriously. People who do not actually use desktop publishing software have trouble understanding why something can be correct in one version of a document and wrong in the next when no changes were made to that particular part of the document.

Here are some of the most common "mystery" errors that you will find in desktop-published text, along with brief explanations of how they occur.

Text that was once there has disappeared. When text vanishes, it is usually near a figure, box of text, or some other graphic element. Desktop programs allow you to create "frames" or "windows," which are like empty boxes into which you can import graphics that were scanned or created in other programs. The software sees all the format elements as separate objects, and it is possible to place one object on top of another and block out the bottom one. If you add a box that is too big for a page without instructing the software to move the text down to make room for it, it will simply cover up the text that is there.

This type of error is often introduced in the final stages of document preparation. Boxes are sometimes put into a document initially as place-holders for graphics and photos that are not yet available; they are later adjusted to the proper size when the graphics are ready to be added. If boxes are made larger but the text is not adjusted, they can cover up text that is actually still in the electronic file but will not show on the page when it is printed.

When you are proofreading a document in which graphics have been added or resized, check the text around them carefully.

Certain characters that appeared on the printout of the word processing file have disappeared from the desktop publishing file, even though the text was supposedly imported directly. One of the wonderful things about desktop publishing is that most programs can accept text that was created in another software program. That means that you can produce a draft with your favorite word processing program, and then someone else can format the text without having to retype it. That means that you do not have to proofread every word; you can just check the formatting—right?

Wrong. Unfortunately, there are a variety of ways that errors can be introduced after the file is converted. The most common is human error, but another has to do with the conversion itself. If the file contains any special characters, such as mathematical symbols or foreign letters, they may not translate directly. If the desktop publishing program does not recognize the code for the symbol that appears in the word processing file, it will either substitute something else or drop the character altogether.

When you are proofreading material that contains special characters, you should look at them very closely and make sure they match the ones in the draft document.

Graphics are no longer in the right place. This problem is related to the disappearing text problem; they both have to do with the way text flows around graphic elements. Desktop programs give you a choice: You can either "anchor" the graphics boxes to a particular spot in the document and have the text flow around the boxes whenever new material is added, or you can "tie" the boxes to the text that refers to them, in which case the boxes move to a different position in the document along with that text whenever new material is added.

Both options can be useful in some situations but cause problems in others. For example, let's say you are producing a brochure that describes a new product that your company is introducing. You want the picture of the product to appear at the bottom of the first page. If you later decide to add text to your introduction, you will not want the picture to move to page 2; you want it to be the first thing the reader sees. In this case, you would "anchor" the graphic box for the picture to the bottom of page 1.

However, suppose that several pages later in your document, you refer to a technical illustration of how the product is constructed. One sentence says "The diagram below shows the internal components of the product." You will want that graphic box to appear right below that sentence no matter what changes you make to the rest of the text. If you add text to the introduction, you want the graphic to move down automatically. In this case, you would "tie" the graphic to the sentence that refers to it by inserting a code into the text.

If the graphics are not correctly tied to their in-text references and changes are made to the document, the graphics may no longer appear on the correct page. Likewise, if graphics are not anchored where you want them, they will float along to other pages when text is added ahead of them.

When you are proofreading a document that you did not create yourself, you will have no way of knowing if the graphics are tied or anchored correctly; the codes are invisible. Be sure to check the positioning of graphics each time a document is revised.

Headings that were once correct are suddenly in the wrong typeface, even though they were not changed. These "wrong font" errors occur when a font (or typeface) is specified on the desktop publishing program's electronic specification sheet but is not available on the printer being used. Different laser printers have different fonts "loaded," or available for use. Just because a document prints a certain way on one printer does not mean it will look the same when printed on another. When the desktop publishing software tries to print a document but encounters a font that is specified in the document but is not available on the current printer, it substitutes a "default" font in its place. Often the default font is plain old-fashioned Courier, which looks like typewriter type, so the error is obvious. Sometimes, though, the default font is whatever happens to be the first one on the alphabetical list of the current printer's available fonts. (This is why the Avant Garde typeface sometimes appears mysteriously in documents where it is not used at all; its name starts with an *A*.)

You may experience this type of error when you set up a document on your computer at the office, print it out, and then take it home to revise on your home computer. You may have the same desktop publishing software in both places, but if your printer at home has fewer fonts than the one at the office, your document may not look the same when you print it out at home.

If you are proofreading a document that someone else created, find out if all versions were output by the same printer. If they were not, you will know to check the typefaces carefully.

All the type throughout the document looks slightly larger (or smaller) than it did in the previous iteration, even though the font specifications were not changed. Even if you have the same fonts on your printer at home as you have on your office printer, you can still run into problems. Fonts are sold under different brand names, and even though they may have the same family name (such as Times Roman), they may look slightly different from one brand to the next. The differences are subtle; at a glance, the typefaces from two different brands look alike. However, even very minor differences in the shapes of the characters can add up to spacing differences, which cause lines of text to wrap differently and pages to flow differently.

If you are proofreading two versions of a document that appear to be printed in the same typeface but do not match up correctly, the problem may be that the documents were printed on printers that contained fonts of different brands.

Footnotes do not fall on the same page as their references in the text. Footnote numbering is an automatic feature that appears as an option in most desktop publishing programs. You can number the footnotes and position them on the pages manually, or you can let the software do it for you. If the automatic feature is not used, the footnotes have to be manually repositioned every time the text reflows.

If you are proofreading a document that contains footnotes, do not take it for granted that the automatic feature was used. Check to be sure the footnotes fall on the pages where they are referenced in the text each time the document is revised.

The document was revised, and now text ends in the middle of a line in some places. One of the very last steps in formatting a document is adjusting the line breaks. The desktop publishing software breaks lines automatically according to the line widths that you specify, but sometimes you have to fine-tune a few of the lines to keep them from looking too spacey or too squashed (for right-justified text) or too jagged (for ragged-right text) by inserting manual line breaks.

Sometimes line breaks are adjusted too soon, before all changes to the text have been incorporated. If changes are made to the text after these manual line breaks are inserted and words end up in new positions on the line, the line breaks do not go away. If a word that was once at the end of a line moves to the center of a line and a manual line-break code appears after the word, the text will jump to a new line after the code.

If you are proofreading a document that was revised late in the production cycle, after it had gone all the way to final formatting, pay special attention to line breaks.

Big gaps appeared between paragraphs after text was added. Desktop publishing programs allow you to specify the amount of space that is to be left between paragraphs in the document by indicating the spacing measurement on the electronic specification sheet. For example, if you want a half inch between paragraphs, you set the specification sheet accordingly and insert an end-of-paragraph code after the last character in every paragraph by hitting the *enter* key. In word processing programs, each time you hit the *enter* key you simply add a single line space. If you have set the paragraph spacing for a half inch and you hit *enter* four times, you will get two full inches of space rather than just four line spaces.

This otherwise helpful feature creates problems if you try to "cheat" when adjusting page breaks. If you try to force a paragraph to the next page by hitting *enter* a few times instead of inserting a page break code, spacing problems will appear if the document is further revised. The pages may look fine the first time the document is printed out, but if text reflows and the two paragraphs you tried to separate appear on the same page, they will have a big gap in between them.

If you are proofreading a document that someone else created and you run across mysterious gaps in the text, it is probably because extra paragraph codes were inserted. The only way to tell for sure is to look at the document on the computer screen.

The table-of-contents page does not match the text, even though it was supposedly created automatically. One of the handiest automatic features of desktop publishing programs (and most word processing programs, for that matter) is the table-of-contents generator. You can insert a code by every heading that should appear in the table of contents, and the software will create it for you automatically. The problem is that you have to remember to regenerate the table of contents each time you make revisions to the document; otherwise the page numbers may be wrong and the headings may not correspond exactly to those in the text.

If you are proofreading a document for which this feature was used, make sure a new table of contents is generated after every revision cycle is complete.

The Difference Between Proportional Type and Monospaced Type

Unless you use a word processing program that allows you to work in WYSIWYG (what you see is what you get) mode, your text looks much different on the computer screen than when it is printed out. The lines break differently, and columns of text align differently. That is because the words on the screen are monospaced, and depending on the font you select, the words on the printed page are likely to be proportionally spaced.

With monospaced type, each letter takes up an equal amount of space on the line. With proportional type, the shape of the letter determines how much space it takes up: An *i* takes very little space, and a *w* takes much more. Most printers have a selection of typefaces that includes both monospaced type and proportional type. Typewriters can produce only monospaced type. For professional-looking documents, proportional type is the better choice.

■ EMERGENCY PROOFREADING: THE BARE MINIMUM

The scenario is a common one: It is noon and you are just about to leave for lunch. Someone rushes into your office carrying a huge stack of pages and says, "Can you proofread my report? It has to go out the door by 6:00 p.m." You estimate by looking at the size of the stack that the report is about 300 single-spaced pages long. Normally it would take about 60 hours to do a thorough word-for-word proofreading of a document this size. When you advise your panic-stricken colleague of this fact, the response is hysterical laughter. What do you do next?

How Much Time Do You Have?

Assuming that it is not within your power to renegotiate the deadline, you have to do whatever you can within the time available. The first step is to figure out exactly how much time that is.

It is fairly safe to assume that any proofreading you do will reveal some errors that need to be fixed. To figure out how much time you have to proofread, you also have to consider how much time it will take to make revisions and check those revisions to be sure they were made correctly. Here is a rule of thumb: It will take approximately 1 hour to revise, print out, and check corrections on the amount of material you can review in 2 hours. (Of course, this time varies depending upon the condition of the manuscript—the revisions may go much more quickly, but when calculating revision time, it is best to assume the worst case.) In this scenario, you have from noon until 6:00 p.m.—a total of 6 hours (assuming you are skipping lunch). That means that you should spend no more than 4 hours reviewing the document before you turn it over to the person who has to make the revisions.

What Do You Look For?

Assuming that the panic-stricken person who brought you the document gave you no specific instructions about what to look for and what to ignore, here is a list of things to check, in order of importance:

1. Check the pagination. Make sure that the pages are numbered sequentially. If the document is to be copied double-sided, check to see that blank pages have been inserted properly and that all odd-numbered pages will fall on a right-hand page.

2. Proofread the cover page and title page word for word. Make sure that the date is correct and that the company's and author's names are spelled correctly on both pages.

3. Flip each page and look for any glaring errors such as a missing figure or printer glitches such as grossly uneven toner coverage.

4. Flip each page again (make a separate pass) and look at the format to see that heads and subheads are the correct size and typeface, spacing and indention are consistent, running heads are correct, and margins are the right size.

5. Check the table of contents against the text. Make sure that all of the chapters or sections (and subsections, if appropriate) are included and that the wording in the table of contents matches the text. Check the page numbers against the text.

6. Scan the chapter or section numbers to see that they are in order and that none were omitted. Also check anything else that is sequentially numbered, such as subsections or lists.

7. Look at the graphics and tables. Make sure they are numbered correctly and that their titles correctly describe what appears.

You have probably noticed that none of the seven items listed so far involve actually proofreading text. You should check these items first and then start reading word for word only if there is time left.

8. Read the preface, executive summary, or any other introductory material that the reader is likely to look at first.

9. Read the conclusion or final summary section.

10. Read the last line on each page and the first line of the page that follows to ensure that text has not been dropped or repeated.

11. Read the heads and subheads.

12. Read the first sentence (or first paragraph, if there is time) of each chapter or section.

How many of the items on this list you can cover will depend on your experience with emergency proofreading and—more importantly—the condition of the document. The more errors you find, the longer it will take you to move on to the next step. You may find it useful to keep a list of the items you checked so that if the deadline is extended and the document comes back to you for a closer look, you will know where you left off.

WORKING WITH THE AUTHOR

After you spend a couple of hours looking through the document, you will have some idea of its overall condition. You will not have had the chance to find every typographical error, format inconsistency, or other glitch, but the number of things you *did* find is probably indicative of what else remains. At this point you should confer with the person who asked you to check the document—let's assume it is the author of the material—and show him or her the kinds of things you found. If there are many errors, the author may decide to change the schedule and take the time to fix them and give the document a more detailed review. If the errors are what the author considers minor (maybe this is just a first draft), he or she may opt to ignore your marks for this round but incorporate your changes in the next cycle. In either case, it is up to you as the designated proofreader to give the author a quick status report at this point. If you don't, you may spend time making changes that are not wanted and jeopardize the deadline unnecessarily.

THE ASSEMBLY LINE APPROACH

One option under emergency circumstances is to set up an "assembly line." That means that you sit right beside the person who will make the revisions and hand pages to him or her as you find errors. The problem with working this way is that it is very likely that you will find errors late in the game that affect pages that have already been revised once, necessitating that those pages be revised again and printed out again.

This duplication of effort can be avoided (or at least minimized) if you start the assembly line only after you have spent the initial two-thirds of the total time reviewing the document and after you have conferred with the author. Then you can begin working directly with the person making the revisions by checking them as the pages come out of the printer.

THE FINAL HOUR

In an emergency situation, the biggest mistakes are often made in the final stage because everyone is rushing to beat the clock. Here are some silly but typical glitches to watch out for:

- When you are checking final corrections and replacing the marked-up pages in the document, be sure to pull out the incorrect pages. Also, be sure to insert the correct pages once you have checked them. It is easy to pull out the marked-up page, carefully check it against the corrected page, and then throw the good page in the trash can and reinsert the page with the error.

- Watch for text reflow on corrected pages. Even if you are checking a change that involved only one word, it is possible that the addition of that single word could cause text to reflow in a way that affects many pages. Scan the last word in each line on the corrected page and look to see that the lines end the same way on the marked-up page. If the text has reflowed, check every page that was reprinted.

- Make sure that all the corrections you marked were actually made. It is best to flag marked pages with a Post-it or paper clip so you and the person making the corrections can find them easily. It is easy to skip over a mark or two when you are in a hurry.

- Be sure that new errors are not introduced when corrections are made. Do not take it on faith that the revisions were made accurately—check them carefully. Where words were inserted, read several words on either side of the insertion. Where words were deleted, read the entire sentence to be sure it still makes sense.

- Before handing over the document to your now much-relieved colleague, check the page sequence one last time to spot any marked-up pages that were not put aside when the corrected pages were inserted.

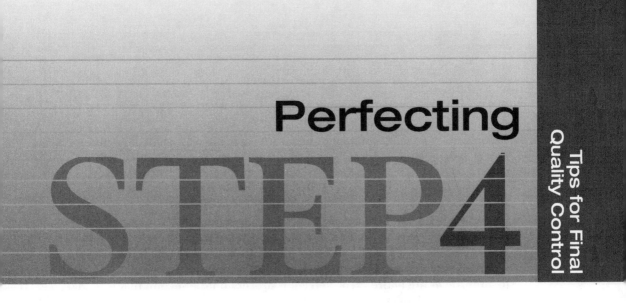

Perfecting

STEP 4

▪ ONE LAST LOOK: THE FINAL QUALITY CONTROL REVIEW

The fourth step in the error-prevention process—the quality control review—is the most critical. Unfortunately, it is also the step that most people skip. Proofreading has traditionally been the last step in the publications process before printing, but there is plenty of evidence to indicate that even several rounds of thorough, careful proofreading are not enough. We've said that there is no magical way to prevent errors, but if there is indeed a secret to high-quality publications, this is it: *Add one more review even though you think everything is perfect.*

THE DIFFERENCES BETWEEN EDITING, PROOFREADING, AND THE QUALITY CONTROL REVIEW

The final quality control review is entirely different from editing and proofreading. Instead of looking at the meaning of the words, as an editor does, or looking at each individual character of the text, as a proofreader does, the quality control reviewer looks at the document *as a whole,* as the readers will. The editor does not always see the document in finished form, and the proofreader frequently does not have the entire document at once, so there are still some errors that can slip through.

Making Changes—When Is It Too Late?

Technically, it is never too late to make changes to a document. The question is, how much you are willing to sacrifice in terms of cost, quality, and time to incorporate the change?

The trouble with changes is that in the process of making them, you may introduce new errors and inconsistencies. For example, the editor may have taken great pains to ensure that the number style was consistent throughout the document, but if at the last minute someone adds a sentence that contains a number, the addition may not conform to the style the editor enforced throughout. To be sure changes do not introduce errors, you have to go through the entire error-detection process on the section that is being changed: The changes have to be checked for editorial correctness and consistency, incorporated into the existing text (which may necessitate some reworking of the layout), and proofread (including checking any text that has reflowed). If the document has already received its final quality control review, this step should be repeated as well.

How much do changes cost? Your actual costs will depend upon your particular publication process and your general costs of doing business, but here is a rule of thumb: If it costs $1 to make a change to draft text, it will cost $10 to make the change after the document has been edited and laid out, and it will cost $100 to make the change after the document has been edited, laid out, proofread, corrected, and quality-control checked.

What kinds of errors can the quality control review unearth? Both large and small:

- an introduction that mentions a glossary that does not appear in the document
- a subtitle on the title page that no longer reflects the content of the document
- a figure without a caption
- a running head that does not match its chapter title
- an empty box that was supposed to contain a photo
- a format inconsistency between the preface and the rest of the document.

These errors, and many more, occur when a document is being prepared on a tight schedule, when changes are being made at the last minute, or when the text is divided among several proofreaders and no one person sees the entire document at once.

There are two requirements that must be met for the quality control review to be most effective:

- The document must be complete and all together. The cover and title page must be included, all graphics must be in place, the index must be complete, and every last error marked by the proofreader must be corrected and checked. The quality control review will not accomplish its intended goal if the document is given to the reviewer incomplete or in pieces.

- The review must be performed by someone who has never seen the document before. This "fresh pair of eyes" is the key to this step. This review should never be performed by the person who has shepherded the document through all the steps in the process and is intimately familiar with it. The bigger the error, the less likely this person is to see it at this stage of production.

When It Absolutely, Positively Has to Be Perfect

We all would like our documents to be absolutely error-free, but sometimes a typographical error could be a matter of life or death (not the life or death of a proofreader, but the life or death of someone using the document). For example, in medical books that instruct doctors and pharmacists on dosage levels, one incorrect number could result in a fatality.

Obviously, achieving the highest possible level of accuracy is an expensive proposition; many review cycles are required. Here is an approach that is used by some professional publishers of critical data:

- The document is proofread separately by four professional proofreaders. Their marks are compiled onto one copy, and the revisions are made.

- The document is completely proofread again by another proofreader—one who has not seen the document before.

- If errors are found, the corrections are made and the document is completely proofread again by yet another proofreader.

- Once the document is proofread and no errors are found, it is proofread two more times.

WHO SHOULD PERFORM THE QUALITY CONTROL REVIEW?

Ideally, the quality control review should be performed by someone with strong editorial skills, a sharp eye for detail, and a familiarity with document production methods and conventions. Under less-than-ideal circumstances, when such a wizard is not available, the review can be performed by any reasonably alert person who has not seen the document before.

One company began enforcing a strict "fresh pair of eyes" policy after a startling experience taught them the importance of the final quality control review. The company's editorial staff had spent several long days and nights producing a newsletter under a tight deadline. When the printer's truck was on its way to pick up the camera-ready pages, the company's mailroom clerk, who had no editorial experience, was looking at the pages as he was putting them in the envelope and found an error that had been missed by entire team of exhausted professional editors and proofreaders. The moral of the story is that you should not skip the final quality control review just because there is no quality control expert on hand; any review is better than none.

HOW TO "QC" A DOCUMENT

What do you look for when you are performing the quality control review? The answer depends on the time available and the level of quality desired. As a general rule, check the most basic elements first; then move on to the details as time allows. You will not receive congratulations for finding an extra space between two words on page 322 if there is a typo on the cover of the document. Here are some additional pointers:

- Ask the person who is responsible for the document to point out any special areas of concern. For example, maybe the proofreader found a lot of errors in the graphics, so they should get a close look. Also, ask the person to define the priorities if time is short. ("We know the sizing of the figures is not consistent; don't worry about that. Just be sure they are all numbered consecutively—we had to add a few at the last minute.")

- Look at the document as the reader would. Start at the beginning, and glance at each page to become familiar with the document before you take a closer look.

- Look at the pages for their overall visual effect before you read the words.

- Mark everything you find—except the most egregious errors—on Post-its that can be removed easily if it turns out that the page is acceptable as is. There may not be time to fix everything, and some decisions may have to be made about what can be fixed and what cannot.

- Flag anything that looks odd or seems confusing to you. Do not get too bogged down trying to figure out what was intended. If something is not obvious to you, it is likely that the readers of the document will react the same way.

- Speak up the minute you find a major problem. For example, if the first thing you notice is that the running head that appears on every page of the document contains a typographical error, let someone know immediately. If time is critical, corrections can begin while you continue your review.

- Use a checklist, particularly if you do not perform quality control reviews on a regular basis. Customize the checklist to reflect the priorities established for the document at hand.

Designing a Checklist—An Example

If you have a particular type of publication that you produce regularly, a checklist can be an excellent aid to the quality control review process. To design a customized checklist for your own publication, simply identify the elements that should be consistent and the areas where errors tend to occur. Update your checklist whenever you start seeing a new kind of recurring error.

Here is an example of a checklist for a monthly newsletter:

1. Are the date and issue number correct?
2. Are the running heads correct?
3. Are the company logo and address correct?
4. Are cross-references correct?
5. Is the table of contents correct?
6. Are the "continued from" lines correct?
7. Are the "continued on" lines correct?
8. Are the graphics positioned correctly?
9. Are the end-of-article dingbats used consistently?
10. Are the head sizes consistent, and are the heads free of typos?
11. Are the page numbers correct?

AFTER THE QUALITY CONTROL REVIEW

The most important thing to remember when planning for the quality control step is to allow time to fix any errors that are found. This seemingly obvious point is often overlooked. The tendency is to schedule the quality control review for the day the document is scheduled to go out the door, but then there is no time to make final revisions and check them one last time. The assumption, of course, is that everything will be perfect before this last review or that the corrections will be so minor that they will take only a short time to make. Ideally, this is the case, but you have to be prepared in case something major turns up. As a rule of thumb, you should allow one-fourth of the total time it took to lay out or format the document to make final changes. For example, if the layout step took 4 days, schedule the quality control review for 2 days before the final deadline, allowing 1 day for final corrections.

HOW TO FIND AT LEAST ONE ERROR THAT EVERYONE ELSE HAS MISSED

Not all offices have professional proofreaders and editors on staff, and very few have full-time quality control specialists who are responsible for the quality of final published products. However, most people who produce documents understand the value of a review by a "fresh pair of eyes." So even if you are not the company's resident eagle eye, you may be called upon to give someone else's document a final look. You may wonder what you could possibly find that all the other reviewers overlooked, particularly if you are not familiar with the subject matter of the document.

If you have never seen the document before, you have an advantage when it comes to catching errors: Your eyes will take nothing for granted. Even the most carefully prepared documents may still contain a few subtle but significant errors. Look at the following elements, and you may become the hero that saves the entire team from embarrassment.

- Check all pagination. If the front matter is paginated with roman numerals, are they in the proper sequence? If the document will be printed double-sided, will all odd-numbered pages fall on the right and all even-numbered pages fall on the left? Do all new chapters or sections begin on a right-hand page? Have blank pages been inserted in the proper places, and have they been accounted for in the pagination?

■ Check the table of contents against the text. Are all the head levels listed? Is the wording exactly the same as it is in the text? Are the page numbers correct?

■ Read all running heads and running footers; do not read only the first one and assume that they were generated automatically and therefore must be correct. Do the running heads reflect the correct chapter title, and is the wording of the title exactly the same as it appears on the first page of the chapter (or suitably abbreviated)? Has the same typeface been used throughout?

■ Read all heads. Chances are they have been only skimmed by everyone along the way and may still contain errors.

■ Read the first few lines after each head.

■ Read page transitions to look for dropped or duplicated text.

■ Check anything that is in alphabetical order. An index, a list of references, acknowledgments with a list of names—these are the places where alphabetization errors lurk.

■ Check the order of numerical listings. If the text says that there are five steps to assemble the product, make sure that five steps are actually given and that they are numbered consecutively. Likewise, if the head levels are numbered, make sure the numbering tracks throughout the document.

■ Check all endnotes and footnotes. Are they mentioned in the text? Are they numbered consecutively?

■ Look for pairs. Parentheses, brackets, and double and single quotation marks must come in pairs. Read all equations—even if you don't understand the meaning, you can look for pairs.

■ Look for "placeholders"—symbols or letters used to hold the place for information that will be filled in later. For example, XXX might be used in cross-references ("see page XXX for a more detailed description of this item") until the pagination is final. These placeholders are often forgotten and can be easy to spot. Once the cross-references have been filled in, check them to be sure they are accurate. Is the detailed description really on page 29 as promised?

**The Five Most Common Problems
That Are Discovered at the Last Minute,
Even After Everyone Has Checked Everything**

1. Incorrect pagination
2. Table of contents that does not match the text
3. Incorrectly numbered graphics or tables
4. A typo in a running head
5. A typo on the cover or the title page

AFTER "CAMERA-READY": WHAT TO LOOK FOR WHEN CHECKING PRINTING AND PHOTOCOPYING

The term *camera-ready* means that a document is ready to be reproduced. Final revisions have been made, the quality control review has been performed, any errors revealed by the quality control review have been fixed, and everyone in the process has signed off on the document. Even after a document is camera-ready, there are still a few more checkpoints in the process. Most documents are reproduced by either offset printing or photocopying, and there are different types of problems that you should watch for, depending on which process is used.

OFFSET PRINTING

The printing process is extremely complex. Although you do not have to be an expert on the process to ensure that your document looks good when it is printed, it helps to have a basic understanding of what you should look for at the checkpoints in the process and the things that can go wrong.

Bluelines and color proofs. If a document is being professionally printed (as opposed to photocopied), you will get an opportunity to see a preview of what the final printed product will look like, in the form of a "proof." There are many different types of printing proofs; the most common type is called a *blueline.*

The blueline is made from the negative films that the printer makes by photographing your camera-ready pages. (Negatives can also be made directly from your electronic file.) These negatives are eventually used to make the printing plates that go on the printing press, but before the plates are made, the images on the negatives must be checked for quality and accuracy. The blueline is created by shining light through the negatives onto special light-sensitive paper. The paper turns blue wherever light hits it, so the text and graphics of your document show up on the page in blue and the background is white. (You will notice that even the background starts to turn light blue once the blueline is removed from its envelope and is exposed to the light of your office.)

At the blueline stage, you do not get to see the actual paper and ink colors of the final printed piece. For documents that are printed in more than one color, especially those in which color is critical (for example, when you are reproducing a photo and the printed piece must match the original), you should also request a set of color proofs.

At the blueline stage you are looking for errors the printer may have made in preparing the document for the press. This is not a time to read the document one more time and change a few words here and there. Changes are extremely expensive to make at this stage, so only the most embarrassing errors should be fixed once the blueline has been made. Even in the unlikely event that you have an unlimited budget and money is no object, making changes at the blueline stage is still inadvisable. Printers schedule their print jobs very carefully to make the most of every hour of available press time. When you make changes, your job has to be rescheduled. The printer may have to rush it through so as not to jeopardize other deadlines, and you may end up with a less-than-perfect product as a result.

When you receive a blueline from the printer, you should also get back your camera-ready pages so that you can check the blueline against them. The camera-ready pages go back to the printer when you return the blueline.

If you are not familiar with the printing process, the best bet is to have the blueline reviewed by someone who understands the process and knows the kinds of things that can go wrong. If an expert is not available, here are some basic things you can look for:

- Is there any broken type?

- Are there any spots, specks, or scratch marks on the pages?

- Are the margins and pagination correct?

- Are the photos and art in the correct position, and are they the proper size?

- Are the color breaks correct as marked? (Everything will appear as blue on the blueline, but the printer should mark any places where color will appear in the final piece.)

- For small documents such as brochures and newsletters, is the piece folded correctly?

Circle any errors or imperfections that you find. Even if you are not sure whether what you see is an actual error or just a flaw in the paper itself, mark it anyway so that the printer can check the negatives.

The printer will probably include a form with the blueline for you to sign, authorizing them to proceed with the job. You must tell the printer either (1) that the blueline is acceptable as is, (2) that they should make the changes indicated and proceed with the job, or (3) that they should make the changes and send you another blueline. If you have marked more than a few errors or changes on the blueline, it is best to request a second blueline so that you can check to be sure the errors were fixed. (Be sure to ask the printer if there is a charge for the second blueline so that you are not surprised when the bill arrives.) Also, when you send the marked-up blueline back, you should include a cover memo that explains the marks you made and summarizes any of your instructions or concerns.

PHOTOCOPYING

As with printing, there are a number of things that can go wrong when a document is being photocopied. Anyone who has ever used a copier knows how temperamental they can be and what problems they can cause when they malfunction. So that you never experience the frustration of polishing a document to near-perfection only to discover that the copies are incomplete or illegible, here are some tips about checking photocopies.

To ensure absolute quality, you will have to check every page of every copy. If the print run is large and it is not practical to check every copy, look at at least three different copies. Do not just pull the first three off the stack; try to check one from early in the run, one from the end of the run, and one from somewhere near the middle. Here are some things to look for:

- Are all the pages there? Flip all pages and look at the page numbers to see that none were missed.

- Do blank pages fall in the appropriate places? For double-sided copies, make sure all even-numbered pages fall on a left-hand page and all odd-numbered pages fall on a right-hand page.

- Are all pages straight? Sometimes paper slips in the copier's feeder, and the resulting copy is crooked.

- Did all pages get even toner coverage? Make sure there are no blobs or light spots.

- Does the left margin allow enough room for the binding? Make sure the binding does not cover up or punch through the text.

FINAL DELIVERY

When your printing or photocopying job is delivered, check it over carefully before you sign the delivery ticket. Once you sign for the job, you have accepted it as is.

- Check documents from several different boxes of the shipment. For large orders, take a random sampling from at least three different boxes.

- If the document was printed rather than photocopied, look for smeared ink. Smears can occur when the print run is packaged before it has time to dry. Also, check the trim. For most documents, the pages are printed on large sheets of paper and then cut apart and assembled. Make sure the pages were cut in the proper place and that there are no ragged edges.

- Check the quantity of your order. If you ordered a large number of copies, you will not be able to tell at a glance if they are all there. You don't have to open every box, but at least open one box and count the number of documents. Then multiply by the number of boxes you received. You will be surprised at how often you do not receive the entire order. Printers usually use the same type of boxes to package all their jobs, so part of your order can be easily left on the truck or on the loading dock. It is your responsibility to make sure you get what you pay for.

- Be sure the shipment includes your originals as well as the copies.

Conclusion

Creating, revising, polishing, and perfecting: Error prevention can be a frustrating task. Sometimes it seems that every time you think you are finished and the document is perfect, some new problem appears. Error prevention can also be fun, though. You are certain to feel enormous personal satisfaction when you find an error that everyone else has missed, saving your company money and embarrassment. Here are some final thoughts to keep in mind as you incorporate the four-step method into your document preparation procedures:

- **Don't abandon the four-step method when time is tight.** When everyone is rushing to meet a deadline, it is more important than ever to look for errors very carefully. When people rush, they make mistakes—lots of them. When the clock is ticking, the boss is yelling, and the client is waiting, the four-step method may seem like a waste of time. Experience has proven that it is not a timewaster but a lifesaver. Remember, you can end up spending much more time when you try to cut corners.

- **Never underestimate the negative impact of even a single error.** You may be tempted to think, "Our stuff may have a typo here and there, but it isn't *that* bad." Remember that your company's reputation is at stake whenever you send out printed material. Don't let people with low standards convince you that a few errors won't matter.

- **Remember that the guidelines presented in this book are just the basics.** There are many more types of errors that aren't covered here. Professional editors and proofreaders study and hone their skills for years to get to the point where they can make a document *virtually* error-free. If your company is producing a document for which quality is critical, and you don't trust your own error-detecting skills, consider hiring a professional.

Appendix A

ABBREVIATIONS

The following guide gives the abbreviations for a selection of business and technical terms. For many abbreviations, there is no one correct choice. For example, some sources list the abbreviation for volume as VOL (all capital letters with no period); others list vol. (lowercase with a period); still others list vol (lowercase with no period). Whichever style you follow, be sure to use a consistent approach.

This list is by no means comprehensive; you will encounter many more abbreviations than appear here, and some may even have different definitions. For a complete, up-to-date list, see the *Acronyms, Initialisms & Abbreviations Dictionary,* published annually by Gale Research and available in most libraries. This three-volume guide contains more than 3,800 pages of abbreviations and their definitions.

μm	micron
μmol	micromole
Ω	ohm
A	ampere
A/D	analog to digital
Å	angstrom
a.	acre
A.B.	*artium baccalaureus* (Latin, bachelor of arts)
A.D.	*anno Domini* (Latin, in the year of our Lord)
a.m.	*ante meridiem* (Latin, before noon)
A.M.	*artium magister* (Latin, master of arts)
aa	author's alteration
AAA	American Automobile Association

aac	average annual cost
aae	average annual earnings
abbr.	abbreviated; abbreviation
ABIOS	Advanced Basic Input-Output System
abr.	abridged
AC	alternating current
ACB	asynchronous communications base
ACL	access control list
ACP	Associate Computer Professional
ACU	automatic calling unit
ad inf.	*ad infinitum* (Latin, to infinity)
ad init.	*ad initium* (Latin, at the beginning)
ad int.	*ad interim* (Latin, in the meantime)
ad lib.	*ad libitum* (Latin, at will)
ad loc.	*ad locum* (Latin, at the place)
ADA	automatic dynamic analyzer
ADE	automatic dialing equipment
adj.	adjective
ADLC	asynchronous data line controller
ADPE	automated data processing equipment
adv.	adverb
aet.	*aetatis* (Latin, aged)
AF	audiofrequency
AFC	automatic frequency control
AFL	American Federation of Labor
AFT	automatic fine tuning
Ag	silver
AI	artificial intelligence
AID	Agency for International Development
AIDS	acquired immunodeficiency syndrome
AIS	automated information systems
Al	aluminum
ALCOA	Aluminum Company of America
ALGOL	algorithmic-oriented language
Alt	alternate
ALU	arithmetic logic unit

Am	americium
AM	amplitude modulation
AMA	American Medical Association
AMEX	American Express Company
AMOCO	American Oil Company
anon.	anonymous
ANSI	American National Standards Institute
AOC	automatic operation controller
APA	all points addressable
API	application program interface
app.	appendix
Ar	argon
ARC	AIDS-related complex
ARPANET	Advanced Research Projects Agency Network
art.	article
As	arsenic
ASAP	as soon as possible
ASCAP	American Society of Composers, Authors, and Publishers
ASCII	American Standard Code for Information Interchange
ASPI	asynchronous serial printer interface
ASR	automatic send-receive
at wt	atomic weight
At	astatine
ATG	arithmetic test generator
atm	standard atmosphere
ATM	automated teller machine
ATV	all-terrain vehicle
Au	gold
aux.	auxiliary
av	average
B	boron
b.	born
B.A.	bachelor of arts
B.C.	before Christ
B.D.	bachelor of divinity

B.S.	bachelor of science
B&B	bed and breakfast
Ba	barium
bar	barometer, barometric
BART	Bay Area Rapid Transit
BASIC	Beginner's All-Purpose Symbolic Instruction Code
BBB	Better Business Bureau
bbl.	barrel
BBS	bulletin board system
BCCD	bar code controller-decoder
BCD	binary coded decimal
BCDIC	binary coded decimal interface code
BCM	basic control monitor
bd ft	board foot
BDOS	basic disk operating system
Be	beryllium
BeV	billion electron volts
BFAS	basic file access system
Bi	bismuth
BIB	Bureau of International Broadcasting
bibl.	*bibliotheca* (Latin, library)
bibliog.	bibliography, bibliographer, bibliographical
biog.	biography, biographer, biographical
biol.	biology, biological, biologist
BIOS	basic input-output system
bit	binary digit
BITNET	Because It's Time Network
BIZNET	American Business Network (database of U.S. Chamber of Commerce)
Bk	berkelium
bk.	block; book
BLT	basic logic test
BMC	bulk media conversion
BOLD	Bibliographic On-Line Display (document retrieval system)
BOT	beginning of tape
bp	boiling point

BPI	bytes per inch
BPM	batch processing monitor
bps	bits per second
Br	bromine
Bros.	Brothers
BSA	Boy Scouts of America
BSC	binary synchronous communications
BSN	block sequence number
BTM	batch time-sharing monitor
Btu	British thermal unit
bu.	bushel
bull.	bulletin
c/o	in care of
C	centigrade, Celsius; carbon
c., ca.	*circa* (Latin, about)
C.	curie
Ca	calcium
CAB	Civil Aeronautics Board
CAD	computer-aided design
CAD/CAM	computer-aided design/computer-aided manufacturing
CADD	computer-aided design and drafting
CAE	computer-aided engineering
CAI	computer-aided instruction
cal, c	calorie
CAL	course authoring language; computer-augmented learning
CAM	computer-aided manufacturing
CARE	Cooperative for American Relief Everywhere
CASE	computer-aided software engineering
CAT	computerized axial tomography; computer-assisted training
Cb	columbium
CBT	computer-based training
cc	cubic centimeter
CCC	Civilian Conservation Corps
CCU	combined card unit
cd	candela

Cd	cadmium
CD	compact disk
CD-ROM	compact disk—read-only memory
CDU	cartridge disk unit
Ce	cerium
CEO	chief executive officer
Cf	californium
cf.	*confer* (Latin, compare)
CFF	common files facility
cg	centigram
CGA	color graphics adapter
CGM	color graphics metafile
cgs	centimeter gram second
ch.	chapter
CIA	Central Intelligence Agency
CIF	central information file
CIO	Congress of Industrial Organizations
CISC	complex instruction set computer
CIU	channel interface unit
cl	centiliter
Cl	chlorine
CLIN	contract line item number
CLM	configuration load manager
CLU	chartered life underwriter
cm, c	centimeter
Cm	curium
CMD	cartridge module disk
CMI	computer-monitored instruction
CML	current mode logic
CMOS	Complementary Metal-Oxide Semiconductor
CNC	communication network configurator
Co	cobalt
Co.	Company
COBOL	Common Business-Oriented Language
COD	cash on delivery
coeff	coefficient

COGO	coordinate geometry
col.	column
colloq.	colloquial, colloquially, colloquialism
COM	communications
COMDEX	Communications and Data Processing Exposition
COMEX	Commodities Exchange (New York)
comp.	compiler; compiled by
compar.	comparative
compd	compound
con.	*contra* (Latin, against)
concd	concentrated
concn	concentration
conj.	conjunction; conjugation
cons.	consonant
const	constant
constr.	construction
cont.	continued
contr.	contraction
COO	chief operating officer
copr.	copyright
cor	corrected
Corp.	Corporation
COTS	commercial off-the-shelf
cp	candlepower
CP	central processor
CP/M	Control Program for Microprocessors
cp.	compare
CPA	certified public accountant
cpi	characters per inch
CPL	console power and logic
CPM	critical path method
cps	characters per second
CPS	cycles per second
CPU	central processing unit
Cr	chromium
CRC	cyclic redundancy check

CRP	capacity requirements planning
CRT	cathode ray tube
CRU	card-reader unit
Cs	cesium
CSCI	computer software configuration item
CSMA	carrier sense multiple access
CSP	Certified Systems Professional
CST	central standard time
CSU	console system unit
CT	computerized tomography
Ctrl	control
Cu	copper
cu. in.	cubic inch
cu. ft.	cubic foot
cwt.	hundredweight
d	deuteron
D	deuterium
d.	died
D.A.	district attorney
D.B.	*divinitatis baccalaureus* (Latin, bachelor of divinity)
D.D.	*divinitatis doctor* (Latin, doctor of divinity)
D.O.	doctor of osteopathy
D.V.M.	doctor of veterinary medicine
D&C	dilatation and curettage
DA	direct access; desk accessory
DAC	direct-access communications
dag	decagram
DAI	direct adaptor interface
dam	decameter
DAR	Daughters of the American Revolution
DAS	direct access storage
DASD	direct access storage device
DAT	digital audio tape; dynamic address translation
dB	decibel
DBA	database administration

DBDL	database definition language
DBMS	database management system
DBSS	direct broadcast satellite service
DBS	database system
DC	direct current; data conversion
DCC	data communications controller
DCD	data communications device
DCL	direct coupled logic
DD/DS	data dictionary/dictionary system
DDL	data definition language
DDP	distributed data processing
DEA	Drug Enforcement Administration
def.	definite, definition
Del	delete
dept.	department
deriv.	derivative
DES	Data Encryption Standard
dg	decigram
DHP	document handler processor
DHU	document handler unit
dial.	dialect
diam	diameter
dict.	dictionary
DIF	data interchange format
dil	dilute
DIP	dual in-line package
dist.	district
distd	distilled
div.	division
dl	deciliter
DLC	data line controller
DLI	direct line interface
dm	decimeter
DMA	direct memory access
DML	Data Management Language; Data Manipulation Language
DMS	data management system

DMU	display monitor unit
DNA	deoxyribonucleic acid
DNC	direct numerical control
do.	ditto
DOA	dead on arrival
DOS	disk operating system; digital operating system
doz.	dozen
DP	data processing
dpi	dots per inch
dr.	dram; drachma
DRAM	dynamic random-access memory
DSAC	distributed system administration and control
DSL	Dynamic Simulation Language
DSM	Distinguished Service Medal
DSO	Distinguished Service Order
DSS	disk storage subsystem
DST	daylight savings time
DTE	data terminal equipment
DTL	diode-transmitter logic
DTP	desktop publishing
DTS	direct timing source
DVI	digital video interactive
DVT	design validation testing
dwt.	pennyweight
Dy	dysprosium
e.g.	*exempli gratia* (Latin, for example)
E-mail	electronic mail
ea.	each
EARN	European Academic Research Network
EBAM	electron beam addressed memory
EBCDIC	Extended Binary Coded Decimal Interchange Code
ECC	error correcting code
ECL	emitter coupled logic; Execution Control Language
ECSL	Extended Control and Simulation Language
ed.	editor, edited by, edition

EDAC	error detection and correction
EDI	electronic data interchange
eds.	editors
EDS	exchangeable disk storage
EEMS	enhanced expanded memory specifications
EEO	equal employment opportunity
EFT	electronic funds transfer
EGA	enhanced graphics adapter
EIS	extended instruction set
EISA	Extended Industry Standard Architecture
EKG	electrocardiogram
EL	electroluminescent
EMI	electromagnetic interference
EMMU	extended main memory unit
EMS	expanded memory specification
encyc.	encyclopedia
ENDEX	Environmental Data Index
Eng.	English
engg.	engineering
engr.	engineer
EOF	end of file
EOJ	end of job
EOL	end of line
EOM	end of message
EOT	end of transmission
EPA	Environmental Protection Agency
EPCOT	Experimental Prototype Community of Tomorrow
EPROM	erasable programmable read-only memory
EPS	encapsulated PostScript
EPU	execution processing unit
EQ	example query
eq.	equation
EQUAL	Extended Query and Update Access Language
equiv	equivalent (math)
Er	erbium
Es	einsteinium

ES	expert system
Esc	escape
ESDI	Enhanced System Device Interface
esp.	especially
Esq.	esquire
ESS	executive support system
EST	eastern standard time
et al.	*et alii* (Latin, and others)
et seq.	*et sequentes* (Latin, and the following)
etc.	*et cetera* (Latin, and so forth)
ETS	extended time-sharing
ETX	end of text
Eu	europium
eV	electron volt
ex.	example
f/t	full time
f/x	special effects (movies)
F	fluorine; Fahrenheit; farad; fermi; formal (concentration)
f.	feminine, female; and following
f.o.b.	free (or freight) on board
f.v.	*folio verso* (Latin, on the back of the page)
FAA	Federal Aviation Administration
FACT	file access control table
FAT	file allocation table
FAQ	frequently asked question
FBI	Federal Bureau of Investigation
FCB	file control block
FCC	Federal Communications Commission
FDA	Food and Drug Administration
FDDL	file data description language
FDIC	Federal Deposit Insurance Corporation
Fe	iron
FEP	front-end processor
ff.	pages following
FF	form feed

FHA	Federal Housing Administration
FIB	file information block
FICA	Federal Insurance Contributions Act (Social Security)
FIFO	first-in/first-out
fig.	figure
FILO	first-in/last-out
FLIP	Federal Loan Insurance Program
Fm	fermium
FM	frequency modulation
FmHA	Farmers Home Administration
FMS	file management supervisor
FNPS	front-end network processor support
FOIA	Freedom of Information Act
fol.	folio
FORTRAN	Formula Translation (programming language)
fp	freezing point
FPL	forms processing language
fps	foot pound second
Fr	francium
fr.	from
Fr.	French
FRS	Federal Reserve System
ft	foot
ft-lb	foot-pound
FTC	Federal Trade Commission
FTF	file transfer facility
FTP	file transfer protocol
fut.	future
FYI	for your information
g	gas; gram; gravity
G	gauss
Ga	gallium
Gael.	Gaelic
gal.	gallon
GAO	General Accounting Office

gb	gigabyte
GCR	group character recording
Gd	gadolinium
Ge	germanium
gen.	genitive; genus
geog.	geography, geographical
geom.	geometry, geometrical
GEOS	geodetic Earth-orbiting satellite
ger.	gerund
Ger.	German
GERT	Graphics Evaluation and Review Technique
GeV	billion electron volts (also, BeV)
GFRC	general file and record control
gi.	gill
GIGO	garbage in, garbage out
GIPSY	General Information Processing System
GMAP	General Macro Assembler Program
GMAT	Graduate Management Admission Test
GMT	Greenwich mean time
GOP	Grand Old Party (Republican Party)
GPI	graphics programming interface
GPIB	general purpose interface bus
GPO	Government Printing Office
GPSS	general purpose systems simulation
gr.	grain; gross
Gr.	Greek
GRE	Graduate Record Examination
GSA	Girl Scouts of America
GSFC	Goddard Space Flight Center
GUI	graphical user interface
h, hr.	hour
H	hydrogen
H.R.	House of Representatives
ha	hectare
HCl	hydrochloric acid

HDBMS	hierarchical database management system
He	helium
hex	hexagonal
Hf	hafnium
HF	high frequency
HFS	Hierarchical File System
hg	hectogram
Hg	mercury
HGC	Hercules graphics card
HHBCR	hand-held bar code reader
hhd.	hogshead
hi-res	high resolution
hist.	history, historical, historian
HIV	human immunodeficiency virus
hl	hectoliter
hm	hectometer
HMS	his/her majesty's ship
Ho	holmium
hp	horsepower
HPF	high-power field
HQ	headquarters
HRH	his/her royal highness
HSLA	high-speed line adapter
HSP	high-speed printer
HTML	hypertext markup language
HUD	(Department of) Housing and Urban Development
Hz	hertz
I	iodine
I/O	input/output
i.d.	inside diameter
i.e.	*id est* (Latin, that is)
IA	international angstrom
IAS	immediate access storage
ibid.	*ibidem* (Latin, in the same place)
IBS	Interactive Business Storage

IC	integrated circuit
ICC	Interstate Commerce Commission
ICCU	intercomputer communications unit
ICU	integrated control unit
id.	*idem* (Latin, the same)
IDI	intelligent device interface
IDP	integrated data processing
IE	Indo-European
IEEE	Institute of Electrical and Electronics Engineers
imper.	imperative
IMS	information management system
in pr.	*in principio* (Latin, in the beginning)
In	indium
in.	inch
Inc.	Incorporated
incl.	inclusive, including, includes
indef.	indefinite
indic.	indicative
inf.	*infra* (Latin, below)
infin.	infinitive
ins	insert
INS	Immigration and Naturalization Service
inst.	instant; institute; institution
instr.	instrumental
interj.	interjection
intrans.	intransitive
intro.	introduction
IOF	Interactive Operation Facility
IOM	input-output multiplexer
IOP	input-output processor
IORB	input-output request block
IP	Internet protocol
IPS	interactive processing system
IQ	intelligence quotient; interactive query
IQF	interactive query facility
IQL	interactive query language

Ir	iridium
IR	infrared
IRA	individual retirement account; Irish Republican Army
IRDS	Information Resource Dictionary System
IRM	inventory record management
irreg.	irregular
IRS	Internal Revenue Service
ISBN	International Standard Book Number
ISO	International Standards Organization
ISR	information storage and retrieval
It.	Italian
ITC	intelligent transaction controller
ITP	integrated transaction processor
IU	international unit
IURP	integrated unit record processor
IV, iv	intravenously
J	joule
J.D.	*juris doctor* (Latin, doctor of laws)
J.H.D.	*litterarum humaniorum doctor* (Latin, doctor of humanities)
J.P.	justice of the peace
JCL	job control language
K	potassium; 1,000; Kelvin
k.	karat
kb	kilobyte
kbar	kilobar
kc	kilocycle; kilocharacter
kcal	kilocalorie
KDS	keyboard/display station
KDT	keyboard/display terminal
kg	kilogram
KHz	kilohertz
kl	kiloliter
km	kilometer
kn	knot

KO	knock out
kph	kilometers per hour
Kr	krypton
KSR	keyboard send/receive
kv	kilovolt
KVDU	keyboard/video display unit
kw	kilowatt
kwh	kilowatt-hour
KWIC	key word in context
l/min	lines per minute
L	liter; Latin
L/s	liters per second
l.	line
L.	left (in stage directions)
l.c.	lowercase
La	lanthanum
LAN	local area network
LANC	local area network controller
lat.	latitude
lb, lb.	pound
LC	Library of Congress
LCD	liquid crystal display
LDM	limited distance modem
LED	light-emitting diode
LF	low frequency; line feed
LFN	logical file number
Li	lithium
LIFO	last-in/first-out
LIPS	laser printer image processing system
LISP	list processing
lit.	literally
Litt.D.	*litterarum doctor* (Latin, doctor of literature)
ll.	lines
LL.B.	*legum baccalaureus* (Latin, bachelor of laws)
LL.D.	*legum doctor* (Latin, doctor of laws)

LNA	low noise amplifier
loc.	locative
loc. cit	*loco citato* (Latin, in the place cited)
long.	longitude
loq.	*loquitur* (Latin, he/she speaks)
LP	linear programming
LPF	low-power field
LPH	line protocol handler
LPM	lines per minute
LPN	licensed practical nurse
Lr	lawrencium
LRC	longitudinal redundancy check
LRN	logical resource number
LSAT	Law School Admission Test
LSD	least significant digit
LSI	large-scale integration
LTD	live test demonstration
Ltd.	Limited
Lu	lutetium
LUD	logical unit designator
LVN	licensed vocational nurse
lx	lux (unit of illuminance)
m	meter
M	molar; mega
m.	married
M.	*meridies* (Latin, noon)
M.A.	master of arts
M.D.	*medicinae doctor* (Latin, doctor of medicine)
m.m.	*mutatis mutandis* (Latin, necessary changes being made)
M.O.	money order; *modus operandi* (Latin, mode of operation)
M.P.	member of Parliament, military police
M.S.	master of science
mA	milliampere
Mac	Macintosh
MADD	Mothers Against Drunk Driving

MARC	machine-readable cataloging
marg.	margin, marginal
masc.	masculine
math.	mathematics, mathematical
max	maximum
mb	megabyte
mc	megacycle, millicycle
MC	master of ceremonies
MCA	microchannel architecture
MCGA	multicolor graphics array
mCi	millicurie
MCP	multi-chip package
Md	mendelevium
MDA	monochrome display adapter
Me	methyl
med.	median; medical; medieval; medium
memo	memorandum
MeV	million electron volts
MFM	modified frequency modulation
MFP	multi-function processor
MFU	multi-function unit
mg	milligram
Mg	magnesium
mgr.	manager
MHz	megahertz
mi.	mile
MICR	magnetic ink character recognition
MIDI	musical instrument digital interface
min.	minute; minimum
MIPS	million instructions per second
MIS	management information system
misc.	miscellaneous
MIU	multiple interface unit
ml	milliliter
mm	millimeter
MM	Maelzel's metronome (tempo indication)

mmHg	millimeters of mercury
mmol	millimole
MMU	main memory unit
Mn	manganese
Mo	molybdenum
mo.	month
MOC	message-oriented communications
Mod. E.	Modern English
modem	modulator/demodulator
mol wt.	molecular weight
mol	mole
MOLTS	mainframe online test subsystem
MOMA	Museum of Modern Art (New York)
MOS	metal oxide semiconductor
mp	melting point
MPC	microprogrammed peripheral controller
mpg	miles per gallon
mph	miles per hour
MPP	microprogrammed peripheral processor
MPS	mathematical programming system
MPU	microprocessing unit
MRI	magnetic resonance imaging
MRS	magnetic reader/sorter
ms, msec	millisecond
ms.	manuscript
MSC	mass storage controller
MSD	most significant digit
MSG	monosodium glutamate
MSI	medium-scale integration
MSL	mean sea level
MSP	mass storage processor
MSR	mass storage resident
MSS	mass storage subsystem
mss.	manuscripts
MSU	mass storage unit
Mt	megaton

MTBF	mean time between failures
MTC	magnetic tape controller
MTP	magnetic tape processor
MTS	magnetic tape subsystem
MTTF	mean time to failure
MTTR	mean time to repair
MTU	magnetic tape unit
MUD	multiuser dialog or dimension
mus.	museum; music, musical
MW	molecular weight
Mx	maxwell
myg	myriagram
myl	myrialiter
mym	myriameter
N/A	not applicable, not available
N	nitrogen; Newton; normal (concentration)
n.	*natus* (Latin, born); note; noun
N.B.	*nota bene* (Latin, note well)
n.d.	no date
n.p.	no place; no publisher
n.s.	new series
N.S.	New Style (dates)
Na	sodium
NAACP	National Association for the Advancement of Colored People
NaCl	sodium chloride
NAFTA	North American Free Trade Agreement
NAM	National Association of Manufacturers
NAPA	National Automotive Parts Association
NARCO	United Nations Narcotics Commission
NASA	National Aeronautics and Space Administration
NASCAR	National Association of Sports Car Racing
NASF	network administrator storage facility
nat.	national; natural
NATO	North Atlantic Treaty Organization

NAU	network administration utilities
Nb	niobium
NCIC	National Crime Information Center
NCS	network control supervisor
Nd	neodymium
NDBMS	network database management system
Ne	neon
neg.	negative
neut.	neuter
ng	nanogram
Ni	nickel
NLQ	near-letter quality
nm	nanometer
NM	nautical mile
No	nobelium
no.	number
NOI	node operator interface
nom.	nominative
NOMAD	Navy oceanographic and meteorological device
non obs.	*non obstante* (Latin, notwithstanding)
non seq.	*non sequitur* (Latin, it does not follow)
NORAD	North American Air Defense
NOW	National Organization for Women
Np	neptunium
NP	notary public
NPS	network processing supervisor
NRA	National Rifle Association
NRC	National Regulatory Commission
ns	nanosecond
NS	not significant
NSC	National Security Council
NSQ	not sufficient quantity
NYPL	New York Public Library
o/t	overtime
O	oxygen

o.d.	outside diameter
o.s.	old series
OAS	office automation system
ob.	*obiit* (Latin, died)
OBCR	optical bar code reader
obs.	obsolete
OCL	Operator Control Language
OCR	optical character recognition
ODESY	On-Line Data Entry System
OEM	original equipment manufacturer
OLTD	online tests and diagnostics
OMR	optical mark read
OMS	office management systems
OOPS	object-oriented programming system
op. cit.	*opere citato* (Latin, in the work cited)
OPEC	Organization of Petroleum Exporting Countries
OPPM	outside principal period of maintenance
ORU	optimum replaceable unit
Os	osmium
OS	operating system
OSHA	Occupational Safety and Health Administration
OSI	open system interconnection
OVE	other vendor equipment
ox	oxidant
Oxon.	*Oxoniensis* (Latin, of Oxford)
oz.	ounce
p	probability
P	phosphorus
p.	page; past
p.m.	*post meridiem* (Latin, after noon); prime minister
p.p.	past participle
P.S.	postscript
P&I	principal and interest
P&L	profit and loss
Pa	protactinium; pascal

PA	public address
PAC	political action committee; Pacific Air Command
para.	paragraph
part.	participle
pass.	*passim* (Latin, throughout); passive
path.	pathology, pathologist, pathological
Pb	lead
PC	personal computer
PCB	printed circuit board
PCF	program checkout facility
PCL	Peripheral Conversion Language; printer command language
PCM	plug-compatible manufacturer
Pd	palladium
PDL	page description language
PDN	Public Data Network
PDSI	peripheral device serial interface
PDU	power distribution unit
PE	phase-encoded
perf.	perfect; perforated
perh.	perhaps
pers.	person, personal
PERT	program evaluation and review technique
PET	parent effectiveness training
pH	measure of acidity
Ph.B.	*philosophiae baccalaureus* (Latin, bachelor of philosophy)
Ph.D.	*philosophiae doctor* (Latin, doctor of philosophy)
Ph.G.	graduate in pharmacy
PIM	personal information manager
PIN	personal identification number; Police Information Network
PIRG	public interest research group
PITI	principal, interest, taxes, and insurance
pk.	peck
pl.	plural; plate
PLN	product line notice

Pm	promethium
PM	preventive maintenance
Po	polonium
POL	Procedure-Oriented Language
POLTS	Peripheral Online Test Subsystem
pos	positive
POS	point of sale
pp.	pages
ppb	parts per billion
pph	pages per hour
ppm	parts per million; pages per minute
PPM	principal period of maintenance
PPP	point-to-point protocol
PPS	*post postscriptum* (Latin, a later postscript)
PPS	Page Printing System
ppt(d)	precipitate(d)
Pr	praseodymium
prep.	preposition
pres.	present
pro tem.	*pro tempore* (Latin, for the time being)
PROM	programmable read-only memory
pron.	pronoun
prox.	*proximo* (Latin, next month)
PrtSc	print screen
PSDN	Packet Switched Data Communication Network
psi	pounds per square inch
PSI	peripheral subsystem interface
Pt	platinum
pt.	part; pint
PTA	Parent-Teacher Association
Pu	plutonium
pub.	publication, publisher, published by
PX	post exchange (military)
q	quintal

Q.E.D.	*quod erat demonstrandum* (Latin, which was to be demonstrated)
q.v.	*quod vide* (Latin, which see)
Q-T-D	quarter-to-date
QA	quality assurance
QBE	query by example
QC	quality control
QLT	Quality Logic Test
qt.	quart
quart.	quarterly
r	roentgen
r/w	read/write
r.	reigned; recto
R.	*rex* (Latin, king), *regina* (Latin, queen); right (in stage direction)
R.A.	Royal Academy
R.I.P.	*requiescat in pace* (Latin, may he/she rest in peace)
R-DAT	rotary head digital audio tape
R&B	rhythm and blues
R&D	research and development
R&R	rest and relaxation (military)
Ra	radium
RAD	rapid access data
RADAR	radio detecting and ranging
RAM	random-access memory
Rb	rubidium
rbi	runs batted in (baseball)
RBM	real-time batch monitor
RBT	remote batch terminal
RBTS	remote batch terminal system
rd.	rod
RDBMS	relational database management system
RDBSQL	Relational Database Structured Query Language
Re	rhenium

READ	real-time electronic access and display
red	reductant
refl.	reflexive
REM	rapid eye movement
repr.	reprint, reprinted
rev.	review; revised, revision
RF	radio frequency
RFD	rural free delivery
RFF	remote file facility
RFI	radio frequency interface (or interference)
RFQ	request for quotation
RGB	red, green, and blue (video)
Rh	rhodium
RIP	raster image processor
RIS	resources information system
RISC	reduced instruction set computing
RJE	remote job entry
RLL	run length limited
RLP	remote line printer
RMC	remote message concentrator
rms	root mean square
RMS	remote maintenance system
Rn	radon
RN	registered nurse
RO	receive-only
ROLTS	Remote Online Test System
ROM	read-only memory
ROTC	Reserve Officers' Training Corps
rpm	revolutions per minute
RR	railroad
RSUF	Remote Software Update Facility
RSVP	*répondez s'il vous plait* (French, respond if you please)
RTE	remote text editor
Ru	ruthenium
Rx	prescription

s	seconds
S	sulfur
s.	substantive
s.a.	*sine anno* (Latin, without year); *sub anno* (Latin, under the year)
s.c.	small capital letters
s.d.	standard deviation; *sine die* (Latin, without setting a day for reconvening)
s.e.	standard error
s.l.	*sine loco* (Latin, without place)
s.v.	*sub verbo, sub voce* (Latin, under the world)
S&L	savings and loan
SAA	System Application Architecture
SAC	Strategic Air Command
SADD	Students Against Driving Drunk
SAF	short address format
SALT	Strategic Arms Limitations Talks
SAM	sequential access method
SASE	self-addressed stamped envelope
SAT	Scholastic Aptitude Test
Sb	antimony
Sc	scandium
sc.	scene; *scilicet* (Latin, namely); *sculpsit* (Latin, carved by)
SCF	System Control Facility
scfh	standard ft^3/h
SCSI	Small Computer System Interface
SCU	System Control Unit
scuba	self-contained underwater breathing apparatus
SD	standard deviation
SDCB	software disk cache buffer
SDI	Strategic Defense Initiative
Se	selenium
SE	standard error of the mean
SEC	Securities and Exchange Commission
sec.	second; section; *secundum* (Latin, according to)

Sen.	Senate
seq.	*sequentes* (Latin, the following)
ser.	series
SF	scalable font
SGML	Standard Generic Markup Language
Si	silicon
SI	International System of Units (Système International)
SIG	special interest group
SIMM	single in-line memory module
sing.	singular
SIP	scientific instruction processor; single in-line packages
SL	Simulation Language
SLIP	serial line interface protocol
SLT	self-loading tape
Sm	samarium
SMD	storage module device
SMS	shared mass storage
Sn	tin
SNA	Systems Network Architecture
SNOBOL	String-Oriented Symbolic Language
sociol.	sociology
SOS	international distress signal
sp ht	specific heat
sp gr	specific gravity
sp vol	specific volume
Sp.	Spanish
SPARC	scalable processor architecture
SPD	shared program display
SPG	sort program generator
sq.	square
SQL	Structured Query Language
Sr	strontium
SRAM	static random access memory
SRB	Software Release Bulletin
SS	Social Security; steamship; supersonic
SSI	small-scale integration

SSLC	synchronous single-line controller
SSU	system support unit
st.	stanza
std	standard
STP	standard temperature and pressure
STPA	standard temperature and pressure, absolute
STPG	standard temperature and pressure, gauge
subj.	subject, subjective
subst.	substantive
sup.	*supra* (Latin, above)
superl.	superlative
suppl.	supplement
syn.	synonym, synonymous
SYSGEN	systems generation
SYSOP	system operator
t	temperature, °C
T	temperature, K
T	ton; telsa; tritium
T.N.T.	trinitrotoluene
T&D	test and diagnostics
T&V	test and verification
Ta	tantalum
TAC	Tactical Air Command; technical assistance center
tb	terabyte
Tb	terbium
tbsp	tablespoonful
Tc	technetium
TCB	task control block
TCL	Transaction Compiler Language
TCP/IP	transfer control protocol/Internet protocol
TD	touchdown (football)
TDG	test data generator
TDP	terminal display processor
Te	tellurium
TED	text editor

temp	temperature
TEMPEST	Transient Electromagnetic Pulse Emanations Standard
TEX	public-domain page description language
Tg	teragram
Th	thorium
theol.	theology, theologian, theological
Ti	titanium
TIFF	tagged-image file format
TIM	terminal interface manager
Tl	thallium
Tm	thulium
TPR	transaction processing routine
trans.	transitive; translated, translator
TRB	task request block
treas.	treasurer
TSA	trap save area
TSM	transaction screen management
tsp	teaspoonful
TSR	terminate and stay resident
TSS	time-sharing system
TTY	teletype
TVA	Tennessee Valley Authority
u	atomic mass unit
U	uranium
u.c.	uppercase
U.N.	United Nations
UART	Universal Asynchronous Receiver/Transmitter
UFO	unidentified flying object
UHF	ultrahigh frequency
ULSI	ultra-large-scale integration
ult.	*ultimo* (Latin, last month)
UM	user's manual
UNESCO	United Nations Educational, Scientific, and Cultural Organization
UNICEF	United Nations International Children's Emergency Fund

univ.	university
UNIVAC	universal automatic computer
UPC	universal product code
UPF	user productivity facility
UPS	universal product code; uninterruptible power supply
URL	universal resource locator
URP	unit record processor
USA	United States Army
USAF	United States Air Force
USCG	United States Coast Guard
USDA	United States Department of Agriculture
USI	user system interface
USIA	United States Information Agency
USMC	United States Marine Corps
USN	United States Navy
USPS	United States Postal Service
USS	United States ship
ut sup.	*ut supra* (Latin, as above)
UT	universal time
UV	ultraviolet
V	vanadium; volt
V/V	volume per volume
v.	verse; verso; *vide* (Latin, see); verb
v.i.	verb intransitive
V.P.	vice president
v.t.	verb transitive
VA	Department of Veterans Affairs (formerly Veterans Administration)
VAN	value-added network
VAR	value-added reseller
VCAM	Virtual Communications Access Method
VDT	video display terminal
VDU	video display unit
VFU	vertical format unit
VFW	Veterans of Foreign Wars

VGA	video graphics array
VHF	very high frequency
VHSIC	very high speed integrated circuit
VIP	very important person; visual information projection
VISTA	Volunteers in Service to America
viz.	*videlicet* (Latin, namely)
VLSI	very large scale integration
voc.	vocative
vol %	volume percent
vol.	volume
VR	virtual reality
VRAM	video random-access memory
vs.	*versus* (Latin, against)
VS	virtual storage
w/v	weight per volume
W	watt; tungsten
W-I-P	work-in-progress
WAC	Women's Army Corps
WAIS	wide area information servers
WAN	wide area network
WASP	white Anglo-Saxon Protestant
WATS	Wide-Area Telecommunications Service
WAVES	Women Accepted for Volunteer Emergency Service (Navy)
Wb	Weber
wgt. pct.	weight percent
WHO	World Health Organization
wk.	week
WORM	write once/read many
WP	word processing
wpm	words per minute
WUDO	Western European Defense Organization
WWW	World Wide Web
WYSIWYG	what you see is what you get

XCMD	external command
Xe	xenon
Y	yttrium
Y-T-D	year-to-date
Yb	ytterbium
yd.	yard
YMCA	Young Men's Christian Association
YMCK	yellow, magenta, cyan, black
YMHA	Young Men's Hebrew Association
yr.	your; year
yuppie	young urban professional
YWCA	Young Women's Christian Association
YWHA	Young Women's Hebrew Association
Z	zinc
ZBR	zone bit recording
ZIP	Zone Improvement Plan (U.S. Postal Service)
Zr	zirconium

UNITED STATES

State	Traditional	Postal
Alabama	Ala.	AL
Alaska	—	AK
Arizona	Ariz.	AZ
Arkansas	Ark.	AR
California	Calif.	CA
Colorado	Colo.	CO
Connecticut	Conn.	CT
Delaware	Del.	DE
Florida	Fla.	FL
Georgia	Ga.	GA
Hawaii	—	HI
Idaho	Ida.	ID
Illinois	Ill.	IL
Indiana	Ind.	IN
Iowa	Ia.	IA
Kansas	Kan.	KS
Kentucky	Ky.	KY
Louisiana	La.	LA
Maine	Me.	ME
Maryland	Md.	MD
Massachusetts	Mass.	MA
Michigan	Mich.	MI
Minnesota	Minn.	MN
Mississippi	Miss.	MS
Missouri	Mo.	MO
Montana	Mont.	MT
Nebraska	Neb.	NE
Nevada	Nev.	NV
New Hampshire	N.H.	NH
New Jersey	N.J.	NJ
New Mexico	N.M.	NM
New York	N.Y.	NY

State	Traditional	Postal
North Carolina	N.C.	NC
North Dakota	N.D.	ND
Ohio	—	OH
Oklahoma	Okla.	OK
Oregon	Ore.	OR
Pennsylvania	Pa.	PA
Rhode Island	R.I.	RI
South Carolina	S.C.	SC
South Dakota	S.D.	SD
Tennessee	Tenn.	TN
Texas	Tex.	TX
Utah	—	UT
Vermont	Vt.	VT
Virginia	Va.	VA
Washington	Wash.	WA
West Virginia	W.Va.	WV
Wisconsin	Wis.	WI
Wyoming	Wyo.	WY
Canal Zone	—	CZ
District of Columbia	D.C.	DC
Guam	—	GU
Puerto Rico	P.R.	PR
Virgin Islands	V.I.	VI

CANADA

Province	Traditional	Postal
Alberta	Alta.	AB
British Columbia	B.C.	BC
Labrador	Labr.	LB
Manitoba	Man.	MB
New Brunswick	N.B.	NB
Newfoundland	Nfld.	NF

Province	*Traditional*	*Postal*
Northwest Territories	N.W.T.	NT
Nova Scotia	N.S.	NS
Ontario	Ont.	ON
Prince Edward Island	P.E.I.	PE
Quebec	P.Q.	PQ
Saskatchewan	Sask.	SK
Yukon Territory	Y.T.	YT

Appendix B

▇ COMPOUNDING GUIDE

Like capitalization, compounding is often a matter of preference: Dictionaries and style guides often differ in the way they hyphenate (or don't hyphenate) compounds. A compound is a term made of two or more words. Whether or not the words are joined together, separated by a hyphen, or separated by a letterspace sometimes depends on how the term is used in the sentence. For example, when the words *common* and *sense* are used to form an adjective (a unit modifier), they are joined:

> *Their **commonsense** approach to the problem saved time and money.*

However, when the term is used as a noun, the words are separated by a letterspace:

> *They solved the problem by using **common sense**.*

This guide, extracted from the *U.S. Government Printing Office Style Manual*, is based on an approach that calls for minimal hyphenation. Whether you follow this guide or use another source, be sure to use one approach consistently.

adv. = adverb
c.f. = combining form
n. = noun
pref. = prefix
u.m. = unit modifier
v. = verb

A

A-bomb
A-flat
A-sharp
able-bodied (u.m.)
able-minded (u.m.)
about-face
above-cited (u.m.)
abovedeck
above-found (u.m.)
above-given (u.m.)
aboveground (u.m.)
above-mentioned (u.m.)
above-named (u.m.)
above-water (u.m.)
above-written (u.m.)
absentminded
acid-treat (v.)
acre-foot
acre-inch
add-on (u.m.)
adeno (c.f., all one word)
afore (c.f., all one word)
after (all one word)
ageless
age-old (u.m.)
age-stricken (u.m.)
age-weary (u.m.)
aide-de-camp
airbag
airbase
airblast
air-blasted (u.m.)
airblown
airbrake

airbrush
airburst
aircargo
air-clear (u.m.)
air-condition (all forms)
air-cool (v.)
air-cooled (u.m.)
aircourse
aircrew
air-dried (u.m.)
air-driven (u.m.)
airdrop
air-dry (u.m., v.)
airfare
air-floated (u.m.)
airflow
airfoil
air-formed (u.m.)
airframe
airfreight
airgap
airhead
airhose
airlift
air line (line for air)
airline (aviation)
airliner
airlink
airlocked
airmail
airmass
airpark
airport
airshow
airship
airsick

airspace

airspeed

airstream

airstrike

airstrip

air time

airwave

all-absorbing (u.m.)

all-aged (u.m.)

all-American

all-clear (n., u.m.)

all-fired (u.m.)

all-inclusive (u.m.)

all-out (u.m.)

allspice

all-star (u.m.)

allo (c.f., all one word)

alongside

alpha-cellulose

alpha-iron

also-ran (n., u.m.)

altocumulus

altostratus

amber-clear (u.m.)

amber-colored (u.m.)

ambi (c.f., all one word)

amino (pref., all one word)

amino acid

ampere-foot

ampere-hour

ampere meter

ampere-minute

ampere-second

amphi (as prefix, all one word)

amylo (c.f., all one word)

anchorhold

anchor light

anchorplate

angelcake

angel-eyed (u.m.)

angel-faced (u.m.)

angelfood

angio (c.f., all one word)

anglehook

anglemeter

anglewing

Anglo (c.f., all one word)

Anglo-American (hyphenate when
    second word is capitalized)

anklebone

ankle-deep (u.m.)

anteater

anthill

ante (prefix, all one word)

ante bellum

ante-Christian

ante mortem

antero (c.f., all one word)

anthra (c.f., all one word)

anthropo (c.f., all one word)

anti (pref., all one word)

anti-American

antichrist

antigod

anti-hog-cholera (u.m.)

anti-icer

anti-imperial

anti-missile-missile (u.m.)

antimissile

antitrust

anti-New Deal

antro (c.f., all one word)

anvil-faced (u.m.)

anvil-headed (u.m.)

anyhow

anyone

any one (one thing or one of a
    group)

anyplace (adv.)

aorto (c.f., all one word)

apo (pref., all one word)

applecart

applejack

applejuice

applesauce

apple-scented (u.m.)

April-fool (v.)

aquaculture

aqualung

aquamarine

aquameter

arc-over (n., u.m.)

arc-weld (v.)

archbishop

archduke

archenemy

arch-Protestant

archeo (c.f., all one word)

archi (pref., all one word)

archo (c.f., all one word)

areo (c.f., all one word)

aristo (c.f., all one word)

armband

armbone

armchair

armhole

armlift

armpit

armplate

armrest

armor-clad (u.m.)

armor-piercing (u.m.)

armorplate

armor-plated (u.m.)

arm's-length (u.m.)

arrowhead

arrowplate

arrow-shaped (u.m.)

arrowshot

arrow-toothed (u.m.)

arseno (c.f., all one word)

arterio (c.f., all one word)

arthro (c.f., all one word)

asbestos-covered (u.m.)

asbestos-packed (u.m.)

ashbin

ashcan

ash-colored (u.m.)

ash-free (u.m.)

ash-gray (u.m.)

ashpile

ashtray

assembly line

assembly room

astro (c.f., all one word)

attorney at law

audiofrequency

audiogram

audiometer

audiotape

audiovisual

authorship

auto (c.f., all one word)

auto-objective

auto-observation
awe-filled (u.m.)
awe-inspired (u.m.)
awesome
ax-grinding (u.m.)
axhammer
ax-shaped (u.m.)
axo (c.f., all one word)
azo (c.f., all one word)
azo-orange
azo-orchil

B

B-flat
babyface (n.)
babysit (v.)
backache
backbite (v.)
backbone
backbreaker
back-country (u.m.)
backdate
backdown (n., u.m.)
backdrop
backflow
back-focus (v.)
background
backhand
back-in (n., u.m.)
backlash
backlist (v.)
backlog
backpacker (n.)
backpaddle (v.)
backpay
backpayment

backpedal (v.)
backrest
backroad
backrun
backscatter
backslide
backspace
backspin
backstage
backstairs
backstich
backstop
backstretch (n.)
backstroke
backswept
backswing
backtalk
backtrack (v.)
backup (n., u.m.)
backwash
bagpipe
bag-shaped (u.m.)
baggage room
bailout (n., u.m.)
bakepan
baldfaced
ball-like
ballpark (nonliteral)
ball park (literal)
ballplayer
ballot box
bandstand
bandwagon
bandwidth
bangup (n., u.m.)
banknote

bantamweight

barpost

bartender

bare-armed (u.m.)

bareback

barebone

barefaced

barefoot

barelegged

bark-tanned (u.m.)

barleycorn

barleymow

barley water

barnstormer

barrelhead

barrel-shaped (u.m.)

baseball

baseball bat

baseline

base line (surveying)

base-minded (u.m.)

basi (c.f., all one word)

basketball

bas-relief

batblind

bat-eyed (u.m.)

batwing

bathmat

bathrobe

bathtub

battleax

battle-fallen (u.m.)

battlefront

battleground

battle-scarred (u.m.)

battleship

beachcomber

beachhead

beadroll

beamfilling

beam-making (u.m.)

beanbag

beanpole

bean-shaped (u.m.)

beanstalk

beauty-blind (u.m.)

beauty shop

bedchamber

bedclothes

bedfellow

bedframe

bedpan

bedpost

bedrail

bedridden

bedrock

bedsheet

bedside

bedsore

bedspread

bedspring

beehive

beechnut

beefeater

beefsteak

beeswax

beeswing

before-cited (u.m.)

beforehand

before-mentioned (u.m.)

before-named (u.m.)

bell-bottomed (u.m.)

bellhop
bellringer
bellyache
bellybutton
belt-driven (u.m.)
bench-hardened (u.m.)
benchmade (u.m.)
benchmark (nonliteral)
bench mark (surveying)
benchwarmer
benzo (c.f., all one word)
berry-brown (u.m.)
best man
bestseller (n.)
beta-glucose
betatron
bi (pref., all one word)
bi-iliac
big-eared (u.m.)
big-leaguer
bigmouthed
bigname (n., u.m.)
billbroker
billfold
billet-doux
bio (c.f., all one word)
bio-aeration
bio-osmosis
birchbark
birdbath
birdcage
birdcall
birdcatcher
bird-faced (u.m.)
birdseed
birdwatcher

bird's-eye
bird's nest (n., literal)
bird's-nest (n., u.m.)
birthday
birthmark
birthplace
birthright
biscuit-shaped (u.m.)
bittersweet
bitter-tongued (u.m.)
blackball (nonliteral)
black-eyed (u.m.)
blackjack
blacklist
blackmail
blackmark
black-market (u.m., v.)
black-marketer
blackout (n., u.m.)
black-robed (u.m.)
blacksnake
blacktop
blasthole
blasto (c.f., all one word)
blight-resistant (u.m.)
blind-flying (u.m.)
blindfold
blindspot
blockbuster
blockhead
blood-alcohol (u.m.)
bloodbath
bloodcurdling
bloodhound
bloodletting
blood-red (u.m.)

bloodshed

bloodstain

bloodstream

bloodsucker

bloodthirsty

blossom-bordered (u.m.)

blowdown (n., u.m.)

blowgun

blowhard (n.)

blowhole

blowout (n., u.m.)

blowpipe

blowtorch

blowup (n., u.m.)

blueblood

bluecoat (n.)

blue-eyed (u.m.)

bluegrass

blue-gray (u.m.)

blue-pencil (v.)

blueprint

blunt-edged (u.m.)

blunt-spoken (u.m.)

boardwalk

boatbuilder

boatcrew

bobcat

bobsled

bobbypin

bodybearer

bodybuilder

bodyguard

boildown (n., u.m.)

boiloff (n., u.m.)

boilout (n., u.m.)

boilerplate

boilerworks

boldface

bold-spirited (u.m.)

boltcutter

bolt-shaped (u.m.)

bombdrop

bombshell

bomb-throwing (u.m.)

boneache

bonebreaker

bone-dry (u.m.)

bone-hard (u.m.)

bonemeal

boneshaker

bone-white (u.m.)

boobytrap

boogie-woogie

bookbinder

bookcase

bookdealer

bookfair

book-learned (u.m.)

book-lined (u.m.)

booklist

booklore

booklover

bookmark

bookmobile

bookplate

bookrack

bookrest

bookseller

bookshelf

bookstand

book-stitching (u.m.)

boomtown

boondoggling

bootlace

bootlick

bootstrap

borehole

boresight

bottle-fed (u.m.)

bottleneck

bottle-nosed (u.m.)

bottom land

bowbent

bowknot

bowlegged

bow-necked (u.m.)

bowstring

boxcar

boxtruck

brainchild

brainstorm

brainwash

brakedrum

brakeshoe

brandywine

brass-bold (u.m.)

brassworks

brave-looking (u.m.)

breadbasket

breadcrumb

breadplate

breadwinner

breakaway (n., u.m.)

breakdown (n., u.m.)

break-even (u.m.)

breakfast

breakfast room

breakfront

break-in (n., u.m.)

breakneck

breakoff (n., u.m.)

breakout (n., u.m.)

breakpoint

breakthrough (n., u.m.)

breakup (n., u.m.)

breastbone

breast-fed (u.m.)

breastpin

breastplate

breathtaking

breeze-borne (u.m.)

breeze-swept (u.m.)

bribegiver

bribetaker

bric-a-brac

brickbat

brick-built (u.m.)

brick-colored (u.m.)

bricklayer

brickmason

brick-red (u.m.)

bridegroom

bridgebuilder

briefcase

bright-colored (u.m.)

bright-eyed (u.m.)

brilliant-cut (u.m.)

brine-soaked (u.m.)

broadacre

broadband (n., u.m.)

broad-beamed (u.m.)

broadcast

broadcloth

broad-leaved (u.m.)

broadloom

broadminded

broadsheet (n.)

broadside

broadwoven

broken-down (u.m.)

broken-legged (u.m.)

bromo (c.f., all one word)

bronchio (c.f., all one word)

bronze-covered (u.m.)

bronze-red (u.m.)

broom-making (u.m.)

broomstick

brotherhood

brother-in-law

browbeat

browpoint

brown-eyed (u.m.)

brownout (n., u.m.)

brush holder

brushoff (n., u.m.)

brush-treat (v.)

buckeye

buckpasser

bucksaw

buckshot

buckskinned

bucktooth

bucket-shaped (u.m.)

buff-yellow (u.m.)

bugbear

bugbite

bug-eyed (u.m.)

buildup (n., u.m.)

built-in (u.m.)

built-up (u.m.)

bulkhead

bulk-pile (v.)

bulkweigh (v.)

bulldog

bulldoze

bull-faced (u.m.)

bullfight

bullfrog

bullpen

bullring

bullwhip

bull's-eye (nonliteral)

bumblebee

burn-in (n., u.m.)

burnout (n., u.m.)

burnup (n., u.m.)

burned-over (u.m.)

busdriver

busfare

bushbeater

bush-grown (u.m.)

bush-leaguer

bushwhacker

bustup (n., u.m.)

busybody

butt-joint (v.)

butt-weld (v.)

butterball

butter-colored (u.m.)

butterfat

butterfingers

buttermilk

butternut

butterscotch

butter-smooth (u.m.)

butter-yellow (u.m.)

button-eared (u.m.)
buttonhole
buttonhook
by-and-by
by-the-way (n., u.m.)

C

C-sharp
C-star
C-tube
cabdriver
cabfare
cab owner
cabstand
cable-laid (u.m.)
caco (c.f., all one word)
cakebaker
cake-eater
cakemixer
cake-mixing (u.m.)
cakepan
cakewalk
calci (c.f., all one word)
calk-weld (v.)
callback (n., u.m.)
calldown (n., u.m.)
call-in (n., u.m.)
callnote
call-off (n., u.m.)
callout (n., u.m.)
call-over (n., u.m.)
callup (n., u.m.)
camshaft
camelback
camel-backed (u.m.)
camel's-hair (u.m.)

campfire
campground
campstool
cannot
canalside
candle-foot
candle-hour
candlelighter
candlelit
candle-meter
candle-shaped (u.m.)
candlestand
candlestick
candlewick
candystick
cane-backed (u.m.)
cannonball
canvas-covered (u.m.)
carbarn
carbuilder
carfare
carhop
carlot
car-mile
carpool
carport
carsick
carwash
carbo (c.f., all one word)
carcino (c.f., all one word)
cardcase
card-index (u.m., v.)
cardplayer
cardstock
cardio (c.f., all one word)
cardio-aortic

carefree

care-laden (u.m.)

caretaker

careworn

carpetbagger

carpetbeater

carpet-cleaning (u.m.)

carpet-covered (u.m.)

carpetfitter

carpetlayer

carpet-sweeping (u.m.)

carrot-colored (u.m.)

carrotjuice

carryall (n., u.m.)

carryback (n., u.m.)

carry-in (n., u.m.)

carryout (n., u.m.)

cartwheel

cash-flow

castaway (n., u.m.)

cast-by (n., u.m.)

castoff (n., u.m.)

cast-weld (v.)

catcall

cat-eyed (u.m.)

catface (n.)

catnap

catnip

cat-o'-nine-tails

catwalk

catchall (n., u.m.)

catch-as-catch-can (u.m.)

catchplate

catchup (n., u.m.)

catercorner

caterwauling

cat's-eye (nonliteral)

cat's-paw (nonliteral)

cattlefeed

cattle-raising (u.m.)

cauliflower-eared (u.m.)

cavedweller

cave-dwelling (u.m.)

cave-in (n., u.m.)

cease-fire (n., u.m.)

cedar-colored (u.m.)

celi (c.f., all one word)

celio (c.f., all one word)

cement-covered (u.m.)

cementmason

cement-temper (v.)

census-taking (u.m.)

center field

centermost

centi (c.f., all one word)

centimeter-gram-second

centri (c.f., all one word)

centro (c.f., all one word)

cephalo (c.f., all one word)

cerato (c.f., all one word)

cerebro (c.f., all one word)

cerebro-ocular

cervico (c.f., all one word)

cervico-occipital

cervico-orbicular

cesspool

chain-driven (u.m.)

chainstitch

chairperson

chair-shaped (u.m.)

chairwarmer

chalk-white (u.m.)

charbroiler

charcoal

charge book

chargeoff (n., u.m.)

chargeout (n., u.m.)

cheapskate

check-in (n., u.m.)

checklist

checkmark

checkoff (n., u.m.)

checkout (n., u.m.)

checkpasser (n.)

checkpoint

checksheet

checkup (n., u.m.)

checker-in

checker-off

checker-out

checker-up

cheekbone

cheerleader

cheeseburger

cheesecake

cheesecloth

cheesecurd

cheeseplate

chemico (c.f., all one word)

chemo (c.f., all one word)

cherry-colored (u.m.)

cherrystone (nonliteral)

cherry stone (literal)

chestnut-colored (u.m.)

chestnut-red (u.m.)

chickenbill

chicken-billed (u.m.)

chicken breast

chickenbreasted

chickenfeed

chickenheart

chickenpox

chicken yard

chief justice

chief-justiceship

chief mate

childbearing

childbed

childbirth

childhood

child-minded (u.m.)

chill-cast (u.m., v.)

chinband

chin-high (u.m.)

chinrest

chinstrap

china-blue (u.m.)

china shop

Chinatown

chipmunk

chiro (c.f., all one word)

chisel-cut (u.m.)

chisel-edged (u.m.)

chitchat

chitter-chatter

chloro (c.f., all one word)

chockablock

chock-full (u.m.)

chocolate-brown (u.m.)

chocolate-coated (u.m.)

chocolate maker

choir master

chokeout (n., u.m.)

chokepoint

chokestrap

chop-chop

chopstick

chowchow

Christ-inspired (u.m.)

chromo (c.f., all one word)

chrono (c.f., all one word)

chuckhole

chuckwagon

churchgoer

cigarcase

cigarcutter

cigar-shaped (u.m.)

cigarette holder

cigarette maker

cigarette-making (u.m.)

cine (c.f., all one word)

circum (pref., all one word)

circum-Saturnal

cirro (c.f., all one word)

city-born (u.m.)

city-bred (u.m.)

cityfolk

cityscape

clambake

clamshell

clampdown (n., u.m.)

clasphook

class-conscious (u.m.)

clawbar

claw-footed (u.m.)

clawhammer

clawhatchet

claw-tailed (u.m.)

claybank

clay-colored (u.m.)

clayworks

clean-cut (u.m.)

cleanhanded

cleanout (n., u.m.)

clean-smelling (u.m.)

cleanup (n., u.m.)

clear-cut (u.m.)

clearcut (forestry—n., v.)

clear-eyed (u.m.)

clear-sighted (u.m.)

clearup (n., u.m.)

cleft-footed (u.m.)

cleft-graft (v.)

cliffdweller

cliff-dwelling (u.m.)

cliffhanger

cliffside

clifftop

clip-clop

clip-edged (u.m.)

clipsheet

clipper-built (u.m.)

cloak-and-dagger (n., u.m.)

clockcase

clockface

clock-minded (u.m.)

clocksetter

clockwatcher

clodhopping

close-connected (u.m.)

close-cut (u.m.)

closedown (n.)

close-fertilize

closefisted

closemouthed

closeout (n., u.m.)

closeup (n., u.m.)

closed-circuit (u.m.)

closed shop

cloth-backed (u.m.)

clothesbag

clothesbasket

clothesbrush

clotheshorse

clothespin

clothespress

clothesrack

cloudbase

cloudburst

cloudcap

cloud-hidden (u.m.)

cloverleaf

club-shaped (u.m.)

co (pref, all one word)

co-op

coachwhip

coalbag

coalbed

coalbin

coal-black (u.m.)

coaldigger

coal-faced (u.m.)

coal-laden (u.m.)

coal loader

coalpit

coalrake

coastside

coathanger

coatrack

coattailed

cobweb

cockeye

cockfight

cocksure

cock-tailed (u.m.)

cocktail

cockleshell

cockscomb

codfishing

coffeebreak

coffeecake

coffee-colored (u.m.)

coffee-growing (u.m.)

coffeepot

cogwheel

coin-operated (u.m.)

coldblooded

cold-chisel (v.)

coldcuts

cold-draw (v.)

cold-flow (v.)

cold-forge (v.)

cold-hammer (v.)

cold-hammered (u.m.)

coldpack

cold-press (v.)

cold-roll (v.)

cold-rolled (u.m.)

cold-shoulder (v.)

coldtype

cold-work (v.)

coleseed

coleslaw

coli (c.f., all one word)

collarband

collarbone

colo (c.f., all one word)

colorbearer

colorblind

color blindness

colorfast

color-free (u.m.)

color line

colortype (n.)

color-washed (u.m.)

comb-toothed (u.m.)

comeback (n., u.m.)

come-between (n.)

comedown (n.)

come-off (n., u.m.)

come-on (n., u.m.)

come-out (n.)

comeuppance

comic book

commander in chief

commonplace

common sense (n.)

commonsense (u.m.)

commonwealth

companionship

cone-shaped (u.m.)

conference room

Congressman at Large

contra (pref., all one word)

contra-acting

contra-approach

contra-ion

cookoff (n., u.m.)

cookout (n., u.m.)

cookstove

cooped-in (u.m.)

cooped-up (u.m.)

cop out (v.)

copout (n.)

copper-bottomed (u.m.)

copper-colored (u.m.)

copperhead

copper-headed (u.m.)

copperplate

copper-plated (u.m.)

copperworks

coral-red (u.m.)

cork-lined (u.m.)

corkscrew

cornbread

corncake

corncob

corn-fed (u.m.)

cornhusk

cornmeal

cornstalk

cornstarch

cornerpost

corpsmember

costo (c.f., all one word)

cotton-clad (u.m.)

cotton-covered (u.m.)

cotton-growing (u.m.)

cotton mill

cottonmouth

cottonseed

countdown (n., u.m.)

counter (c.f., all one word)

country-born (u.m.)

country-bred (u.m.)

countryfolk

countrypeople

countryside

court-martial

courtship

cousinhood

coveralls

coverlet

coverup (n., u.m.)

cowbell

cow-eyed (u.m.)

cowherd

cowhide

cowpath

cowpen

crabcake

crabcatcher

crabfaced

crabmeat

crackdown (n., u.m.)

crackpot

crack-the-whip (n., u.m.)

crackup (n., u.m.)

cradlesong

cranio (c.f., all one word)

crankcase

crank-driven (u.m.)

crankshaft

crashdive (v.)

crawlup (n., u.m.)

creamcake

cream-colored (u.m.)

creditworthiness

creekbed

creekside

crepe de chine

crestfallen

crewcut

crewmember

cribstrap

crimefighter

crimewave

crisscross

crooked-nosed (u.m.)

crooked-toothed (u.m.)

crop-year

cross-appeal

crossband

crossbar

crossbeam

crossbearer

crossbedded

crossbelt

cross-bidding

crossbill (bird)

cross bill (legal)

crossbind

crossbolt

crossbones

cross-bridge (v.)

cross-brush (v.)

cross-carve (v.)

cross-channel (u.m.)

cross-check

cross-claim

cross-compound (v.)

cross-connect (v.)

cross-country (u.m.)

cross-cultivate (v.)

crosscurrent

cross-curve (n.)

crosscut

cross-date (v.)

cross-examine (v.)

cross-eye (n., u.m.)

cross-eyed (u.m.)

crossfall

crossfeed

cross-fertile (u.m.)

cross-fertilize (v.)

cross-fiber (u.m.)

crossfire

cross-grained (u.m.)

crosshair

crosshatch

crosshaul

cross-immunity

cross-index (u.m.)

cross-interrogate (v.)

cross-interrogatory

crosslegged

crosslegs

cross-level (v.)

cross-license (v.)

crosslift (v.)

crossmember

crosspath

crossplow (v.)

cross-pollinate (v.)

cross-purpose (n.)

cross-question

crossrail

cross-reaction

cross-refer (v.)

cross-reference

crossroad

cross-stitch

cross-stratification

cross-sue (v.)

cross-surge (v.)

crosstalk

crosstie

crosstown

crosstrack

crosstrail

crossunder (n., u.m.)

cross-vote

crosswalk

crosswind

crossword

crowbar

crowfoot

crow's-foot (nonliteral)

crow's-nest (nonliteral)

crybaby

crypto (c.f., all one word)

crystal-clear (u.m.)

crystal-smooth (u.m.)

cubbyhole

cumulo (c.f., all one word)

cupbearer

cupcake

cupful

curbside

curbstone

cure-all (n., u.m.)

curlyhead

curlylocks (n.)

cussword

custom-built (u.m.)

custom-made (u.m.)

custom-tailored (u.m.)

cutaway (n., u.m.)

cutback (n., u.m.)

cutglass

cut-in (n., u.m.)

cutoff (n., u.m.)

cutout (n., u.m.)

cutrate (u.m.)

cutthroat
cut-under (u.m.)
cut-up (n., u.m.)
cutter-built (u.m.)
cutter-rigged (u.m.)
cutter-up
cuttlebone
cyano (c.f., all one word)
cyclecar
cysto (c.f., all one word)
cyto (c.f., all one word)

D

D-day
D-major
D-plus-4-day
dairy-fed (u.m.)
dairy-made (u.m.)
dampproofing
damp-stained (u.m.)
damping-off (n., u.m.)
dancehall
danger line
dare-all (n., u.m.)
daredevil
daresay
dark-eyed (u.m.)
darkhorse (nonliteral)
data bank
database
datelined
datemark
daughter-in-law
dawn-gray (u.m.)
dawnstreak
daybeam

daybed
daybreak
day-bright (u.m.)
daydream
day-fly (v.)
day-flying (u.m.)
daygoing
daylighted
daylit
daylong (u.m.)
daymark
daystar
day-to-day (u.m.)
de (pref., all one word)
de-air
deicer
de-ion
deadbeat (n.)
deadborn
dead-burn (v.)
dead-cold (u.m.)
dead-drunk (u.m.)
dead-ender
deadeye (n.)
dead-eyed (u.m.)
deadfall
deadhead
dead-heated (u.m.)
dead-heater
deadlatch
dead load
deadlock
deadpan
deadweight (n., u.m.)
deaf-mute
deaf-muteness

deathbed

deathblow

deathday

death-divided (u.m.)

death house

death-struck (u.m.)

deathtrap

deathwatch

death-weary (u.m.)

deckhand

deep-affected (u.m.)

deep-cut (u.m.)

deep-felt (u.m.)

deep-freeze (u.m., v.)

deep-frying (u.m.)

deepgoing

deep-grown (u.m.)

deep-laid (u.m.)

deepmost

deep-rooted (u.m.)

deep-seated (u.m.)

deep-set (u.m.)

deep-sunk (u.m.)

deep-voiced (u.m.)

deerdrive (n.)

deer-eyed (u.m.)

deerfood

deerherd

deerhorn

deerhound

deermeat

deerstalker

deerstand

dehydr(o) (c.f., all one word)

demi (pref., all one word)

demi-Christian

demi-incognito

dermato (c.f., all one word)

desert-bred (u.m.)

desk room

dessertspoon

deutero (c.f., all one word)

devildog

devil-inspired (u.m.)

devil-ridden (u.m.)

dewbeam

dewcap

dew-clad (u.m.)

dewclaw

dewdamp

dew-drenched (u.m.)

dewdrop

dewfall

dew-fed (u.m.)

dew-laden (u.m.)

dextro (c.f., all one word)

di (pref., all one word)

dia (pref., all one word)

diamondback

diamond-backed (u.m.)

diamond-shaped (u.m.)

diazo (c.f., all one word)

diazo-oxide

dicecup

diceplay

die-away (u.m.)

dieback

diecase

die-cast (u.m., v.)

diecaster

die-cut (u.m., v.)

diecutter

diehard (n., u.m.)

die proof (n.)

diesetter

diesinker

die-square (u.m.)

diesel-driven (u.m.)

diesel-electric (u.m.)

dillydally

dim-lighted (u.m.)

dimlit

dimout (n., u.m.)

dingbat

dingdong

dining room

dip-dye (v.)

dip-grained (u.m.)

diphead

dipstick

direct-connected (u.m.)

direct-indirect

direction-finding (u.m.)

dirt-cheap (u.m.)

dirtfast

dirt-encrusted (u.m.)

dirtplate

dirty-faced (u.m.)

dirty-minded (u.m.)

dirty work

dis (pref., all one word)

dishcloth

dishpan

dishrack

dishwasher

dishwiper

diskjockey

diskpack

diskplow

disk-shaped (u.m.)

ditchbank

ditchdigger

ditchside

dive-bomb (v.)

do-all (n., u.m.)

do-gooder

do-little (n., u.m.)

do-nothing (n., u.m.)

dockhand

dockhead

dockside

dogbite

dog-bitten (u.m.)

dogbreeder

dogcart

dogcatcher

dog-drawn (u.m.)

dog-ear (v.)

dog-eared (u.m.)

dogface

dog-faced (u.m.)

dogfight

dogfood

dog-headed (u.m.)

dogleg

dog owner

dogsled

dog-tired (u.m.)

dogtooth

dog-toothed (u.m.)

dollface

doll-faced (u.m.)

doomsday

doorbell

doorcheck

doorframe

doorhead

doorjamb

doorknob

doormat

doornail

doorplate

doorpost

door-shaped (u.m.)

doorsill

doorstep

doorstop

dopepasser

dopepusher

dopesheet

dorsi (c.f., all one word)

dorso (c.f., all one word)

dorso-occipital

double-barrel (n., u.m.)

double-barreled (u.m.)

double-breasted (u.m.)

double-charge (v.)

doublecheck (n., v.)

doublechecked (u.m., v.)

double-chinned (u.m.)

doublecross (nonliteral)

doubledeal (v.)

double-decker

double-distilled (u.m.)

double-duty (u.m.)

double-dye (v.)

double-edged (u.m.)

double-ender

double-entendre

doublehanded

doubleheader

double-jointed

double-quick (u.m.)

doubletalk

doubletone

doubletree

double-trouble

double-up (u.m., v.)

double work

dough-colored (u.m.)

doughface

dough-faced (u.m.)

doughmixer

doughnut

downbeat

downcast

downcheck

downcoast

down-covered (u.m.)

downcry

downcurved

downcut

downdraft

downdrag

downfall

downfilled

downflow

downfold

downgrade

downgradient

downgrowth

downhanging

downhaul

downhill

downlock (n.)

downmost

downpayment

downpour

downrate

downright

downriver

downshore

downside

downsitting

downslip

downslope

down-soft (u.m.)

downspout

downstage

downstairs

downstate

downstream

downstroke

downswing

downtake

downthrow

downthrust

downtown

downtrampling

downtrend

downtrodden

downturn

downvalley

downweigh

downweight

downwind

draftage (allowance)

draft age

draft-exempt (u.m.)

dragbar

dragbolt

dragnet

dragpipe

dragrope

dragsaw

dragwire

dragger-out

dragger-up

dragon-eyed (u.m.)

dragon piece

draincleaner

drainpipe

drainplug

draintile

draw-arch (n.)

drawarm

drawback

drawbar

drawbeam

drawbench

drawbolt

drawbore

drawbridge

drawcut

drawdown (n., u.m.)

drawfile

drawgate

drawgear

drawglove

drawhead

drawhorse

drawknife

drawknot

drawlink

drawloom

drawnet

drawoff (n., u.m.)

drawout (n., u.m.)

drawpin

drawplate

drawpoint

drawsheet

drawspan

drawstop

drawstring

drawtube

drawer-down

drawer-in

drawing board

drawing room

dream-haunted (u.m.)

dreamlore

dreamworld

dressup (n., u.m.)

dressing room

drift boat

driftbolt

driftmeter

drift-mining (u.m.)

driftpin

driftwind

drillcase

drill-like

drillstock

drip-dry (u.m., v.)

dripsheet

driveaway (n., u.m.)

drivebelt

drivebolt

drivecap

drivehead

drive-in (n., u.m.)

drivepipe

drivescrew

dropaway (n., u.m.)

dropbolt

drop-forge (v.)

dropfront

drophammer

drophead

dropkick

dropleaf (n., u.m.)

dropleg

dropoff (n., u.m.)

dropout (n., u.m.)

dropstitch

drug-addicted (u.m.)

drugmixer

drugpasser

drugpusher

drugseller

drumbeat

drumfire

drumhead

drumstick

drum-up (n., u.m.)

dryclean

dry-cure (v.)

drydock

dry-dye (v.)

dry-farm (v.)

dryfarming (n., u.m.)

drylot

dry-pack (u.m., v.)

dry-rotted (u.m.)

dry-salt (v.)

drywash

duckbill

duck-billed (u.m.)

duckfoot

duck-footed (u.m.)

duck pond

due-in (n., u.m.)

dueout (n., u.m.)

duffelbag

dugout (n.)

dug-up (u.m.)

dull-edged (u.m.)

dull-looking (u.m.)

dull-witted (u.m.)

dumbbell

dumbwaiter

dumpcart

dunderhead

duo (c.f., all one word)

dustbag

dustbin

dustbrush

dustcloth

dust-covered (u.m.)

dustfall

dust-gray (u.m.)

dust-laden (u.m.)

dustpan

duststorm

duty-free (u.m.)

dwelling house

dyemixer

dyestuff

dyeworks

dys (pref., all one word)

E

earache

eardrop

eardrum

earflap

earguard

earhole

earlap

earmark

earphone

ear-piercing (u.m.)

earplug

earring

earscrew

earshot

earsplitting

earwax

earwig

earwitness

earthbank

earthborn

earth-bred (u.m.)

earthfall

earthfast

earth-fed (u.m.)

earthfill

earthgrubber

earth house

earthlit

earthmover

earthquake

earth-shaking (u.m.)

earthslide

earth-stained (u.m.)

earthwall

east-central (u.m.)

eastgoing

east-northeast

east-sider

east-southeast

Eastertide

easygoing

easy-rising (u.m.)

easy-spoken (u.m.)

eavesdrop

ebbtide

edge plane

edgeshot

edgeways

eggbeater

eggcup

egghead (nonliteral)

eggnog

eggplant

egg-shaped (u.m.)

eggshell

egg-white (u.m.)

eight-angled (u.m.)

eightfold

eightpenny

eight-ply (u.m.)

eightscore

eight-wheeler

elbowchair

elder brother

elderbrotherhood

elderbrotherly

electro (c.f., all one word)

electro-optics

electro-osmosis

electro-ultrafiltration

embryo (c.f., all one word)

emptyhanded

empty-looking (u.m.)

en route

encephalo (c.f., all one word)

end-all (n., u.m.)

endbell

endbrain

endgate

endlap

endlong

end-match (v.)

endmatcher

end-measure (v.)

endmost

end-shrink (v.)

endo (c.f., all one word)

engine shop

enginework

engine worker

engine yard

entero (c.f., all one word)

entry book

envelope holder

envelope maker

epi (pref., all one word)

equi (c.f., all one word)

equi-gram-molar

erythro (c.f., all one word)

evenglow

evenhanded

evenminded

even-numbered (u.m.)

even-tempered (u.m.)

eventide

ever-abiding (u.m.)

everblooming

ever-constant (u.m.)

ever-fertile (u.m.)

everglade

evergoing

evergreen

everlasting

evermore

ever-normal (u.m.)

ever-present (u.m.)

ever-ready (u.m.)

eversporting

everyday (n., u.m.)

every day (each day)

everyone (all)

every one (distributive)

every time

evildoer

evil-eyed (u.m.)

evil-faced (u.m.)

evil-looking (u.m.)

evilminded (u.m.)

evilwishing

excommunicate

ex-Governor

ex libris

ex officio

ex post facto

ex-serviceman

extra-alimentary

extra-American

extrabold

extra-Britannic

extra-condensed (u.m.)

extracurricular

extra-fine (u.m.)

extrahazardous

extrajudicial

extra-large (u.m.)

extra-long (u.m.)

extramarginal

extramural

extraordinary

extrapolar

extra-strong (u.m.)

extraterritorial

extravascular

eyeball

eyebank

eyebar

eyeblink

eyebolt

eyebrow

eyecup

eyeflap

eyeglass

eyehole

eyelash

eyelens

eyelid

eyemark

eyeshade

eyeshield

eyeshot

eyesight

eyesore

eyespot

eye-spotted (u.m.)

eyestrain

eyetooth

eyewash

eye weariness

eyewink

eyewitness

F

F-flat

F-horn
F-sharp
fable book
fableteller
faceabout (n., u.m., v.)
face-arbor (v.)
facecloth
face-harden (v.)
face-hardened (u.m.)
facelifting
facemark
face-on (n., u.m.)
faceplate
faceup (n., u.m.)
factfinding
factsheet
fadeaway (n., u.m.)
fade-in (n., u.m.)
fadeout (n., u.m.)
fail-safe
faintheart
faint-voiced (u.m.)
fairground
fair-lead (n., u.m.)
fairminded
fairplay
fair-skinned (u.m.)
fairytale
faithbreaker
fallaway (n., u.m.)
fallback (n., u.m.)
fall-in (n., u.m.)
fallout (n., u.m.)
fall-plow (v.)
fall-sow (v.)
falltrap

fallow land
false-bottomed (u.m.)
false-faced (u.m.)
falsehood
false-tongued (u.m.)
fame-crowned (u.m.)
fame-thirsty (u.m.)
fanbearer
fanfare
fanfold
fan-jet
fan-leaved (u.m.)
fan-shaped (u.m.)
fan-tailed (u.m.)
fancy-free (u.m.)
fancy-woven (u.m.)
fancy-wrought (u.m.)
far-aloft (u.m.)
faraway (n., u.m.)
far-borne (u.m.)
far-distant (u.m.)
far-eastern (u.m.)
farfetched
farflung (u.m.)
far-off (u.m.)
far-reaching (u.m.)
farseeing
far-seen (u.m.)
farsight
farm-bred (u.m.)
farmhand
farmhold
farmpeople
farmplace
farmstead
fashion-led (u.m.)

fashion piece
fashion-setting (u.m.)
fast-anchored (u.m.)
fastback
fast-dyed (u.m.)
fastgoing
fasthold
fast-moving (u.m.)
fast-read (v.)
fast-reading (u.m.)
fast time
fatback
fat-bellied (u.m.)
fat-free (u.m.)
fathead
fat-soluble (u.m.)
father-confessor
father-in-law
faultfinder
faultslip
faux pas
fear-free (u.m.)
fear-pursued (u.m.)
fear-shaken (u.m.)
featherbed (v.)
featherbone
featherbrain
featheredge
feather-leaved (u.m.)
featherstitch
feather-stitched (u.m.)
feather-stitching
feather-tongue (v.)
featherweight
featherwing
fed-up (u.m.)

feeble-bodied (u.m.)
feebleminded (u.m.)
feedback (n., u.m.)
feedbag
feedbin
feedpipe
fellowcraft
fellowship
feltcutter
felt-lined (u.m.)
fencepost
fern-clad (u.m.)
fernleaf
fern-leaved (u.m.)
ferro (c.f., all one word)
ferro-carbon-titanium
ferro-uranium
feverless
fever-stricken (u.m.)
fevertrap
fever-warm (u.m.)
Fiberglas (copyright)
fiberglass
fiberstitch
fibro (c.f., all one word)
fibro-osteoma
fickleminded (u.m.)
fiddle-faddle
fiddlehead
fiddle-shaped (u.m.)
fiddlestick
fiddlestring
fieldball
fieldglass
fieldgoal
field-strip

fierce-eyed (u.m.)

fierce-looking (u.m.)

fiery-flaming (u.m.)

fiery-hot (u.m.)

fiery-red (u.m.)

fiery-tempered (u.m.)

figbar

figleaf

figurehead

figure work

filecard

file-hard (u.m.)

filesetter

file-soft (u.m.)

fill-in (n., u.m.)

fillout (n., u.m.)

fill-up (n., u.m.)

fillercap

filler-in

filler-out

filler-up

filmcutter

filmgoer

filmgoing

filmstrip

film-struck (u.m.)

fine-cut (u.m., v.)

fine-draw (v.)

fine-drawn (u.m.)

fine-featured (u.m.)

fine-looking (u.m.)

fine-set (u.m.)

fingerbreadth

finger-cut (u.m.)

fingerhold

fingerhole

fingerhook

fingermark

fingernail

fingerparted

fingerprint

fingerspin

fingertip

firearm

fireback (n.)

fireball

firebell

firebomb

firebrand

firebrick

firecoat

firecracker

fire-cure (v.)

fire-eater

firefall

firefighter

fireguard

fire-hardened (u.m.)

firehose

firelit

firepit

fireplace

fireplow

fire-polish (v.)

fire-red (u.m.)

fire-resistant (u.m.)

firesafe

fireside

firetrap

firetruck

firewall

firm-footed (u.m.)

firm-set (u.m.)
firm-up (n., u.m.)
first-aider
first-born (u.m.)
first-class (u.m.)
firstcomer
firsthand (u.m.)
first-made (u.m.)
first-named (u.m.)
first-nighter
first-rate (u.m.)
first-rater
fishback
fishbed
fish-bellied (u.m.)
fishbone
fishcake
fisheye
fish-eyed (u.m.)
fish-fed (u.m.)
fishfood
fishhook
fishmouth
fishpond
fishpool
fishpot
fishtrap
fishworks
fisherfolk
fisherpeople
fivebar
fivefold
five-ply (u.m.)
five-pointed (u.m.)
five-reeler
fivescore

five-shooter
flagbearer
flagpole
flagpost
flag-raising (u.m.)
flagship
flag-signal (v.)
flagstaff
flagstick
flame-cut (v.)
flameout (n.)
flamethrower
flannelmouth
flapcake
flap-eared (u.m.)
flapjack
flareback (n., u.m.)
flareout (n., u.m.)
flareup (n., u.m.)
flashback (n., u.m.)
flashbulb
flashcard
flashcube
flashgun
flashlamp
flashpan
flashpoint
flatback
flatbed
flat-bottomed (u.m.)
flatcar
flat-compound (v.)
flatfold
flatfoot (n.)
flathat
flathead

flatiron

flatnose

flatout (n., u.m.)

flat-rolled (u.m.)

flattop

flat-topped (u.m.)

flax-leaved (u.m.)

flax-polled (u.m.)

flaxseed

fleabite

flea-bitten (u.m.)

fleetfoot

fleet-footed (u.m.)

fleshhook

flesh-pink (u.m.)

fleshpot

fleur-de-lis

flightcrew

flight-hour

flightpath

flight-test (v.)

flimflam

flip-flop

flip-up (n., u.m.)

floodflow

floodgate

floodlamp

floodlighting

floodmark

floodtide

floodwall

floorbeam

floorcloth

floorlamp

floormat

floormop

floorspace

floorstain

floorwalker

floor-waxing (u.m.)

flourbin

flour mill

floursack

flowchart

flowmeter

flowoff (n., u.m.)

flowsheet

flowthrough

flowerbed

flowerbud

flower grower

flower-hung (u.m.)

flowerpot

flower-scented (u.m.)

flower shop

fluid-compressed (u.m.)

fluidextract (n.)

fluidglycerate

fluo (c.f., all one word)

fluoro (c.f., all one word)

flush-cut (u.m.)

flush-decked (u.m.)

flush-decker

flushgate

fluvio (c.f., all one word)

flyaway

flyback

flyball

fly-bitten (u.m.)

flyblown

fly-by-night (n., u.m.)

flycatcher

flyeater
fly-fish (v.)
fly-fisher
fly-fisherman
fly fishing
flyflap
fly-free (u.m.)
flyleaf
flypaper
flysheet
flyspeck
fly-specked (u.m.)
flytrap
flywheel
flying boat
flying fish
foam-crested (u.m.)
foam-white (u.m.)
fogeater
fog-hidden (u.m.)
foghorn
fog-ridden (u.m.)
fold-in
foldup (n., u.m.)
folklore
folksong
follow-on
followthrough (n., u.m.)
followup (n., u.m.)
follower-up
foodpacker
foodsick
foodstuff
foolhardy
foolscap
foot-and-mouth (u.m.)

football
footband
footbath
footblower
footbrake
footbreadth
footbridge
foot-candle
footfall
foot-free (u.m.)
footgear
foot-grain
foothill
foothold
footlocker
footloose
footmark
footnote
footpad
footpath
footplate
foot-pound
foot-pound-second
footprint
footrail
footrest
foot-second
footsore
footstep
footstool
foot-ton
footwalk
footwall
footworn
for (pref., all one word)
fore (pref., all one word)

fore-age

fore-and-aft (n., u.m.)

fore-and-after (n.)

fore-edge

fore-end

fore-exercise

forest-covered (u.m.)

forest land

forestside

forkhead

forklift

fork-pronged (u.m.)

fork-tailed (u.m.)

formfitting

form work

forthcoming

forthright

forthwith

fortuneteller

forty-niner

foul line

foul-looking (u.m.)

foulmouthed

foul-spoken (u.m.)

foul-tongued (u.m.)

foulup (n., u.m.)

foundry proof

fountainhead

four-bagger

four-ball (u.m.)

four-eyed (u.m.)

fourflusher

fourfold

four-footed (u.m.)

four-in-hand (n., u.m.)

four-masted (u.m.)

four-master

fourpenny

four-ply (u.m.)

fourscore

foursome

foursquare

four-wheeler

fox-faced (u.m.)

foxhole

foxhound

foxtailed

foxtrot

fracto (c.f., all one word)

frameup (n., u.m.)

freeborn

freedrop

free-for-all (n., u.m.)

free-grown (u.m.)

freehand

freehanded

freehold

freelance

freeloader

free-minded

freemasonry

free-spoken (u.m.)

freestanding (u.m.)

freethinker

freetrader

freewheel (u.m., v.)

freewheeler (n.)

free will (n.)

freewill (u.m.)

freezedown (n., u.m.)

freezeout (n., u.m.)

freezeup (n., u.m.)

freight house
freight-mile
freight room
fresh-looking (u.m.)
fresh-painted (u.m.)
frog-eyed (u.m.)
frogface
frogpond
front-end (u.m.)
front-focused (u.m.)
frontrunner
frontstall
front-wheel (u.m.)
fronto (c.f., all one word)
fronto-occipital
fronto-orbital
frostbite
frost-free (u.m.)
frost-hardy (u.m.)
frost-heaving (u.m.)
frost-killed (u.m.)
frostlamp
fruitcake
fruit fly
fruitgrowing
fruit shop
frying pan
fuel line
fuel oil
fullback
full-bellied (u.m.)
fullface
full-fashioned (u.m.)
full-flowering (u.m.)
full-grown (u.m.)
full-handed (u.m.)

full-headed (u.m.)
full load
full-strength (u.m.)
full-time (u.m.)
fundraising
funlover
funnel-shaped (u.m.)
fur-clad (u.m.)
furcoat
fur-lined (u.m.)
fur-trimmed (u.m.)
fuseplug

G

G-major
G-man
G-minor
G-sharp
gabfest
gadabout (n., u.m.)
gadfly
gag-check (v.)
gaugepin
gainsay
gain-sharing (u.m.)
galact(o) (c.f., all one word)
gallbladder
galley proof
galley-west (u.m.)
galvano (c.f., all one word)
gamebag
gamecock
gangboss
gangplank
gangsaw
garnet-brown (u.m.)

gasbag

gasbomb

gas-driven (u.m.)

gas-fired (u.m.)

gasfiring

gasfitter

gas-heated (u.m.)

gas-laden (u.m.)

gaslamp

gaslighted

gasline (auto)

gas line (people queue)

gaslock

gasmeter

gasworks

gastro (c.f., all one word)

gastro-omental

gateleg (u.m.)

gatepin

gatepost

gateworks

gearcase

gear-driven (u.m.)

gearfitter

gear-operated (u.m.)

gearset

gearshift

gearwheel

gelatin-coated (u.m.)

gelatin-making (u.m.)

gelatinobromide

gelatinochloride

gemcutter

gem-set (u.m.)

gem stone

genito (c.f., all one word)

gentlefolk

gentle-looking (u.m.)

gentle-mannered (u.m.)

gentle-spoken (u.m.)

geo (c.f., all one word)

germ-free (u.m.)

gerrymander

getaway (n., u.m.)

getoff (n., u.m.)

get-together (n., u.m.)

getup (n., u.m.)

ghost-haunted (u.m.)

ghostwrite (v.)

giddy-paced (u.m.)

gilt-edge (u.m.)

gin-run (u.m.)

gingerbread

ginger-colored (u.m.)

gingersnap

gingerspice

give-and-take (n., u.m.)

giveaway (n., u.m.)

glacio (c.f., all one word)

glad-cheered (u.m.)

glassblower

glasscutter

glass-eyed (u.m.)

glass-hard (u.m.)

glassworks

glauco (c.f., all one word)

glidepath

globetrotter

glosso (c.f., all one word)

glowlamp

glowmeter

gluc(o) (c.f., all one word)

gluepot

gluestick

glycero (c.f., all one word)

glyco (c.f., all one word)

go-ahead (n., u.m.)

go-around (n., u.m.)

go-as-you-please (u.m.)

go-back (n., u.m.)

go-between (n.)

gocart

go-getter

go-getting (n., u.m.)

go-off (n., u.m.)

goalpost

goat-bearded (u.m.)

goat-eyed (u.m.)

goatherd

goat's-hair

goat's-horn

God-conscious (u.m.)

God-fearing (u.m.)

God-forsaken (u.m.)

God-given (u.m.)

God-ordained (u.m.)

God-sent (u.m.)

God-sped (u.m.)

Godspeed

godchild

goddaughter

godfather

godless

godmother

godparent

godsend

godson

godsonship

goggle-eyed (u.m.)

goings-on

goldbeater

goldbrick (swindle)

gold brick (of real gold)

gold-bright (u.m.)

gold-brown (u.m.)

golddigger

gold-filled (u.m.)

goldfoil

gold-inlaid (u.m.)

goldleaf

goldplate (v.)

gold-plated (u.m.)

gold-plating (u.m.)

goldsmithing

gold-wrought (u.m.)

golden-fingered (u.m.)

golden-headed (u.m.)

goodbye

good-fellowship

good-for-nothing (n., u.m.)

good-looker

good-looking (u.m.)

good-natured (u.m.)

good will (kindness)

goodwill (salable asset)

goose-eyed (u.m.)

gooseflesh

gooseneck

goosepimples

goosestep

goosewing

gospellike

gospel-true (u.m.)

Government-in-exile (U.S. or foreign)

Government-owned (U.S. or foreign, u.m.)

governmentwide (State, city, etc.)

grab-all (n., u.m.)

grabhook

grabrope

gradefinder

grademark

grain-cut (u.m.)

grain-laden (u.m.)

grainmark

gram-fast (u.m.)

gram-meter (u.m.)

gram-molecular

gram-negative (u.m.)

gram-positive (u.m.)

grandaunt

grandchild

grandfather

grandmother

grandparent

grandstand

grant-in-aid

grapefruit

grapejuice

grape-leaved (u.m.)

grapeseed

grapestalk

grapevine

graphalloy

grapho (c.f., all one word)

grass-covered (u.m.)

grasscutter

grass-green (u.m.)

grasshopper

grassnut

grassplot

grassroots (nonliteral)

grass roots (literal)

gravedigger

graveside

gravel-blind (u.m.)

grayback (n., u.m.)

graybeard (n.)

graycoat (n.)

gray-eyed (u.m.)

gray-haired (u.m.)

grayhead

gray-headed (u.m.)

great-aunt

greatcoat

great-eared (u.m.)

great-grandchild

great-grandfather

great-grandmother

great-headed (u.m.)

greenback (n., u.m.)

greenbelt

green-clad (u.m.)

green-eyed (u.m.)

greengrocer

greenhorn

green-leaved (u.m.)

green wood (literal)

greenwood (forest)

greyhound

gridiron

griddlecake

gripwheel

groundhog

groundmass

groundnut

groundpath
groundplot
ground-sluicer
groundspeed
groundwave
ground water
group-connect (v.)
grownup (n., u.m.)
guardplate
guardrail
guestchamber
guidepost
guided-missile (u.m.)
gumchewer
gumdrop
gum-saline (n.)
gumshoe
gunbearer
gunblast
gundeck
gunfight
gunflint
gunlock
gunplay
gunpoint
gunpowder
gunrack
gun-rivet (v.)
gunrunner
gunshot
gun-shy (u.m.)
gunsight
gunstock
gunwale
gutless
gutstring

gutterspout
gymno (c.f., all one word)
gyneco (c.f., all one word)
gyro horizon
gyro mechanism
gyro pelorus

H

H-bar
H-beam
H-bomb
H-hour
H-piece
hackhammer
hacksaw
hailstorm
hairband
hairbreadth
hairbrush
hair-check (n.)
haircloth
haircut (n.)
hairdo
hairdresser
hair-fibered (u.m.)
hairpin
hairspace
hairsplitting
hairstreak
hairstroke
half-and-half (n., u.m.)
half-alive
half-angry
halfback
half-backed (u.m.)
half-baked (u.m.)

halfblood (n.)

half-bound (u.m.)

half-bred (u.m.)

halfbreed

half-clear

halfcock (v.)

halfcocked (nonliteral)

half-dark

halfdeck

half-decked (u.m.)

half-decker

half-feed (v.)

half-hourly (u.m.)

half-life

half load

half-loaded (u.m.)

half-mast

half-miler

half-monthly (u.m.)

half-on (n., u.m.)

halfpace

halfpenny

half-ripe

half-sole (v.)

halfstaff

halfstitch

half-strength (u.m.)

halftitle

halftone

halftrack

half-true

half-truth

half-weekly (u.m.)

halfwit

half-witted (u.m.)

half-yearly

hallmark

hamstring

hammercloth

hammer-hard (u.m.)

hammer-harden (v.)

hammer-hardened (u.m.)

hammerhead

hammerlock

hammertoe

hammer-weld (v.)

hammer-wrought (u.m.)

handbag

handball

handbill

hand-bound (u.m.)

handbow

handbrake

handbreadth

handbrush

hand-built (u.m.)

handcar

hand-carry (v.)

handcart

hand-carve (v.)

handclap

handclasp

hand-clean (v.)

handcrank

handcuff

hand-cut (v.)

hand-embroidered (u.m.)

hand-fed (v.)

handfold

handgrasp

handgrenade

handgrip

handguard
handgun
hand-high (u.m.)
handhold
handhole
hand-in-hand (u.m.)
handkerchief
hand-knit (v.)
hand-knitter
handlaid
hand-letter (v.)
handlift
handliner
handmade
hand-me-down (n., u.m.)
handmix (v.)
handmold (v.)
handmower
handoff (n., u.m.)
handout (n., u.m.)
handpick (v.)
handpress
handprint
handrail
handreading
handsaw
handscrape (v.)
handset
handshake
handspring
handspun
hand-stamp (v.)
handstand
handstitch
handstroke
hand-tailored (u.m.)

handtool
hand-tooled (u.m.)
hand-tooling (u.m.)
handtruck
handweave
handwheel
handworked
handwoven
handwrite (v.)
handwritten
handlebar
hangdog
hangnail
hangnet
hangout (n., u.m.)
hangup (n.)
hanger-back
hanger-on
hanger-up
happy-go-lucky
harborside
hard-and-fast (u.m.)
hardback
hard-baked (u.m.)
hard-bitten (u.m.)
hard-boiled (u.m.)
hardcase
hardcore
hardfist (n.)
hardhanded
hardhat (n.)
hardhead
hard-hit (u.m.)
hard-looking (u.m.)
hardmouthed
hardnose

hardpan

hard-pressed (u.m.)

hard-set (u.m.)

hardspun

hardtack

hardtop

hard-won (u.m.)

hard work

hard-working (u.m.)

hardwrought

harebrain

harefoot

harehound

harelip

harness-making (u.m.)

has-been (n.)

hashmark

hatband

hatbrim

hatbrush

hatcleaner

hatpin

hatrack

hatrail

hatstand

hatchet-faced (u.m.)

haulabout (n., u.m.)

haulaway (n., u.m.)

haulback (n.)

have-not (n., u.m.)

hawk-nosed (u.m.)

haycart

haycock

hayfork

hayloft

haymarket

haymow

hayrake

hay-scented (u.m.)

hayseed

haystack

haywire

hazel-eyed (u.m.)

hazelnut

he-man

headache

headachy

headband

headbander

headblock

headcap

headcheese

headcloth

headdress

head-ender

headfirst

headframe

headgate

headgear

headhunter

headlamp

headlighting

headliner

headlock

headlong

headmost

headnote

head-on (u.m.)

headphone

headplate

headpost

headquarters

headrail
headrest
headset
headshake
headspace
headspin
headspring
headstand
headstart
headstrong
headwall
headwaiter
headwind
header-up
heal-all (n., u.m.)
heartache
heartaching
heartbeat
heartblock
heartblood
heartbreak
heartburn
heartdeep
heartfelt
heartfree (u.m.)
heartgrief
heartheavy
heartleaf
heart-leaved (u.m.)
heartsick
heartsore
heartstring
heartstruck
heartthrob
heart-throbbing (u.m.)
heart-weary (u.m.)

hearthrug
hearthwarming
heatdrops
heat-resistant (u.m.)
heatstroke
heattreat (v.)
heat-treating (u.m.)
heaven-inspired (u.m.)
heaven-sent (u.m.)
heavyback
heavy-duty (u.m.)
heavy-eyed (u.m.)
heavy-footed (u.m.)
heavyhanded
heavy-looking (u.m.)
heavy-set (u.m.)
heavy water
heavyweight (n., u.m.)
hecto (c.f., all one word)
hedgebreaker
hedgehog
hedgehop
hedgepig
hedgerow
heelball
heelband
heelblock
heelcap
heelgrip
heelpad
heelplate
heelprint
heelstrap
heeltap
helio (c.f., all one word)
hellbender

hellbent

hellborn

hellbred

hellcat

hell-dark (u.m.)

helldog

hellfire

hellhole

hellhound

hell-red (u.m.)

hellship

helpmeet

helter-skelter

hemstitch

hema (c.f., all one word)

hemato (c.f., all one word)

hemi (pref., all one word)

hemo (c.f., all one word)

hempseed

hempstring

hencoop

hen-feathered (u.m.)

henpecked

henroost

henceforth

henceforward

hepato (c.f., all one word)

hepta (c.f., all one word)

hereabout

hereafter

hereat

hereby

herefrom

herein

hereinabove

hereinafter

hereinto

hereof

hereon

hereto

heretofore

hereunder

hereunto

hereupon

herewith

herringbone

hetero (c.f., all one word)

hetero-ousia

hexa (c.f., all one word)

hi-fi

hijack

hide-and-seek (n., u.m.)

hideaway (n., u.m.)

hideout (n., u.m.)

highball

highbrow (nonliteral)

high-caliber (u.m.)

high-class (u.m.)

highflier (n.)

highflying (u.m.)

high-foreheaded (u.m.)

highhanded

high-hat (v.)

hijinks

highlander

high light (literal)

highlight (nonliteral)

high-minded (u.m.)

high-power (u.m.)

high-pressure (u.m., v.)

high-priced (u.m.)

high proof

high-reaching (u.m.)

high-rigger (n.)

highrise

highroad

high seas

high-speed (u.m.)

highstepper

high-tension (u.m.)

high water

higher-up (n.)

hillbilly

hillculture

hillside

hilltop

hindgut (n.)

hindhead

hindleg

hindmost

hindquarter

hindsaddle

hindsight

hipbone

hipmold

hipshot

hippo (c.f., all one word)

histo (c.f., all one word)

hit-and-miss (u.m.)

hit-and-run (u.m.)

hit-or-miss (u.m.)

hitchhiker

hoary-haired (u.m.)

hobgoblin

hobnail

hobnob

hobbyhorse

hocus-pocus

hodgepodge

hogback

hog-backed (u.m.)

hogfat

hoghide

hognose

hog-nosed (u.m.)

hogpen

hogsty

hog-tie (v.)

hogwash

hog-wild (u.m.)

hogshead

hoistaway

holdall (n., u.m.)

holdback (n., u.m.)

hold-clear (n., u.m.)

holddown (n., u.m.)

holdfast (n., u.m.)

holdoff (n., u.m.)

holdout (n., u.m.)

holdup (n., u.m.)

holder-forth

holder-on

holder-up

hollow-eyed (u.m.)

hollowfaced

hollow-ground (u.m.)

holo (c.f., all one word)

home-baked (u.m.)

homebody

homeborn

homebred

homebrew

homebuilder

homecomer

home-fed (u.m.)

homefolk

homefront

homefurnishings (n.)

homegrown

homelander

homelife

homemade

homeplate

homeseeker

homesick

homespun

homestead

homestretch

hometown

homewoven

homeo (c.f., all one word)

homo legalis

homo sapiens

homo (c.f., all one word)

homo-ousia

honey-colored

honeycomb

honeydew

honeydrop

honey-laden (u.m.)

honeymoon

honeypot

honeysweet

hoodcap

hoodmold

hoodwink

hoofbeat

hoofmark

hoofprint

hoof-printed (u.m.)

hookladder

hooknose

hook-nosed (u.m.)

hookup (n., u.m.)

hooker-up

hoopstick

hopabout (n., u.m.)

hopoff (n., u.m.)

hopscotch

hoptoad

horehound

hormono (c.f., all one word)

hornbill

hornblower

horn-eyed (u.m.)

hornpipe

horseback

horsebreaker

horsecar

horsecloth

horsedealer

horsefight

horsehair

horsehead

horseherd

horsehide

horsehoof

horse-hour

horsejockey

horselaugh

horsemeat

horseplay

horsepower-hour

horsepower-year

horserace

horse sense (n.)

horseshoe

horsethief

horsewhip

hotbed

hotblood

hot-blooded (u.m.)

hotbrain

hotcake

hot-cold

hotdog

hotfoot

hothead (n.)

hot-mix (u.m.)

hotpack

hotpatch

hotplate

hot-press (v.)

hotrod (nonliteral)

hot-roll (v.)

hot-rolled (u.m.)

hotspot

hot-work (v.)

houndshark

hourglass

housebreaking

housebroken

housebuilder

housecleaner

house-cleaning (u.m.)

housecoat

housedress

housefather

housefurnishing(s) (n.)

houseguest

household

househusband

housemother

houseparent

housepest

house-raising (u.m.)

housetop

housetrailer

housewares

housewarming

housewife

how-do-you-do (n.)

however

howsoever

hubcap

humankind

humble-looking (u.m.)

humble-spirited (u.m.)

humdrum

humero (c.f., all one word)

humero-olecranal

humpback

hump-shouldered (u.m.)

humpty-dumpty

hunchback

hundredfold

hundred-legged (u.m.)

hundred-percenter

hundred-pounder

hundredweight

hung-up (u.m.)

hunger-worn (u.m.)

hurly-burly

hush-hush

hushup (n., u.m.)

hydro (c.f., all one word)

hydro station

hygro (c.f., all one word)

hyper (pref., all one word)
hyper-Dorian
hypo (c.f., all one word)
hystero (c.f., all one word)
hystero-oophorectomy
hystero-salpingo-oophorectomy

I

I-bar
I-beam
I-iron
I-rail
iceberg
iceblind
ice blindness
iceblock
icebreaker
icecap
ice-cold (u.m.)
ice-cooled (u.m.)
ice-covered (u.m.)
icefall
ice fishing
ice-free (u.m.)
icemelt
icepack
iceplant
iceplow
ice water
ichthyo (c.f., all one word)
ideo (c.f., all one word)
ideo-unit
idleheaded
idle-looking (u.m.)
idle-minded
ileo (c.f., all one word)

ilio (c.f., all one word)
ill-advised (u.m.)
ill-being (n.)
ill-born (u.m.)
ill-bred (u.m.)
ill breeding (n.)
ill-doing (n., u.m.)
ill-fated (u.m.)
ill-humored (u.m.)
ill-looking (u.m.)
ill-treat (v.)
ill-use (v.)
ill-wisher
ill-wishing (u.m.)
in-and-out (u.m.)
in-and-outer
in-being (u.m.)
in-flight (u.m.)
in-house
in-law (n.)
inactive (u.m.)
inasmuch
indepth (u.m.)
inservice (u.m.)
inch-deep (u.m.)
inch-long (u.m.)
inchmeal
inch-pound
inch-ton
index-digest
indigo-blue (u.m.)
indigo-carmine (u.m.)
Indochinese
Indo-European
infra (pref., all one word)
infra-auricular

infra-axillary
infra-esophageal
infra-umbical
inguino (c.f., all one word)
ink-black (u.m.)
inkmixer
inkpot
inkspot
ink-spotted (u.m.)
inkstain
inkstand
inkwell
inner-city (u.m.)
innerspring
ino (c.f., all one word)
insect-borne (u.m.)
inter (pref., all one word)
inter-American
intra (pref., all one word)
intra-atomic
intro (pref., all one word)
Irish-American (u.m.)
Irish-born (u.m.)
ironback
iron-braced (u.m.)
ironclad
ironfisted
iron-free (u.m.)
ironhanded
ironhard
iron-lined (u.m.)
ironmold
iron-red (u.m.)
ironshod
ironshot (mineral, u.m.)
iron shot (golf)

ironside
ironworks
ironer-up
island-born (u.m.)
island-dotted (u.m.)
iso (c.f., all one word)
iso-octane
iso-oleic
iso-osmosis
ivory-tinted (u.m.)
ivory-white (u.m.)
ivy-covered (u.m.)

J

J-bolt
jackass
jackhammer
jackhead
jack-in-the-box
jackknife
jack-of-all-trades
jack-o'-lantern
jack-plane (v.)
jackpot
jackrabbit
jackscrew
jackshaft
jampacked
jawbone
jawbreaker
jawfoot
jaw-locked (u.m.)
jayhawk
jaywalk
jellybean
jellyroll

jetblack (u.m.)

jetliner

jetport

jet-powered (u.m.)

jetprop

jet-propelled (u.m.)

jetstream

jetwash

jewel-bright (u.m.)

jewel-studded (u.m.)

jibhead

jib-o-jib

jibstay

jig-drill (v.)

jigsaw

jobseeker

job shop

joint owner

joulemeter

joyride

joystick

jumpoff (n., u.m.)

jumprock

jungle-covered (u.m.)

jungleside

junkpile

jury box

jury-fixing (u.m.)

juxta (c.f., all one word)

juxta-ampullar

juxta-articular

K

K-ration

K-term

keelblock

keelhaul

keel-laying (u.m.)

keel line

keepsake

kerato (c.f., all one word)

kettledrum

kettlestitch

keybolt

keyhole

keylock

keynote

keypunch

keyring

keyseat

keystop

keyword

kickabout (n., u.m.)

kickback (n., u.m.)

kick-in (n., u.m.)

kickoff (n., u.m.)

kickout (n., u.m.)

kickup (n., u.m.)

killjoy

kiln-dry (u.m., v.)

kilo (pref., all one word)

kilogram-meter

kilovoltampere

kilowatthour

kindheart

kingbolt

kinghood

kingpin

kinsfolk

kinspeople

kiss-off (n., u.m.)
kiteflier
kiteflying
knapsack
knee-braced (u.m.)
kneebrush
kneecap
knee-deep (u.m.)
knee-high (u.m.)
kneehole
kneepad
kneestrap
knickknack
knickpoint
knight-errant
knighthood
knitback
knobstick
knockabout (n., u.m.)
knockaway (n., u.m.)
knockdown (n., u.m.)
knock-knee (n.)
knock-kneed (u.m.)
knockoff (n., u.m.)
knock-on (n., u.m.)
knockout (n., u.m.)
knothole
know-all (n., u.m.)
know-how (n., u.m.)
know-it-all (n., u.m.)
know-little (n., u.m.)
know-nothing (n., u.m.)
knucklebone
knuckle-deep (u.m.)
knuckle-kneed (u.m.)

Ku Klux Klan

L

L-bar
L-beam
L-block
L-shaped
labio (c.f., all one word)
laborsaving
lace-edged (u.m.)
lace edging
lacewing
lace-winged (u.m.)
laceworked
lackluster
ladder-backed (u.m.)
ladybeetle
ladyfinger
ladykiller
ladyship
lakebed
lakefront
lakeshore
lakeside
lameduck (nonliteral, n., u.m.)
lamp-blown (u.m.)
lamp-foot
lamp-hour
lamp house
lamplighter
lamplit
lamppost
lampshade
lampstand
lampwick

land base
land-based (u.m.)
land bird
landfall
landflood
landgrabber
land-grant (u.m.)
landholding
landlady
landlocked
landlook
landlubber
landmark
landmass
landmine
land-poor (u.m.)
landright
landscape
landside
landslide
landstorm
landwash
landwire
lantern-jawed (u.m.)
lapbelt
laprobe
lapweld (v.)
lap-welded (u.m.)
lap-welding (u.m.)
large-eyed
large-handed (u.m.)
large-minded (u.m.)
largemouthed
large-scale (u.m.)
larkspur
laryngo (c.f., all one word)

last-born (u.m.)
last-cited (u.m.)
last-ditcher
last-named (u.m.)
latchbolt
latchkey
latchstring
late-born (u.m.)
latecomer
late-lamented (u.m.)
late-maturing (u.m.)
latero (c.f., all one word)
lathe-bore (v.)
latter-day (u.m.)
lattermost
laughingstock
laundry room
law-abiding (u.m.)
lawbreaker
law-fettered (u.m.)
lawgiver
lawsuit
lawnmower
layaway (n., u.m.)
layback (n., u.m.)
lay-by (n.)
laydown (n., u.m.)
lay-minded (u.m.)
layoff (n., u.m.)
layon (n., u.m.)
layout (n., u.m.)
layup (n., u.m.)
layer-on
layer-out
layer-over
layer-up

lazybones
lead-alpha
lead-burn (v.)
lead-filled (u.m.)
lead-gray (u.m.)
lead-in (n., u.m.)
leadline
lead line (medical, nautical)
leadoff (n., u.m.)
leadout (n., u.m.)
leaden-eyed (u.m.)
leaden-souled (u.m.)
leader line
leafbud
leaf-clad (u.m.)
leaf-eating (u.m.)
leaf-shaped (u.m.)
leafstalk
lean-faced (u.m.)
lean-looking (u.m.)
lean-to (n., u.m.)
leapfrog
leaseback (n., u.m.)
leasehold
leatherback
leather-backed (u.m.)
leather-bound (u.m.)
leather-brown (u.m.)
leather-covered (u.m.)
leatherhead
leatherneck
leavetaking
lee-bow (v.)
left-bank (v.)
left field
left-hand (u.m.)

left-handed (u.m.)
left-hander
leftmost
left-sided (u.m.)
leftwing (political)
legband
legpuller
legrope (v.)
lend-lease
lepto (c.f., all one word)
letdown (n., u.m.)
letoff (n., u.m.)
letup (n., u.m.)
letterdrop
lettergram
letterhead
letter-perfect (u.m.)
letterpress
letterspace
leuc(o) (c.f., all one word)
liberal-minded (u.m.)
lieutenant colonel
lieutenant-colonelcy
lieutenant governor
lieutenant-governorship
lifebelt
lifeblood
lifefloat
lifegiver
lifeguard
lifehold
lifejacket
lifelong
liferaft
lifering
lifesaver

life-size (u.m.)

life-sized (u.m.)

lifespan

lifespring

lifestyle

lifevest

lift-off (n., u.m.)

light-armed (u.m.)

light-clad (u.m.)

light-colored (u.m.)

light-draft (u.m.)

lightface

light-footed (u.m.)

lighthanded

lighthouse keeping (nautical)

light housekeeping (domestic)

light-producing (u.m.)

lightship

light-struck (u.m.)

lightweight (n., u.m.)

light-year

lighter-than-air (u.m.)

like-looking (u.m.)

like-minded (u.m.)

lily-shaped (u.m.)

lily-white (u.m.)

limejuice

limelighter

linchbolt

linchpin

line-bred (u.m.)

line-breed (v.)

linecasting

linecrew

linecut

linefinder

lineup (n., u.m.)

linewalker

linkup (n., u.m.)

link up (v.)

lion-headed (u.m.)

lipread

lipservice

lipstick

litho (c.f., all one word)

litho-offset

little-known (u.m.)

littleneck

little-used (u.m.)

live load

livelong

livestock

live wire

livewire (nonliteral)

liver-brown (u.m.)

liver-colored (u.m.)

liverwurst

living room

loadmeter

loblolly

lobster-tailed (u.m.)

lockfast

lockjaw

locknut

lockout (n., u.m.)

lockpin

lockring

lockstep

lockstitch

lockup (n., u.m.)

lockwasher

locker room

logjam

logroll

logsheet

loggerhead

logo (c.f., all one word)

long-awaited (u.m.)

longbeard (n.)

long-bearded (u.m.)

long-billed (u.m.)

long-distance (u.m.)

long-drawn (u.m.)

longfelt

longhair (n.)

long-haired (u.m.)

longhand (nonliteral)

long-handed (u.m.)

long-handled (u.m.)

longhead (n.)

longhorn

long-horned (u.m.)

longleaf

long-leaved

long-legged (u.m.)

longlegs (n.)

long-lived (u.m.)

longmouthed

long-necked (u.m.)

longnose (n.)

long-nosed (u.m.)

long-past (u.m.)

longplay

longplaying (u.m.)

longrun (u.m.)

longspun

longstanding (u.m.)

longstitch

longwave

longways

longwool

lookdown (n., u.m.)

look-in (n., u.m.)

lookout (n., u.m.)

lookthrough (n., u.m.)

looker-on

loophole

loopstitch

looseleaf (u.m.)

loosemouthed

loose-tongued (u.m.)

lop-eared (u.m.)

lopsided

loudmouthed

loudspeaker

loud-voiced (u.m.)

love-inspired (u.m.)

lovelorn

loveseat

lovesick

lowbrow (nonliteral)

lowbrowed (nonliteral)

low-built (u.m.)

lowdown (n., u.m.)

low-lander

low-lived (u.m.)

low-lying (u.m.)

low-power (u.m.)

low-pressure (u.m.)

low water

lowercase

lowermost

lugbolt

lukewarm

lumberjack
lumber room
lumbo (c.f., all one word)
lumbo-ovarian
lumen-hour
lying-in (n., u.m.)

M

M-day
macebearer
machine-finished (u.m.)
machinegun
machine-hour
machine-made (u.m.)
machine shop
machine work
macro (c.f., all one word)
madcap
made-over (u.m.)
made-up (u.m.)
magneto (c.f., all one word)
magneto-optics
mahjong
maid of honor
maidservant
maidenhair
mailbag
mailclad
mailclerk
mailguard
mail-order (u.m.)
mailpouch
mailtruck
mainframe
mainmast
mainpin

mainsail
mainsheet
mainspring
mainstay
mainstream (nonliteral)
maintop
maintopmost
main yard
major-domo
major-leaguer
major-minor
make-believe (n., u.m.)
makefast (n.)
makeready
makeshift
makeup (n., u.m.)
maker-off
maker-up
making up
mal (c.f., all one word)
man-child
man-created (u.m.)
man-day
maneater
man-fashion (u.m.)
man-grown (u.m.)
manhandle
manhater
man-high (u.m.)
manhole
manhood
man-hour
mankiller
mankind
manmade (u.m.)
man-minute

man-of-war

manservant

man-size (u.m.)

manslaughter

man-woman

man-year

manic-depressive

manifold

mantelshelf

many-colored (u.m.)

many-folded (u.m.)

many-sided (u.m.)

mapreader

maptack

marblehead

marble-looking (u.m.)

marble-topped (u.m.)

marble-white (u.m.)

mare's-nest

mare's-tail

markdown (n., u.m.)

markoff (n., u.m.)

markshot

markup (n., u.m.)

marketplace

marrowbone

marshmallow (confection)

marsh mallow (plant)

mass-minded (u.m.)

mass-produce (v.)

masthead

master at arms

mastermind

master of ceremonies

mastership

mat-covered (u.m.)

matchhead

match-lined (u.m.)

matchmark

matchsafe

matchstick

maxi (pref., all one word)

May Day

May-day (u.m.)

Maypole

Maytide

maybe (adv.)

maybeetle

mayday (distress call)

mealymouthed

mean-acting (u.m.)

mean-spirited (u.m.)

meantime (meanwhile)

mean time (astronomical)

meantone (u.m.)

meanwhile

meatball

meatcutter

meat-eater

meat-fed (u.m.)

meathook

meat-hungry (u.m.)

meatpacker

meatworks

meatwrapper

mechanico (c.f., all one word)

medico (c.f., all one word)

medio (c.f., all one word)

medium-brown (u.m.)

medium-size(d) (u.m.)

mediumweight (n., u.m.)

meek-spirited (u.m.)

meetingplace

megalo (c.f., all one word)

melon-shaped (u.m.)

meltdown (n., u.m.)

menfolk

menkind

meningo (c.f., all one word)

merry-go-round

merry-minded (u.m.)

meshbag

meso (c.f., all one word)

messhall

messkit

messtin

mess-up (n., u.m.)

meta (pref., all one word)

metalammonium

metal-clad (u.m.)

metal-coated (u.m.)

metal-lined (u.m.)

metalworks

meter-amperes

metergram

meter-kilogram

meter-kilogram-second

meter-millimeter

metro (c.f., all one word)

mezzograph

mezzorelievo

mezzosoprano

mezzotint

micro (c.f., all one word)

micro-organism

mid (c.f., all one word)

mid-American

mid-April

mid-decade

mid-1958

mid-Pacific

mid-Victorian

middle-aged (u.m.)

middle-burst (v.)

middlemost

middle-of-the-roader

middle-sized (u.m.)

middlesplitter

middleweight

midi (pref., all one word)

mighty-handed (u.m.)

mil-foot

mild-cured (u.m.)

mild-spoken (u.m.)

mile-long (u.m.)

mile-ohm

milepost

mile-pound

mile-ton

mile-wide (u.m.)

milk-fed (u.m.)

milkhead

milkshake

milkshed

milksop

milk-white (u.m.)

millcake

millfeed

millhand

mill-headed (u.m.)

millpond

millstream

millwright

milli (c.f., all one word)

milligram-hour
mincemeat
mind-healing (u.m.)
mindreader
mindset (n.)
mindsight
minelayer
mineship
minesweeper
mineworks
mini (pref., all one word)
minor-leaguer
minute book
mirror-faced (u.m.)
mirrorscope
mis (pref., all one word)
mist-covered (u.m.)
mistfall
miter box
miter-lock (v.)
mixup (n.)
mixing room
mock-heroic (u.m.)
mockup (n., u.m.)
mocker-up
mockingstock
mocking-up (u.m.)
moldmade (u.m.)
mold shop
molecatcher
mole-eyed (u.m.)
molehead
moleheap
molehill
moneybag
moneychanger

moneygetter
moneylender
money-mad (u.m.)
moneysaver
monkey-faced (u.m.)
monkeypod
monkeypot
monkeyshine
mono (c.f., all one word)
mono-ideistic
mono-iodo
mono-iodohydrin
mono-ion
mono-ousian
monthend
monthlong (u.m.)
moonbeam
moonblind
moon blindness
moonborn
moon-bright (u.m.)
mooncalf
moondown
mooneye
moonface
moongazing
moonglow
moonlighter
moonlit
moon-mad (u.m.)
moonrise
moonsail
moonset
moonshade
moonshine
moonstruck

moontide

moonwalker

moon-white (u.m.)

moosecall

mophead

mopstick

mopup (n., u.m.)

mopper-up

mopping-up (u.m.)

morningtide

mosquito-free (u.m.)

mossback

moss-clad (u.m.)

moss-green (u.m.)

moss-grown (u.m.)

mosshead

moss-lined (u.m.)

most-favored-nation (u.m.)

mothball

moth-eaten (u.m.)

mothhole

motherhood

mother-in-law

mother-of-pearl

moto (c.f., all one word)

motorbike

motorbus

motorcab

motorcade

motorcar

motorcoach

motorcycle

motor-driven (u.m.)

motorjet

motor-minded (u.m.)

motorship

motortruck

motorvan

moundbuilder

mountain-high (u.m.)

mountainside

mountaintop

mountain-walled (u.m.)

mouse-brown (u.m.)

mouse-eared (u.m.)

mouse-eaten (u.m.)

mousehole

mousetrap

mouth-filling (u.m.)

mouth-made (u.m.)

mouthwash

muckrake (v.)

muco (c.f., all one word)

mudbank

mudbath

mud-colored (u.m.)

mudflat

mudflow

mudguard

mudhole

mudlark

mudslinger

mud-splashed (u.m.)

mudstain

mudsucker

mudtrack

muddlehead

muleback

muleskinner

multi (c.f., all one word)

multiple-purpose (u.m.)

music-mad (u.m.)

musico (c.f., all one word)

muskrat

mutton chop (meat)

muttonchop (shape)

muttonhead

myria (c.f., all one word)

mytho (c.f., all one word)

myxo (c.f., all one word)

N

nailbin

nailbrush

nailhead

nail-headed (u.m.)

nailprint

nailpuller

nail-shaped (u.m.)

nail-studded (u.m.)

name-calling (u.m.)

name-dropping (u.m.)

nameplate

namesake

narco (c.f., all one word)

narrow-mouthed (u.m.)

narrowminded

naso (c.f., all one word)

naso-occipital

naso-orbital

native-born (u.m.)

navy-blue (u.m.)

near-acquainted (u.m.)

near-bordering (u.m.)

nearby

near-miss

nearsighted

neat's-foot (u.m.)

neckband

neckbone

neck-breaking (u.m.)

neck-deep (u.m.)

neckguard

neck-high (u.m.)

neckhole

necklace

necktie

necro (c.f., all one word)

needlecase

needle-made (u.m.)

needlepoint

needle-shaped (u.m.)

needle-sharp (u.m.)

needleworked

ne'er-do-well

neo (c.f., all one word)

neo-Greek

nephro (c.f., all one word)

nerve-celled (u.m.)

nerve-racked (u.m.)

netball

netbraider

net-veined (u.m.)

nettlefoot

nettlesome

neuro (c.f., all one word)

never-ending (u.m.)

nevermore

nevertheless

newborn

new-car (u.m.)

newcomer

newfangled

new-fashioned (u.m.)

new-front (v.)

new-made (u.m.)

new-mown (u.m.)

new-rich (u.m.)

newlywed

newscase

newscast

newsclip

newsdealer

news-greedy (u.m.)

newsletter

newspaper

newspaper work

newspaper worker

newsphoto

newsprint

newsreader

newsreel

newssheet

newsstand

newsstory

newsteller

nickname

nickelplate (v.)

nickel-plated (u.m.)

nickel-plating (u.m.)

nickeltype

night-black (u.m.)

nightcap

night-clad (u.m.)

nightclothes

nightclub

nightdress

nightfall

night-fly (v.)

night-flying (u.m.)

night-grown (u.m.)

nighthawk

nightlong (u.m.)

nightmare

nightshade

nightshirt

nighttide

night-veiled (u.m.)

nightwalker

nimble-fingered (u.m.)

nimblefooted

nimbostratus

ninefold

nine-lived (u.m.)

ninepenny

ninepin

ninescore

nitro (c.f., all one word)

nitro-hydro-carbon

no-account (n., u.m.)

no-fault

no-good (n., u.m.)

no-hitter (n.)

nohow

no man's land

no-par (u.m.)

no-par-value (u.m.)

no-show (n., u.m.)

no-thoroughfare (n.)

noble-born (u.m.)

noble-featured (u.m.)

nobleheartedness

noble-looking (u.m.)

noble-minded (u.m.)

non (pref., all one word)

non-civil-service (u.m.)

non-European

non sequitur

non-tumor-bearing (u.m.)

nonesuch

nonetheless

noonday

noontide

north-central (u.m.)

northeast

northgoing

northmost

north-northeast

north-sider

nosebag

nosebleed

nosebone

nosedive

nosedown (n., u.m.)

nosegay

noseguard

nose-high (u.m.)

nosehole

nose-led (u.m.)

nosepipe

nosering

nose-thumbing (u.m.)

noseup (n., u.m.)

notehead

notwithstanding

novel-reading (u.m.)

novel writer

novel-writing (u.m.)

nucleo (c.f., all one word)

nutbreaker

nut-brown (u.m.)

nutcake

nutcracker

nuthatch

nutpick

nut-shaped (u.m.)

nutshell

nutsweet

O

oak-beamed (u.m.)

oak-green (u.m.)

oak-leaved (u.m.)

oarlock

oatbin

oatcake

oat-fed (u.m.)

oatmeal

oatseed

oathbreaker

oblong-elliptic (u.m.)

oblong-leaved (u.m.)

oblong-linear (u.m.)

oblong-ovate (u.m.)

oblong-shaped (u.m.)

oblong-triangular (u.m.)

occipito (c.f., all one word)

occipito-otic

ocean-born (u.m.)

ocean-girdled (u.m.)

oceangoing

oceanside

ocean-spanning (u.m.)

octo (c.f., all one word)

odd-jobber

odd-looking (u.m.)

odd-numbered (u.m.)

off-and-on (u.m.)

offbeat

offcast

offcenter (u.m.)

offcolor (u.m.)

off-colored (u.m.)

offday

off-fall (v.)

off-flavor (n., u.m.)

off-flow

off-go (n.)

offgoing

offgrade

offhand

off-hours

offloading

offlook

off-lying (u.m.)

offpeak

offprint

offput

off-reckoning (n.)

off-season

offset

offshoot

offshore

offside

off-sorts (n.)

offstage

offstreet

offtake

off-the-record (u.m.)

offtype

off-wheel (n.)

off-wheeler (n.)

off-white (u.m.)

officeseeker

office-seeking (u.m.)

office worker

oftentimes

ohm-ammeter

ohmmeter

ohm-mile

oilcake

oilcan

oilcloth

oilcoat

oilcup

oil-driven (u.m.)

oil-fed (u.m.)

oil-forming (u.m.)

oil-harden (v.)

oilhole

oilpaper

oilproofing

oilseed

oilskinned

oil-soaked (u.m.)

oilspill

oilstove

oil-temper (v.)

old-fashioned (u.m.)

old-fogy (u.m.)

old-growing (u.m.)

old-looking (u.m.)

old maid

old-maidish (u.m.)

old man

old-new

oldstyle

oldtimer

old woman

old-young

oleo (c.f., all one word)

oleo butter

oleo oil

olive-brown (u.m.)

olive-drab (u.m.)

olive-growing (u.m.)

olive-skinned (u.m.)

olivewood

olive wood (color)

omni (c.f., all one word)

omni-ignorant

on-and-off (n., u.m.)

on-go (n.)

ongoing

once-over (n.)

once-run (u.m.)

one-acter

one-armed (u.m.)

one-decker

one-eyed (u.m.)

onefold

one-half

one-handed (u.m.)

oneness

one-piece (u.m.)

oneself

one-sided (u.m.)

one-sidedness

onesigned (u.m.)

one-step

one-striper

onetime (formerly, u.m.)

one-time (one action, u.m.)

one-two-three

one-way (u.m.)

onion peel

open-air

open-armed (u.m.)

open-back (u.m.)

open-backed (u.m.)

openband

opencast

opencut

open-faced (u.m.)

openhanded

open house

openminded

openmouthed

open shop

openside (u.m.)

open-sided (u.m.)

operagoer

operagoing

opera house

ophthamalo (c.f., all one word)

orangeade

orange-colored (u.m.)

orangepeel

orange-red (u.m.)

orangestick

orchard house

orderly room

organo (c.f., all one word)

ornitho (c.f., all one word)

osteo (c.f., all one word)

oto (c.f., all one word)

out (pref., all one word)

out-and-out (u.m.)

out-and-outer (n.)

out-loud (u.m.)

outmigration

out-of-date (u.m.)

out-of-door(s) (u.m.)
out-of-State (u.m.)
out-of-the-way (u.m.)
out-to-out (u.m.)
outer-city (u.m.)
outermost
outward-bound (u.m.)
outward-bounder
ovate-acuminate (u.m.)
ovate-oblong (u.m.)
ovato (c.f., all one word)
ovato-oblong
ovato-orbicular
ovenbaked
ovendried
over (c.f., all one word)
overage (surplus)
over-age (older, n., u.m.)
overall (all meanings)
over-the-counter (u.m.)
owl-eyed (u.m.)
oxblood
oxbow
oxcart
oxhorn
oxy (c.f., all one word)
oystershell
oyster-white (u.m.)

P

pace-setting (u.m.)
pachy (c.f., all one word)
packbuilder
packcloth
packhorse
pack-laden (u.m.)

packsack
packsaddle
packstaff
packthread
packup (n., u.m.)
packing box
padcloth
padlock
paddlefoot
page-for-page (u.m.)
page proof
painkiller
painstaking
paintbox
paintbrush
paintmixer
paintstained (u.m.)
pale-blue (u.m.)
pale-cheeked (u.m.)
paleface (n.)
pale-faced (u.m.)
pale-looking (u.m.)
pale-reddish (u.m.)
paleo (c.f., all one word)
paleo-Christian
pallbearer
palm-green (u.m.)
palm-shaded (u.m.)
palmi (c.f., all one word)
pan-broil (v.)
pan ice
Pan American Union
Panhellenic
panel-lined (u.m.)
panic-stricken (u.m.)
panto (c.f., all one word)

panty hose

paperback (n.)

paper box

papercutter

paperhanger

papershell (n., u.m.)

paper-shelled (u.m.)

paper-thin (u.m.)

paperweight

paper-white (u.m.)

papier mache

para (c.f. or pref., all one word)

para-aminobenzoic

para-analgesia

para-anesthesia

parcel-plate (v.)

parchment-covered (u.m.)

parchment maker

parchment-making (u.m.)

parieto (c.f., all one word)

parieto-occipital

parimutuel

part-finished (u.m.)

part owner

part-time (u.m.)

part-timer (n.)

part way

parti (c.f., all one word)

party line

parvi (c.f., all one word)

passback (n.)

passkey

passout (n., u.m.)

passport

passthrough

password

passenger-mile

passer(s)-by

passion-driven (u.m.)

passion-feeding (u.m.)

passion-filled (u.m.)

pastedown (n., u.m.)

pastepot

pasteup (n., u.m.)

patent-in-fee

pathbreaker

pathfinder

patho (c.f., all one word)

patri (c.f., all one word)

pattycake

pawnbroker

payback (n., u.m.)

paycheck

payday

paydirt

payoff (n., u.m.)

payout (n., u.m.)

payroll

paysheet

pay-TV

peacoat

pea-green (u.m.)

peajacket

peanut

peashooter

pea-sized (u.m.)

peace-blessed (u.m.)

peacebreaker

peace-loving (u.m.)

peachbloom

peach-colored (u.m.)

pear-shaped (u.m.)

pearl-eyed (u.m.)

pearl-pure (u.m.)

pearl-set (u.m.)

pearl-studded (u.m.)

pearl-white (u.m.)

peat moss

peat-roofed (u.m.)

pebble-paved (u.m.)

pebble-strewn (u.m.)

peeloff (n., u.m.)

peephole

peepshow

pegleg

pellmell

pen-cancel (v.)

penknife

penmanship

penpoint

penpusher

penrack

penscript

pen-shaped (u.m.)

penstock

pencil box

pencil-mark (v.)

penny-a-liner

pennypincher

pennyweight

pennyworth

pent-up (u.m.)

penta (c.f., all one word)

penta-acetate

peptalk

peppercorn

peppermint

pepperpot

pepper-red (u.m.)

percent

per centum

percompound

percurrent

per diem

persalt

per se

persulfide

peri (pref., all one word)

peri-insular

permafrost

pesthole

pest-ridden (u.m.)

petro (c.f., all one word)

petro-occipital

pharmaco (c.f., all one word)

pharmaco-oryctology

pharyngo (c.f., all one word)

pharyngo-esophageal

pharyngo-oral

phasemeter

phaseout (n., u.m.)

phase-wound (u.m.)

pheno (c.f., all one word)

philo (c.f., all one word)

philo-French

phlebo (c.f., all one word)

phono (c.f., all one word)

phospho (c.f., all one word)

photo (c.f., all one word)

photo-offset

photo-oxidation

photo-oxidative

phreno (c.f., all one word)

phrasemark

phyllo (c.f., all one word)

physico (c.f., all one word)

physio (c.f., all one word)

phyto (c.f., all one word)

pianoforte

pianograph

pianoplayer

pickax

picklock

pick-me-up (n., u.m.)

pickoff (n., u.m.)

pickover (n., u.m.)

pick over (v.)

pickpocket

pickup (n., u.m.)

picker-up

picket line

pickle-cured (u.m.)

picture book

picture writing

piecrust

pie-eater

pie-eyed

piemarker

piepan

pie-stuffed (u.m.)

piece-dye (v.)

piecemeal

piecemold

piezo (c.f., all one word)

piezo-oscillator

pig-back (v.)

pig-backed (u.m.)

pig-bellied (u.m.)

pig-eyed (u.m.)

pigface

pig-faced (u.m.)

pigfoot

pig-footed (u.m.)

pigheaded

pigpen

pigsty

pigtailed

pigeongram

pigeonhole

pigeon-toed (u.m.)

pigeonwing

piggyback

pike-eyed (u.m.)

piledriver

pile-driving (u.m.)

pilehammer

pileup (n., u.m.)

pillpusher

pillrolling

pilltaker

pillowcase

pillowslip

pilot boat

pilot light

pinball

pinblock

pinbone

pincase

pinchback

pinchbar

pinch-hit (v.)

pinch-hitter

pinchpenny

pincushion

pin-eyed (u.m.)

pineapple

pine-bearing (u.m.)

pine-fringed (u.m.)

pine-shaded (u.m.)

pinfall

pinfeather

pinhead

pinhold

pinhole

pinhook

pink-blossomed (u.m.)

pinkeye (n.)

pink-eyed (u.m.)

pinlock

pinpaper

pinpoint

pinprick

pinrail

pinsetter

pinspot

pinstripe

pin-tailed (u.m.)

pinup (n., u.m.)

pinwheel

pipe-drawn (u.m.)

pipedream

pipefitter

pipelayer

pipelined

pipe-shaped

pipestem

pipewalker

pipewelder

pisci (c.f., all one word)

pistol-whip (v.)

pistonhead

pit-eyed (u.m.)

pitfall

pithead

pit-headed (u.m.)

pithole

pitmark

pit-marked (u.m.)

pit-rotted (u.m.)

pitsaw

pitside

pitch-black (u.m.)

pitch box

pitch-colored (u.m.)

pitch-dark (u.m.)

pitchfork

pitchhole

pitch-lined (u.m.)

pitch-marked (u.m.)

pitchout (n., u.m.)

pitchup (n., u.m.)

placecard

placekick

plague-infested (u.m.)

plainback

plain-bodied (u.m.)

plainclothes (u.m.)

plain-headed (u.m.)

plain-spoken (u.m.)

plainwoven (u.m.)

plane-mile

plane-parallel (u.m.)

planetable

plani (c.f., all one word)

plano (c.f., all one word)

plantlife

platelayer

platemark

plate proof

plate-roll (v.)

plate-rolled (u.m.)

platy (c.f., all one word)

play-act (v.)

playback (n., u.m.)

playbill

playbroker

playday

playdown (n., u.m.)

playgoer

playgoing

playground

playoff (n., u.m.)

playpen

playreader

playscript

playsuit

plaything

playwright

play yard

pleasure-bent (u.m.)

pleasure boat

pleasure-seeking (u.m.)

pleo (c.f., all one word)

pleuro (c.f., all one word)

plowback (n., u.m.)

plow-bred (u.m.)

plowhand

plowhorse

plowpan

plowpoint

plow-shaped (u.m.)

plowshare

plowshoe

plowsole

plowstaff

plow tail

plowwright

plughole

plug-in (n., u.m.)

plugtray

plume-crowned (u.m.)

pluri (c.f., all one word)

pluto (c.f., all one word)

pneumato (c.f., all one word)

pneumato-hydato-genetic

pneumo (c.f., all one word)

pockmark

pock-marked (u.m.)

pock-pit (v.)

pocketbook (purse)

pocket book (book)

pocket-eyed (u.m.)

pocketknife

pocket-sized (u.m.)

pocket-veto (v.)

poet-artist

poet-painter

pointblank

poison-dipped (u.m.)

polearm

pole-armed (u.m.)

poleax

polecat

pole-dried (u.m.)

polehorse

pole-pile (v.)

polesetter

pole-shaped (u.m.)

polesitter

pole-stack (v.)

polestar

poletimber

poletrap

pole-vault (v.)

politico (c.f., all one word)

politico-orthodox

poly (c.f., all one word)

poor-blooded (u.m.)

poorfarm

poor-spirited (u.m.)

popcorn

popeye

popgun

popup (n., u.m.)

poppy-bordered (u.m.)

poppycock

poppy-red (u.m.)

poppyseed

portfire

portfolio

porthole

portmanteau

port-mouthed (u.m.)

portside

post (pref., all one word)

post bellum

postcard

post-Christian

post diem

post-free (u.m.)

posthaste

post hospital (military)

post meridiem

post mortem (literal)

postmortem (nonliteral)

post partum

post school (military)

postgraduate

potash

potbellied

potboil

poteye

pothanger

pothole

pothook

potlatch

potlid

potluck

potpie

potpourri

potrack

potshot

potwhiskey

potato field

poultry house

poultry keeper

poultry-keeping (u.m.)

poultry raiser

poultry-raising (u.m.)

poultry yard

poundcake

pound-foolish (u.m.)

pound-foot

poundworth

powder-blue (u.m.)

powder house

powder mill

powder room

powder-scorched (u.m.)

power-driven (u.m.)

power-operated (u.m.)

powerpack

powerplant
praise-deserving (u.m.)
praise-spoiled (u.m.)
praiseworthiness
pre (pref., all one word)
pre-Incan
president-elect
president pro tempore
press agent
press-agentry
pressfeeder
press-forge (v.)
press-made (u.m.)
pressmark
presspack (v.)
pressplate
press proof
preter (pref., all one word)
price cutter
price-cutting (u.m.)
price fixer
price-fixing (u.m.)
pricelist
price-support (u.m.)
priesthood
priest-prince
prime minister
prime-ministerial (u.m.)
prime-ministership
prime-ministry
princehood
prince-priest
printcloth
printout
printscript
printing-in (n., u.m.)

printing-out (n., u.m.)
prison-free (u.m.)
prison-made (u.m.)
prisoner-of-war (u.m.)
prizefighter
prizetaker
prizewinner
prize-winning (u.m.)
pro (pref., all one word)
pro-Ally
pro forma
pro rata
pro tem
pro tempore
procto (c.f., all one word)
profit-and-loss (u.m.)
profit-sharing (u.m.)
proofread
proofsheet
propjet
propwash
proso (c.f., all one word)
proto (c.f., all one word)
proto-Egyptian
proud-looking (u.m.)
proud-minded (u.m.)
pseudo (c.f., all one word)
pseudo-Messiah
pseudo-occidental
pseudo-official
pseudo-owner
psycho (c.f., all one word)
psycho-organic
ptero (c.f., all one word)
public-minded (u.m.)
public-spirited (u.m.)

pugnose

pullback (n., u.m.)

pull box

pulldown (n., u.m.)

pull-in (n., u.m.)

pulloff (n., u.m.)

pull-on (n., u.m.)

pullout (n., u.m.)

pull-push (u.m.)

pullthrough (n., u.m.)

pullup (n., u.m.)

puller-in

puller-out

punchbowl

punchcard

punch-drunk (u.m.)

punchmark

punch-marked (u.m.)

punchout (n.)

pureblood

purebred

pure line

purple-blue (u.m.)

purple-colored (u.m.)

purpleheart (wood)

pushbutton

pushcard

pushcart

pushoff (n., u.m.)

push-pull (u.m.)

pushup (n., u.m.)

pussycat

pussyfoot

putback (n., u.m.)

putoff (n., u.m.)

put-on (n., u.m.)

putout (n., u.m.)

put-put (n.)

put-up (n., u.m.)

putter-forth

putter-in

putter-off

putter-on

putter-out

putter-through

putter-up

pyo (c.f., all one word)

pyro (c.f., all one word)

Q

Q-boat

Q-fever

quadri (c.f., all one word)

quadri-invariant

quarter-angled (u.m.)

quarterback

quarter-bloom (u.m.)

quarter-bound (u.m.)

quarter-breed (u.m.)

quarter-cast (u.m.)

quarter-cut (u.m.)

quarterdeck

quarter-miler

quarterpace

quarter-phase (u.m.)

quartersaw (v.)

quarterstaff

quarterstretch

quartermaster

quartermaster general

quartermaster-generalship

quasi- (all hyphenated)

queen bee
quick-change (u.m., v.)
quick-draw (u.m., v.)
quickfreeze (u.m., v.)
quicklime
quicksand
quickset
quicksilver
quickstep
quick time
quick-witted (u.m.)
quin (c.f., all one word)
quitclaim
quitrent

R

rabbit-backed (u.m.)
rabbit-eared (u.m.)
rabbitmouth
rabbitmouthed (u.m.)
raceabout (n., u.m.)
racecourse
racegoer
racehorse
racetrack
radarscope
radiofrequency
radiumtherapy
ragbolt
rag-made (u.m.)
ragsorter
ragtag
railcar
railguard
rail-ridden (u.m.)
railroad

railsetter
railsplitter
railway maker
rainband
rain-beaten (u.m.)
rainbow
raincheck
raincoat
raindrop
rainfall
rain-soft (u.m.)
rainspout
rainstorm
rainwash
rakeoff (n., u.m.)
ramjet
ramrod
ramshackle
ranch hand
rangefinder
range light
rangerider
rash-headed (u.m.)
rash-hearted (u.m.)
rash-minded (u.m.)
ratbite
ratcatcher
rathole
rat-infested (u.m.)
rat-tailed (u.m.)
rat-tight (u.m.)
rattrap
rate-cutting (u.m.)
rate-fixing (u.m.)
ratepayer
rate-raising (u.m.)

ratesetting

rattlebrain

rattlesnake

rattletrap

rawboned

raw-edged (u.m.)

rawhide

raw-looking (u.m.)

razorback

razor-billed (u.m.)

razoredge

razor-keen (u.m.)

razor-sharp (u.m.)

razzle-dazzle

re (pref., all one word)

re-cover (cover again)

re-create (create again)

re-cross-examination

re-ice

re-ink

re-redirect

reading room

readout (n.)

ready-built (u.m.)

ready-handed (u.m.)

readymade (u.m.)

ready-mix (u.m.)

ready-witted (u.m.)

rearguard

rearmost

rearview (u.m.)

reception room

recordbreaker

recti (c.f., all one word)

recto (c.f., all one word)

red-billed (u.m.)

red-blooded (u.m.)

redbone

redcap (porter)

redcoat (n.)

redeye (n.)

red-eyed (u.m.)

red-faced (u.m.)

red-haired (u.m.)

redhanded

redhead (n.)

red-hot (u.m.)

red-legged (u.m.)

red line (literal)

redout (n., u.m.)

redtape (nonliteral)

red tape (literal)

red-throated (u.m.)

red-yellow (u.m.)

religio (c.f., all one word)

repair shop

representative at large

representative-elect

research worker

resino (c.f., all one word)

retro (c.f., all one word)

retro-ocular

retro-omental

retro-operative

retro-oral

rheo (c.f., all one word)

rhino (c.f., all one word)

rhizo (c.f., all one word)

rhod(o) (c.f., all one word)

rhomb(o) (c.f., all one word)

ricegrowing

rice water

rich-bound (u.m.)

rich-looking (u.m.)

ridgeband

ridgepole

ridgetop

riffraff

rifleshot

rigout (n., u.m.)

rig-up (n., u.m.)

rightabout

rightabout-face

right-angle (u.m., v.)

right-angled (u.m.)

right field

right-handed (u.m.)

right-hander

right-headed (u.m.)

rightmost

right-of-way

rightwing (political)

rim-deep (u.m.)

rimfire

rimlock

rimrock

ring-adorned (u.m.)

ring-banded (u.m.)

ring-billed (u.m.)

ringbolt

ringgiver

ring-in (n., u.m.)

ringlead (v.)

ring-necked (u.m.)

ring-off (n., u.m.)

ringpin

ring-porous (u.m.)

ring-shaped (u.m.)

ringside

ringsight

ringstand

ringstick

ring-tailed (u.m.)

ring-up (n., u.m.)

riverbank

riverbed

riverflow

river-formed (u.m.)

riverfront

riverhead

riverscape

riverside

riverwash

river-worn (u.m.)

roadbank

roadbed

roadblock

roadbuilder

roadhead

roadhog

roadmap

roadside

road-test (v.)

road-weary (u.m.)

rockabye

rockbottom (nonliteral)

rock-climbing (u.m.)

rockfall (n.)

rock-fallen (u.m.)

rockfill

rockfirm

rockpile

rockshaft

rockslide

rod-shaped (u.m.)

roebuck

roentgeno (c.f., all one word)

rollabout (n., u.m.)

rollback (n., u.m.)

rollcall

roll-fed (u.m.)

rollfilm

rolloff (n., u.m.)

roll-on (n., u.m.)

rollout (n., u.m.)

rolltop

rollup (n., u.m.)

roller-made (u.m.)

roller-milled (u.m.)

roofgarden

rooftop

rootcap

root-cutting (u.m.)

rootfast

roothold

ropelayer

ropestitch

ropewalk

rose-bright (u.m.)

rosebud

rosehead

rose-headed (u.m.)

rose-scented (u.m.)

rose-sweet (u.m.)

rose water

rotorship

rotten-dry (u.m.)

rotten-minded (u.m.)

rough-and-ready (u.m.)

rough-and-tumble (n., u.m.)

roughcast (u.m., v.)

rough-coat (v.)

rough-cut (u.m.)

roughdraw (v.)

roughdress (v.)

roughdry (u.m., v.)

rough-face (v.)

rough-faced (u.m.)

roughhew

rough-looking (u.m.)

roughneck

roughrider

roughsetter

roughshod

rough-sketch (v.)

roughstuff

roughtailed

rough work (n.)

roughwork (v.)

roughwrought

rougher-up

roughing-in (u.m.)

roundabout (n., u.m.)

roundabout-face

round-faced (u.m.)

roundhead

round-made (u.m.)

roundmouthed

roundnose (tool)

roundout (n., u.m.)

roundrobin (petition)

roundseam

roundtable (panel)

round-tailed (u.m.)

round-topped (u.m.)

round-tripper

roundup (n., u.m.)
rub-a-dub
rubdown (n., u.m.)
rubberband
rubber-down
rubber-lined (u.m.)
rubberneck
rubber-off
rubber-set (u.m.)
rubberstamp (nonliteral, n., u.m., v.)
rubber stamp (n.)
rubber-stamped (u.m.)
ruby-hued (u.m.)
ruby-red (u.m.)
ruby-throated (u.m.)
rudderhead
rudderhole
rudderpost
rule of thumb
rumrunner
rumseller
rumpus room
runabout (n., u.m.)
runaround (n., u.m.)
runaway (n., u.m.)
runback (n., u.m.)
runby (n.)
rundown (n., u.m.)
run-in (n., u.m.)
runoff (n., u.m.)
run-on (n., u.m.)
runout (n., u.m.)
runthrough (n., u.m.)
runup (n., u.m.)
runner-up
rush-bottomed (u.m.)

rust-brown (u.m.)
rust-eaten (u.m.)
rustproofing
rust-resistant (u.m.)
rust-stained (u.m.)
rye field

S

S-bend
S-brake
S-iron
S-ray
S-shaped
S-trap
S-wrench
saber-legged (u.m.)
sabertooth
saber-toothed (u.m.)
sable-cloaked (u.m.)
Sabrejet
saccharo (c.f., all one word)
sackbearer
sackcloth
sack coat
sack-coated (u.m.)
sack-making (u.m.)
sack-shaped (u.m.)
sacro (c.f., all one word)
sad-eyed (u.m.)
sadiron
sad-voiced (u.m.)
saddleback
saddle-backed (u.m.)
saddlebag
saddlebow
saddlecloth

saddle-making (u.m.)

saddlesore

saddle-stitched (u.m.)

saddle-wire (u.m.)

safeblower

safecracker

safe-deposit (u.m.)

safeguard

safehold

sagebrush

sageleaf

sage-leaved (u.m.)

sailcloth

sail-dotted (u.m.)

sailflying

salesclerk

salesmanship

salespeople

salesperson

salmon-colored (u.m.)

salmon-red (u.m.)

saltcellar

salt-cured (u.m.)

saltpeter

saltpit

saltshaker

saltspoon

saltsprinkler

saltworks

salver-shaped (u.m.)

sample book

sample box

sample-making (u.m.)

sandbag

sandbank

sandbar

sandbath

sandbin

sandblast

sandblown

sand-built (u.m.)

sand-buried (u.m.)

sand-cast (u.m., v.)

sandfill

sandflea

sandhill

sandhole

sandlot

sandpaper

sandpile

sandpipe

sandpit

sand-pump (u.m., v.)

sandshoe

sandspit

sandstorm

sandweld (v.)

sand-welded (u.m.)

sand-welding (u.m.)

sandy-bottomed (u.m.)

sangfroid

sans serif

sans souci

sapphire-blue (u.m.)

sapphire-colored (u.m.)

sarco (c.f., all one word)

sashcord

satin-lined (u.m.)

satin-smooth (u.m.)

saucedish

saucepan

sauerbraten

sauerkraut

save-all (n., u.m.)

sawback

saw-billed (u.m.)

sawbones (n.)

sawbuck

sawdust

saw-edged (u.m.)

sawtimber

sawtooth

saw-toothed (u.m.)

saxcornet

saxhorn

saxtuba

say-nothing (n., u.m.)

say-so (n.)

scaledown (n., u.m.)

scale-reading (u.m.)

scapegoat

scapulo (c.f., all one word)

scarface

scar-faced (u.m.)

scarecrow

scarfpin

scarlet-breasted (u.m.)

scarlet-red (u.m.)

scatterbrain

sceneshifter

scenewright

schisto (c.f., all one word)

schizo (c.f., all one word)

schoolbag

school board

schoolbookish

schoolbus

schoolchildren

schoolday

school-made (u.m.)

schoolteacher

school-trained (u.m.)

scientifico (c.f., all one word)

scissorbill

scissor-tailed (u.m.)

scissor-winged (u.m.)

scissorshold

scissors-shaped (u.m.)

scissors smith

sclero (c.f., all one word)

sclero-oophoritis

sclero-optic

scorecard

scoresheet

scouthood

scrapbasket

scrapworks

scratchbrush

scratch-brusher

scratch-coated (u.m.)

screenout (n., u.m.)

screenplay

screwball

screwbolt

screwcap

screwdown (u.m.)

screw-driven (u.m.)

screwdriver

screwhead

screwnut

screw-threaded (u.m.)

screw-turned (u.m.)

scrollhead

scuttlebutt

scythe-shaped (u.m.)

sea base

sea-based (u.m.)

sea-bathed (u.m.)

seabeach

sea-beaten (u.m.)

seabed

sea bird

sea-blue (u.m.)

sea boat

sea-born (u.m.)

sea-bred (u.m.)

seacoast

sea-deep (u.m.)

seadog

sea-driven (u.m.)

seadrome

sea-encircled (u.m.)

seafare (food)

seafighter

seafolk

seafood

seafront

seagoer

seagoing

seahound

sealift

seaport

sea room

seascape

sea scout

seascouting

seashell

seashine

seashore

seasick

seaside

seastroke

sea time (clock)

seawall

seaworn

seaworthiness

sea-wrecked (u.m.)

seamblasting

seamstitch

seamweld (v.)

seam-welded (u.m.)

seatbelt

seat-mile

second-class (u.m.)

second-degree (u.m.)

second-foot

second-guess (v.)

secondhand (adv., u.m.)

second-rate (u.m.)

secretary general

secretary-generalcy

secretary-generalship

section person

seesaw

seedbed

seedcake

seedcase

seedcoat

seedstalk

seerhand

seersucker

seismo (c.f., all one word)

selfhood

selfless

selfness

selfsame

selloff (n., u.m.)

sellout (n., u.m.)

semiannual

semiarid

semi-armor-piercing (u.m.)

semi-Christian

semi-idleness

semi-indirect

sendoff (n., u.m.)

sendout (n., u.m.)

senso (c.f., all one word)

septi (c.f., all one word)

septo (c.f., all one word)

serio (c.f., all one word)

sero (c.f., all one word)

serrate-ciliate (u.m.)

serrate-dentate (u.m.)

service-connected (u.m.)

servoaccelerometer

servoamplifier

servocontrol

servomechanism

servomotor

servosystem

sesqui (c.f., all one word)

set-aside (n., u.m.)

setback (n., u.m.)

setbolt

setdown (n., u.m.)

set-fair (n.)

set-in (n., u.m.)

setoff (n., u.m.)

set-on (n., u.m.)

setout (n., u.m.)

setpin

setscrew

set-stitched (u.m.)

set-to (n., u.m.)

setup (n., u.m.)

setter-forth

setter-in

setter-on

setter-out

setter-to

setter-up

sevenfold

sevenpenny

sevenscore

seven-shooter

seven-up (v.)

severalfold

shade-giving (u.m.)

shade-grown (u.m.)

shadowboxing

shadowgram

shadowgraph

shadow line

shagbark

shag-haired (u.m.)

shakedown (n., u.m.)

shakeout (n., u.m.)

shakeup (n., u.m.)

shallow-draft (u.m.)

shame-crushed (u.m.)

shamefaced

shankbone

shank mill

shapeup (n., u.m.)

sharp-angled (u.m.)

sharp-cut (u.m.)

sharp-edged (u.m.)

sharp-freeze (u.m., v.)

sharp-freezer
sharp-looking (u.m.)
sharp-set (u.m.)
sharpshooter
sharp-tailed (u.m.)
sharp-witted (u.m.)
sheepdip
sheepfaced
sheepgate
sheepherder
sheepnose
sheepshank
sheepshear (v.)
sheepshearer (n.)
sheepshed
sheepstealer
sheeroff (n., u.m.)
sheerup (n., u.m.)
sheetblock
sheetflood
sheetrock
shellburst
shellfire
shellfishery
shellhole
shell-like
shellshocked
shelterbelt
shield-shaped (u.m.)
shinbone
shinguard
shinplaster
shiner-up
shipbreaker
shipbroken
shipbroker

shipbuilder
shiplap
shipmast
shipowning
ship-rigged (u.m.)
shipshape
shipside
shipwreck
shipping master
shipping room
shirtband
shirtwaist
shoeblack
shoebrush
shoehorn
shoelace
shoepack
shoescraper
shoeshine
shoestring
shoetree
shootoff (u.m.)
shopbreaker
shopfolk
shoplifter
shop-made (u.m.)
shopmark
shop-soiled (u.m.)
shoptalk
shopwalker
shopwindow
shore bird
shore boat
shorefast
shoregoing
shoreside

short-armed (u.m.)

shortbread

shortcake

shortchange (v.)

shortchanger

short-circuited (u.m.)

shortcoming

shortcut (n., u.m., v.)

shortfall (n.)

short-fed (u.m.)

shorthand (writing)

short-handed (u.m.)

shorthead

shorthorn (n., u.m.)

short-horned (u.m.)

short-lasting (u.m.)

shortleaf (u.m.)

short-lived (u.m.)

shortrib

shortrun (u.m.)

shortsighted

shortstaff

shortstop

shortwave (radio)

shotgun

shothole

shotput

shotstar

shoulder-high (u.m.)

shovel-headed (u.m.)

shovel-nosed (u.m.)

showcard

showcase

showdown (n., u.m.)

showoff (n., u.m.)

showplace

showthrough (n., u.m.)

showup (n., u.m.)

shredout (n., u.m.)

shroud-laid (u.m.)

shroudplate

shunt-wound (u.m.)

shutaway (n., u.m.)

shutdown (n., u.m.)

shuteye (n., u.m.)

shut-in (n., u.m.)

shut-mouthed (u.m.)

shutoff (n., u.m.)

shutout (n., u.m.)

shutup (u.m.)

shuttlecock

sickbay

sickbed

sicklist

sidearms

sideband

sidebone

sideburns

sidecar

sidecheck

side-cut (u.m.)

sidedress (v.)

sideflash

sidehead

sidehill

sidehook

sidekick

sidelap

side light (literal)

sidelight (nonliteral)

side line (literal)

sideline (nonliteral)

sidelong

sidenote

sideplate

sideplay

sidesaddle

sideshow

sideslip

sidesplitting

sidestep

sidestitch

side-stitched (u.m.)

sidesway

sideswipe

sidetrack

sidewalk

sidewall

side-wheeler

sidewinder

sighthole

sightread

sightsaver

sightseeing

sightsetter

signoff (n., u.m.)

sign-on (n., u.m.)

signpost

signup (n., u.m.)

silico (c.f., all one word)

silk-stockinged (u.m.)

silkworks

siltpan

silver-backed (u.m.)

silverbeater

silver-bright (u.m.)

silver-gray (u.m.)

silver-haired (u.m.)

silver-lead (u.m.)

silver-leaved (u.m.)

silverplate (v.)

silver-plated (u.m.)

silverpoint

silverprint

silvertip

silver-tongued (u.m.)

silvertop

simon-pure (u.m.)

simple-headed (u.m.)

simple-minded (u.m.)

simple-rooted (u.m.)

simple-witted (u.m.)

simulcast

sin-born (u.m.)

sin-bred (u.m.)

singsong

singlebar

single-breasted (u.m.)

single-decker

single-edged (u.m.)

singlehanded

singlehood

single-loader

single-minded (u.m.)

single-phase (u.m.)

single-seater

singlestick

singletree

sinkhead

sinkhole

sisterhood

sister-in-law

sitdown (n., u.m.)

sit-downer

sitfast (n., u.m.)

situp (n., u.m.)

sitter-by

sitter-out

sitting room

six-cylinder (u.m.)

sixfold

sixpenny

six-ply (u.m.)

sixscore

six-shooter

six-wheeler

sizeup (n., u.m.)

skidlift

skidroad

skindeep

skindiver

skinflint

skin-graft (v.)

skipjack

skirtmarker

skullcap

skunkhead

skunktop

sky-blue (u.m.)

skygazer

sky-high (u.m.)

skyjacker

skylift

skylook (v.)

skyrocket

skysail

skyscape

skyscraper

skyshine

skywave

slab-sided (u.m.)

slack-bake (v.)

slack-filled (u.m.)

slack water

slambang

slapbang

slapdash

slapdown (n., u.m.)

slaphappy

slapjack

slapstick

slap-up (n., u.m.)

slate-blue (u.m.)

slate-colored (u.m.)

slateworks

slaughterpen

slaughter-born (u.m.)

slaughter worker

Slavo-Hungarian

sledge-hammered (u.m.)

sledgemeter

sleep-filled (u.m.)

sleeptalker

sleepwalker

sleepy-eyed (u.m.)

sleepyhead

sleepy-looking (u.m.)

sleetstorm

sleeveband

sleuthhound

slidefilm

slideknot

slingball

slingshot

slipalong (u.m.)

slipback

slipband

slipcase

slipcover

slipknot

slip-on (n., u.m.)

slip proof (printing)

slipproof

slipring

slipsheet

slipshod

slipsole

slipstep

slipstitch

slipstream

slip-up (n., u.m.)

slipwasher

slit-eyed (u.m.)

slitshell

slop-molded (u.m.)

slopseller

slope-faced (u.m.)

slopeways

slowbelly

slowdown (n., u.m.)

slow-footed (u.m.)

slowgoing

slow-motion (u.m.)

slowmouthed

slowpoke

slow time

slowup (n., u.m.)

slow-witted (u.m.)

slug-cast (v.)

slugcaster

slumdweller

slumgullion

slumlord

slumber-bound (u.m.)

small businessman

small-hipped (u.m.)

smallmouthed

smallpox

small-scale (u.m.)

smallsword

smalltalk

smalltown (u.m.)

smart-alecky (u.m.)

smart-looking (u.m.)

smart-tongued (u.m.)

smashup (n., u.m.)

smearcase

smoke-blinded (u.m.)

smokebomb

smokechaser

smoke-dried (u.m.)

smoke-dry (v.)

smoke-dyed (u.m.)

smoke-filled (u.m.)

smokejack

smokejumper

smoke-laden (u.m.)

smokepot

smokescreen

smokestack

smoking room

smoothbore

smooth-browed (u.m.)

smooth-cast (u.m.)

smoothmouthed

smooth-tongued (u.m.)

smooth-working (u.m.)

snackbar

snail-paced (u.m.)

snail-slow (u.m.)

snail's pace

snakebite

snake-bitten (u.m.)

snake-eyed (u.m.)

snakehead

snakehole

snakepit

snapback

snapdragon

snaphead

snaphook

snap-on (n., u.m.)

snapout (n.)

snapring

snaproll

snapshooter

snapshot

snap-up (u.m.)

snapper-back

snapper-up

snipebill

snipe-nosed (u.m.)

sniperscope

snooperscope

snowball

snowbank

snowberg

snowblind

snow blindness

snowblink

snowblock

snow-blocked (u.m.)

snowblower

snowbreak

snowcapped

snow-choked (u.m.)

snowclad (u.m.)

snow-covered (u.m.)

snowdrift

snowfall

snowflake

snowmelt

snow-melting (u.m.)

snowmobile

snowpack

snowpit

snowplow

snowscape

snowshade

snowshed

snowshoe

snowsled

snowslide

snowsuit

snow-topped (u.m.)

snow water

snow-white (u.m.)

so-and-so

so-called (u.m.)

so-seeming (u.m.)

so-so

soapbubble

soapdish

soapflakes

soaprock

soapstock

soapsuds

sober-minded (u.m.)

sobersides

social work

social worker

socio (c.f., all one word)

socio-official

socioeconomic

sodbuster

sodculture

sod house

sodajerk

soda water

sofa maker

sofa-making (u.m.)

softball

soft-boiled (u.m.)

softhead

soft-pedal (v.)

soft-shelled (u.m.)

soft-soap (nonliteral, v.)

soft-soaper (nonliteral, n.)

soft-spoken (u.m.)

softtack

soldier-fashion (u.m.)

solecutter

soleplate

somato (c.f., all one word)

someday

somehow

someone (anyone)

some one (distributive)

someplace

sometime (adv., u.m.)

some time (some time ago)

somewhat

son-in-law

songfest

songwright

sonobuoy

soothfast

soothsayer

sore-eyed (u.m.)

sorefoot (n.)

sorefooted (u.m.)

sorehead (n., u.m.)

sorry-looking (u.m.)

soul-deep (u.m.)

soul-searching (u.m.)

soulsick

sound-absorbing (u.m.)

sound field

soundfilm

sound-minded (u.m.)

soundoff (n., u.m.)

soundtrack

soupbone

soupspoon

sourbelly

sourbread

sourdough (n.)

sourfaced

sour-natured (u.m.)

sour-sweet

south-born (u.m.)

south-central (u.m.)

southeast

southgoing

southlander

southpaw

south-sider

south-southeast

southwest

soybean

sowback

sowbelly

spaceband

spacebar

space-cramped (u.m.)

spacemark

spaceship

space time

spade-dug (u.m.)

spadefoot

spade-footed (u.m.)

spade-shaped (u.m.)

span-long (u.m.)

span-new (u.m.)

Spanish-born (u.m.)

Spanish-speaking (u.m.)

spare-bodied (u.m.)

sparerib

spare room

spark plug (literal)

sparkplug (nonliteral)

speakeasy

spearhead

spear-high (u.m.)

spear-shaped (u.m.)

spectro (c.f., all one word)

speech-bereft (u.m.)

speech-read (v.)

speedboating

speedletter

speedtrap

speedup (n., u.m.)

spellbinding

spelldown (n., u.m.)

spell-free (u.m.)

spend-all (n.)

spendthrift

spermato (c.f., all one word)

spermo (c.f., all one word)

spheno (c.f., all one word)

spheno-occipital

spicecake

spice-laden (u.m.)

spider-legged

spider-spun (u.m.)

spider web (n.)

spiderweb (u.m., v.)

spikehorn

spike-kill (v.)

spike-pitch (v.)

spinback

spinoff

spindle-formed (u.m.)

spindlehead

spindle-legged (u.m.)

spindlelegs

spindleshanks

spinebone

spine-broken (u.m.)

spine-pointed (u.m.)

spino (c.f., all one word)

spino-olivary

spirit-born (u.m.)

spirit-broken (u.m.)

spirit writing

spitball

spitfire

spitstick

splayfooted

splaymouthed

spleen-born (u.m.)

spleen-swollen (u.m.)

spleno (c.f., all one word)

splitfinger

splitfruit

splitmouth

splitsaw

split-tongued (u.m.)

splitup (n., u.m.)

spoilsport

spongecake

spongediver

sponge-diving (u.m.)

sponge-shaped (u.m.)

spoolwinder

spoon-beaked (u.m.)

spoon-billed (u.m.)

spoonbread

spoon-fed (u.m.)

spoon-shaped (u.m.)

spoonways

sporeformer

sporo (c.f., all one word)

spot-checked (u.m.)

spot-face (v.)

spotweld (v.)

spotwelded (u.m.)

spot-welding (u.m.)

spray-washed (u.m.)

spread-eagle (u.m., v.)

spreadhead

spreadout (n., u.m.)

spread-set (v.)

springback

springbok

spring-born (u.m.)

springbuck

spring-clean (v.)

springfinger

spring-grown (u.m.)

springhalt

springhead

spring-plow (v.)

spring-plowed (u.m.)

springtide

springtrap

spur-clad (u.m.)

spur-driven (u.m.)

spurgall

spur-galled (u.m.)

spur-heeled (u.m.)

spyglass

spyhole

spytower

square-bottomed (u.m.)

square-built (u.m.)

square-faced (u.m.)

squareflipper

squarehead

square-headed

square-rigged (u.m.)

square-set (u.m.)

squareshooter

squeeze-in (n., u.m.)

squeezeout (n., u.m.)

squeezeup (n., u.m.)

squirrel-headed (u.m.)

stackup (n., u.m.)

staff-herd (v.)

stag-handled (u.m.)

staghead

stag-headed (u.m.)

staghorn

stag-horned (u.m.)

staghound

staghunter

stagecoach

stagehand

stage-struck (u.m.)

staircase

stairhead

stairstep

stakehead

stakeout (n.)

stale-worn (u.m.)

stall-fed (u.m.)

stall-feed (v.)

standby (n., u.m.)

standdown (n., u.m.)

standfast (n., u.m.)

stand-in (n., u.m.)

standoff (n., u.m.)

standoffish

standout (n., u.m.)

standpat

standpipe

standpoint

standpost

standstill (n., u.m.)

standup (n., u.m.)

standardbred

standard time

staphlyo (c.f., all one word)

starblind

starbright

stardust

stargazer

star-led (u.m.)

starlit

starlite (gem)

starnose

starshake

starshine

sharshoot

star-spangled (u.m.)

starstroke

star-studded (u.m.)

star time

starchworks

stark-blind (u.m.)

stark-mad (u.m.)

stark-naked (u.m.)

stark-raving (u.m.)

starter-off

startup (n., u.m.)

stat (pref., all one word)

State-aided (u.m.)

State line

State-owned (u.m.)

statehood

statequake

stateside

station house

stato (c.f., all one word)

statute-barred (u.m.)

statute book

stay-at-home (n., u.m.)

staybar

staybolt

stayboom

staylace

staylog

staypin

stayplow

staysail

staywire

steamboating

steamcar

steam-cooked (u.m.)

steam-driven (u.m.)

steamfitter

steampipe

steamplant

steampower (n.)

steam powerplant

steam-pocket (v.)

steam-propelled (u.m.)

steamroll (v.)

steamroller (u.m., v.)

steamship

steamtable

steamtightness

steamer line

steel-blue (u.m.)

steel-bright (u.m.)

steel-cased (u.m.)

steelclad

steel-framed (u.m.)

steel-hard (u.m.)

steelhead

steelplate

steelworks

steep-rising (u.m.)

steep-to (u.m.)

steep-up (u.m.)

steep-walled (u.m.)

steeplechase

steeple-high (u.m.)

steeplejack

steepletop

stemhead

stempost

stemwinder

stencil-cutting (u.m.)

steno (c.f., all one word)

stepaunt

stepchild

stepdown (n., u.m.)

step-in (n., u.m.)

stepladder

stepoff (n., u.m.)

step-on (n., u.m.)

step-up (n., u.m.)

stepping-off (u.m.)

stepping-out (u.m.)

stereo (c.f., all one word)

sterncastle

stern-faced (u.m.)

stern-heavy (u.m.)

stern-looking (u.m.)

sternmost

sternpost

stern wheel

stern-wheeler

sterno (c.f., all one word)

stetho (c.f., all one word)

stewpan

stewpot

stick-at-it (n., u.m.)

stickfast (n.)

stick-in-the-mud (n., u.m.)

stickout (n., u.m.)

stickpin

stick-to-it-iveness (n.)

stickup (n., u.m.)

sticker-in

sticker-on

sticker-up

stiff-backed (u.m.)

stiffneck

stiff-necked (u.m.)

still-admired (u.m.)

stillbirth

stillborn

still-burn (v.)

still-fish (v.)

still-hunt (v.)

still-recurring (u.m.)

stillstand

stinkball

stinkbomb

stinkpot

stirabout (n., u.m.)

stirfry

stir-up (n., u.m.)

stitchdown (n., u.m.)

stitchup (n., u.m.)

stockbreeder

stockbroker

stockfeeder

stockholding

stockjobber

stockjudging

stocklist

stockpile

stockpot

stockraiser

stockrack

stock-still (u.m.)

stocktaker

stocktruck

stockwright

stokehold

stokehole

stomach-filling (u.m.)

stomach-shaped (u.m.)

stomach-sick (u.m.)

stomato (c.f., all one word)

stonebiter

stoneblind

stonebrash

stonebreaker

stonebroke

stonebrood

stonecast

stone-cold (u.m.)

stonecrusher

stone-dead (u.m.)

stone-deaf (u.m.)

stone-eyed (u.m.)

stonehand

stonehead

stonelayer

stonelifter

stonemason

stone proof

stoneshot

stone wall (n.)

stonewall (u.m., v.)

stone writing

stony-eyed (u.m.)

stony land

stopback (n.)

stopblock

stopclock

stopgap

stophound

stoplist

stoplog

stop-loss (u.m.)

stopoff (n., u.m.)

stopwatch

storage room

storefront

storeship

storm-beaten (u.m.)

stormflow

storm-laden (u.m.)

storm-swept (u.m.)

storm-tossed (u.m.)

stormwind

storyteller

stout-armed (u.m.)

stoutheartedness

stout-minded (u.m.)

stovebrush

stove-heated (u.m.)

stovepipe

stowaway (n., u.m.)

stowdown (n., u.m.)

straddleback

straddle-face (v.)

straddle-legged (u.m.)

straightaway

straight-backed (u.m.)

straight-cut (u.m.)

straightedge

straight-edged (u.m.)

straight-faced (u.m.)

straightforward

straighthead

straight-legged (u.m.)

straight line

straight-lined (u.m.)

straight-out (n., u.m.)

straight-spoken (u.m.)

straight time

straight-up (u.m.)

straight-up-and-down (u.m.)

strainslip

strait-chested (u.m.)

straitjacket

straitlaced

stranglehold

strap-bolt (v.)

straphanger

straphead

strap-shaped (u.m.)

strapwatch

strato (c.f., all one word)

strawberry field

strawboss

straw-built (u.m.)

strawhat

straw-roofed (u.m.)

strawsplitting

strawstack

straw-stuffed (u.m.)

strawwalker

straw-yellow (u.m.)

strayaway (n., u.m.)

stray line

straymark

streambank

streambed

streamflow

streamhead

streamlined

streamside

street-bred (u.m.)

streetcar

streetcleaner

street-cleaning (u.m.)

streetsweeper

streetwalker

strepto (c.f., all one word)

stretchout (n., u.m.)

strikebreaker

strike-in (n., u.m.)

strikeout (n., u.m.)

striker-in

striker-out

stringcourse

stringhalt

string proof (density)

stringways

stripcropping

striptease

strong-arm (u.m., v.)

strongback (nautical)

strong-backed (u.m.)

stronghold

strong man

strong-minded (u.m.)

strongpoint (n.)

stubrunner

stub-toed (u.m.)

stubwing

stubble field

stubble-mulch (u.m.)

stubbornminded

stucco-fronted (u.m.)

stuckup (n., u.m.)

stuck-upper

stuck-uppish (u.m.)

studbolt

studhorse

studmare

stupidhead

stupid-headed (u.m.)

stupid-looking (u.m.)

sturdy-limbed (u.m.)

stylo (c.f., all one word)

sub (pref., all one word)

sub rosa

sub specie

sub-subcommittee

subject-object

subject-objectivity

subter (pref., all one word)

such-and-such

suckhole

suck-in (n., u.m.)

sugarcake

sugarcane

sugar-coat (v.)

sugar-coated (u.m.)

sugar-cured (u.m.)

sugarloaf

sugarplum

sugarspoon

sugarsweet

sugar water

sugarworks

sulfa (c.f., all one word)

sulfo (c.f., all one word)

sulfon (c.f., all one word)

sullenhearted

sullen-natured (u.m.)

summer-clad (u.m.)

summer-dried (u.m.)

summer-fallow (v.)

summer-made (u.m.)

summertide

summertime (season)

summer time (daylight savings)

sun-baked (u.m.)

sunbath

sun-bathed (u.m.)

sunbeam

sunblind

sun blindness

sunbonnet

sunbow

sunbreak

sunburn

sunburst

sun-cured (u.m.)

sundial

sundog

sundown

sundress

sun-dried (u.m.)

sun-dry (v.)

sunfall

sunfast

sunglade

sunglare

sunglasses

sunglow

sunlamp

sunlit

sunquake

sunray

sunrise

sunscald

sunset

sunshade

sunshine

sun-shot (u.m.)

sunshower

sunspot

sunstricken

sunstroke

sunstruck

suntan

sun time (measure)

suntime (dawn)

sunup

sunny-looking (u.m.)

sunny-natured (u.m.)

super (pref., all one word)

super high frequency

super-superlative

superhighway

supermarket

Super Bowl

supra (pref., all one word)

supra-abdominal

supra-angular

supra-auditory

supra-Christian

sur (pref., all one word)

sure-fire (u.m.)

sure-footed (u.m.)

sure-slow

surf-battered (u.m.)

surf fish

surf-swept (u.m.)

swallowpipe

swallow-tailed (u.m.)

swampside

swan-bosomed (u.m.)

swandive

swanherd

swanmark

swanneck

swansong

swansdown

swashbuckler

swashplate

swayback (n., u.m.)

sway-backed (u.m.)

swaybar

sway-brace (v.)

swearer-in

sweatband

sweatsuit

sweepback (aviation, n., u.m.)

sweepforward (aviation, n., u.m.)

sweepstake

sweepthrough (n., u.m.)

sweepwasher

sweetbread

sweet-breathed (u.m.)

sweetbrier

sweetfaced

sweetheart

sweetmeat

sweetmouthed

sweet-pickle (v.)

sweet-sour

swellhead

swelltoad

swelled-headed (u.m.)

sweptback (n., u.m.)

sweptforward (n., u.m.)

sweptwing (n., u.m.)

swiftfoot

swift-footed (u.m.)

swift-handed (u.m.)

swift-running (u.m.)

swillbowl

swilltub

swimsuit

swine-backed (u.m.)

swinebread

swinehead

swineherd

swinepox

swinesty

swingback (n., u.m.)

swingbar

swingstock

swingtree

switchback

switchblade

switchgear

switchplate

switchplug

switchrail

switchtender

swiveleye

swivel-eyed (u.m.)

swivel-hooked (u.m.)

sword-armed (u.m.)

swordbearer

swordbill

swordfishing

swordplay

sword-shaped (u.m.)

swordstick

syn (pref., all one word)

synchrocyclotron

synchroflash

synchromesh

synchrotron

T

T-bandage

T-beam

T-boat

T-bone

T-cloth

T-iron

T-rail

T-scale

T-shape

T-shaped

T-shirt

T-square

tablecloth

table-cut (u.m.)

tablecutter

table-cutting (u.m.)

tablefellow

table-formed (u.m.)

table-shaped (u.m.)

tablespoon

tabletalk

tabletop

tachy (c.f., all one word)

tag-affixing (u.m.)

taglock

tagrag

tagsore

tailband

tail-cropped (u.m.)

tail-ender

tailfirst

tailforemost

tailgate

tailhead

tail-heavy (u.m.)

tailhook

taillamp

tailpin

tailpipe

tailrace

tailspin

tailstock

tail-tied (u.m.)

tailtwister

tail-up (n., u.m.)

tailwheel

tailwind

tailor-cut (u.m.)

tailormade (u.m.)

tailor-suited (u.m.)

take-all (n.)

takedown (n., u.m.)

take-home (n., u.m.)

take-in (n., u.m.)

takeoff (n., u.m.)

takeout (n., u.m.)

takeup (n., u.m.)

taker-down

taker-in

taker-off

taker-up

talebearer

talecarrier

taleteller

talkfest

talking-to (n.)

tall-built (u.m.)

tall-looking (u.m.)

tallow-faced (u.m.)

tallow-pale (u.m.)

tally board

tallyho

tally room

tame-grown (u.m.)

tame-looking (u.m.)

tanbark

tanworks

tangent-cut (v.)

tangent-saw (v.)

tanglefoot

tangle-haired (u.m.)

tankship

tanktown

tapbolt

tapdance

taphole

tapnet

tapoff (n., u.m.)

tap-riveted (u.m.)

taproot

tap-tap

tapestring

tape-tied (u.m.)

taperbearer

taper-fashion (u.m.)

taper-headed (u.m.)

tapestry-covered (u.m.)

tapestry maker

tapestry-making (u.m.)

tapestry work

tapper-out

tar-brand (v.)

tarbrush

tar-coal (u.m.)

tar-dipped (u.m.)

tar-paved (u.m.)

tarpot

tar-roofed (u.m.)

tarworks

tariff-protected (u.m.)

tarpaulin-covered (u.m.)

tarpaulin maker

tarpaulin-making (u.m.)

tarso (c.f., all one word)

tasksetter

tattletale

tauro (c.f., all one word)

tax-burdened (u.m.)

taxeater

tax-exempt (u.m.)

tax-free (u.m.)

taxgatherer

tax-laden (u.m.)

taxpaid

taxpayer

tax-supported (u.m.)

taxibus

taxicab

taximeter

taxistand

teaball

teacake

teacart

tea-colored (u.m.)

teacup

teadish

teakettle

teapot

tea-scented (u.m.)

teaspoon

teataster

teamplay

tearbomb

tear-dimmed (u.m.)

teardown (n., u.m.)

teardrop

tear-off (n., u.m.)

tear-out (n., u.m.)

tearpit

tearsheet

tearstain

tear-stained (u.m.)

teenage (u.m.)

teenager

teeter-totter

tele (c.f., all one word)

teleo (c.f., all one word)

telltale

telltruth

telo (c.f., all one word)

tempest-rocked (u.m.)

temporo (c.f., all one word)

temporo-occipital

tenfold

tenpenny

tenpins

tender boat

tender-faced (u.m.)

tenderfoot

tender-footed (u.m.)

tenderfootish

tender-handed (u.m.)

tenderheart

tenderloin

tender-looking (u.m.)

tenement house

tent-dotted (u.m.)

tentpole

tent-sheltered (u.m.)

terneplate

terra cotta

terra firma

terramara

terrace-fashion (u.m.)

test-fly (v.)

tetra (c.f., all one word)

thanksgiving

thatch-roofed (u.m.)

theatergoer

theatergoing

thenceforth

theo (c.f., all one word)

theologico (c.f., all one word)

thereabout(s)

thereabove

thereacross

thereafter

thereagainst

thereamong

therearound

thereat

thereaway

therebefore

therebetween

thereby

therefor

therefore

therefrom

therein

thereinafter

thereinbefore

thereinto

thereof

thereon

therethrough

thereto

theretofore

thereunder

thereuntil

thereunto

thereupon

therewith

thermo (c.f., all one word)

thick-blooded (u.m.)

thickhead

thick-looking (u.m.)

thickset (n., u.m.)

thickskinned

thickskull (n.)

thickskulled

thick-tongued (u.m.)

thickwit

thick-witted (u.m.)

thick-wooded (u.m.)

thick-woven (u.m.)

thin-clad (u.m.)

thindown (n., u.m.)

thinset (u.m.)

thin-voiced (u.m.)

thio (c.f., all one word)

third-class (u.m.)

third-degree (u.m.)

thirdhand (adv., u.m.)

third house

third-rate (u.m.)

third-rater

thistledown

thoraco (c.f., all one word)

thornback

thornbill

thorn-covered (u.m.)

thorn-set (u.m.)

thorn-strewn (u.m.)

thorough-bind (v.)

thoroughbred

thorough-dried (u.m.)

thoroughfare

thoroughgoing

thorough-made (u.m.)

thoroughpaced

thoroughpin

thought-free (u.m.)

thought-out (u.m.)

thought-provoking (u.m.)

thousandfold

thousand-headed (u.m.)

thousand-legged (u.m.)

thousandlegs

thrallborn

thralldom

thrall-less

threadbare

thread-leaved (u.m.)

threadworn

three-cornered (u.m.)

three-dimensional (u.m.)

threefold

three-in-hand

three-master

threepenny

three-piece (u.m.)

three-ply (u.m.)

threescore

threesome

three-square

throatcutter

throatlatch

throatstrap

thrombo (c.f., all one word)

throughout

throughput

throwaway (n., u.m.)

throwback (n., u.m.)

throw-in (n., u.m.)

throw line

throwoff (n., u.m.)

throw-on (n., u.m.)

throwout (n., u.m.)

throw-weight

thrust-pound

thumb-made (u.m.)

thumbmark

thumb-marked (u.m.)

thumbnail

thumbprint

thumbscrew

thumbstall

thumbstring

thumbsucker

thumbtack

thumbworn

thunderbearer

thunderblast

thunderbolt

thunderclap

thundercloud

thunderhead

thunderpeal

thundershower

thunderstorm

thunderstruck

thymo (c.f., all one word)

thyro (c.f., all one word)

tibio (c.f., all one word)

tickseed

ticktacktoe

ticktock

ticket-selling (u.m.)

ticket writer

tiddlywink

tideflat

tidehead

tidemark

tide-marked (u.m.)

tiderace

tidetable

tide-tossed (u.m.)

tidewater

tide-worn (u.m.)

tieback (n.)

tiedown (n., u.m.)

tie-in (n., u.m.)

tie-on (n., u.m.)

tie-out (n., u.m.)

tiepin

tie-plater

tieup (n., u.m.)

tierlift

tigereye

tiger-striped (u.m.)

tight-belted (u.m.)

tightfisted

tight-fitting (u.m.)

tightlipped

tightrope

tight-set (u.m.)

tight-tie (v.)

tightwad

tightwire

tile-clad (u.m.)

tile-red (u.m.)

tilesetter

tileworks

tilewright

tilthammer

tiltup (n.)

timber-built (u.m.)

timberhead

timber-headed (u.m.)

timberjack

timber-propped (u.m.)

timberwright

timeborn

timecard

timeclerk

timeclock

time-consuming (u.m.)

timeframe

time-honored (u.m.)

timekeep (v.)

timekiller

timelag

timelock

timeouts (n., u.m.)

timepleaser

timesaver

timeserver

timesheet

timeslip

timeslot

timespan

time-stamp (v.)

timestudy

timetable

timetaker

timewaster

timeworn

tin-bearing (u.m.)

tin-capped (u.m.)

tin-clad (u.m.)

tincup

tin fish (torpedo)

tinfoil

tinhorn

tinkettle

tin-lined (u.m.)

tinpan

tinplate

tin-plated (u.m.)

tinpot

tin-roofed (u.m.)

tintype

tin-white (u.m.)

tinsel-bright (u.m.)

tinsel-clad (u.m.)

tinsel-covered (u.m.)

tintblock

tipburn

tipcart

tip-curled (u.m.)

tiphead

tip-in (n., u.m.)

tipmost

tipoff (n., u.m.)

tipstaff

tipstock

tiptank

tip-tap

tiptoe

tiptop

tip-up (u.m.)

tirechanger

tiredresser

tirefitter

tire-mile

tireshaper

tiresome

titano (c.f., all one word)

tithe-free (u.m.)

tithepayer

titheright

title-holding (u.m.)

titlewinner

title-winning (u.m.)

to-and-fro

to-do (n.)

toadback

toad-bellied (u.m.)

toadblind

toadfish

toad-green (u.m.)

toadstool

tobacco grower

tobacco-growing (u.m.)

tobacco shop

toecap

toe-in (n., u.m.)

toe-mark (v.)

toenail

toeplate

toeprint

toil-beaten (u.m.)

toilsome

toil-stained (u.m.)

toil-weary (u.m.)

toilworn

toilet room

tollbar

tollgate

tollgatherer

toll line

tollpayer

tollpenny

tolltaker

tomcat

tomfoolery

tom-tom

tommygun

tommyrot

ton-hour

ton-kilometer

ton-mile

ton-mileage

ton-mile-day

tone-deaf (u.m.)

tonedown (n., u.m.)

tone-producing (u.m.)

toneup (n., u.m.)

tongue-baited (u.m.)

tongue-bound (u.m.)

tongue-free (u.m.)

tongue-lash (v.)

tongue lashing

tongue-shaped (u.m.)

tongueshot

tonguesore

tonguetack

tonguetied

tonguetip

tongue-twisting (u.m.)

toolbag

toolbuilder

toolcrib

tooldresser

toolfitter

tool-grinding (u.m.)
toolhead
toolholding
toolkit
toolmark
toolplate
toolpost
toolrack
toolsetter
toolshed
toolslide
toolstock
toothache
tooth and nail
tooth-billed (u.m.)
toothbrush
toothmark
tooth-marked (u.m.)
toothpaste
toothpick
toothplate
toothpowder
toothpuller
tooth-pulling (u.m.)
tooth-set (u.m.)
tooth-shaped (u.m.)
toothsome
toothwash
topcap (n.)
topcoat
topcutter
top-drain (v.)
topdress (v.)
topflight (u.m.)
topfull
topgallant (n., u.m.)

top-graft (v.)
tophat
top-hatted (u.m.)
topheavy
topkick
topknot
topliner
topmark
topmast
topmilk
topmost
topnotch (nonliteral)
toprail
toprope
topsail
top-secret (u.m.)
top-shaped (u.m.)
topside (nautical)
topsoil
topo (c.f., all one word)
topsy-turvy
torchbearer
torch holder
torchlighted
torchlit
torpedo boat
torpedo room
torquemeter
tosspot
tossup (n., u.m.)
touch and go
touchback (n., u.m.)
touchdown (n., u.m.)
touchhole
touchpan
touchreader

touchup (n., u.m.)

tough-headed (u.m.)

tough-looking (u.m.)

tough-skinned (u.m.)

towaway

towhead

towmast

tow-netter

towpath

towrope

tower-high (u.m.)

tower-shaped (u.m.)

town-bred (u.m.)

town-dotted (u.m.)

townfolk

towngate

towngoing

townhall

townlot

township

townside

towntalk

town-weary (u.m.)

townsfellow

townspeople

toy-sized (u.m.)

toytown

tracheo (c.f., all one word)

trachy (c.f., all one word)

trackbarrow

trackhound

tracklayer

trackmark

track-mile

trackside

trackwalker

tractor-trailer

trade board

trade-in (n., u.m.)

trade-laden (u.m.)

trade-made (u.m.)

trademark

tradeoff

tradespeople

traffic-mile

tragico (c.f., all one word)

trailblazer

trailbreaker

trail-marked (u.m.)

trailside

trailsight

trail-weary (u.m.)

trainbearer

trainbolt

traincrew

train-mile

trainshed

trainstop

tram-borne (u.m.)

tramcar

tramrail

tramroad

trans (pref., all one word)

transalpine

transatlantic

trans-Canadian

transpacific

transit time

trapdoor

trapfall

trapshoot

trashrack

travel-bent (u.m.)

travel-tired (u.m.)

travel-worn (u.m.)

trawlnet

treadwheel

treasure-filled (u.m.)

treasure house

treasure-laden (u.m.)

treatybreaker

treaty-sealed (u.m.)

tree-clad (u.m.)

tree line

tree-lined (u.m.)

treenail

tree-ripe (u.m.)

treescape

treetop

trellis-covered (u.m.)

trenchback

trenchcoat

trenchfoot

trenchmouth

trench-plowed (u.m.)

tri (c.f., all one word)

tri-iodide

tri-ply (u.m.)

tristate

tribespeople

tribo (c.f., all one word)

tricho (c.f., all one word)

trim-cut (u.m.)

trim-dressed (u.m.)

trim-looking (u.m.)

trinitro (c.f., all one word)

trip-free (u.m.)

triphammer

tripwire

triple-acting (u.m.)

tripleback

triplebranched (u.m.)

triple-edged (u.m.)

triplefold

triple-tailed (u.m.)

tripletree (n.)

trolley line

troopship

tropho (c.f., all one word)

tropo (c.f., all one word)

trouble-free (u.m.)

trouble-haunted (u.m.)

troubleshooter

troublesome

trucebreaker

truce-seeking (u.m.)

truckdriver

truck-mile

truckstop

true-aimed (u.m.)

true-blue (u.m.)

trueborn

truebred

true-eyed (u.m.)

true-false

truelove (n., u.m.)

truepenny (n.)

true time

trunkback

trunknose

trustbreaking

trustbuster

trust-controlled (u.m.)

trust-ridden (u.m.)

truth-filled (u.m.)

truthlover

truthseeker

truth-seeking (u.m.)

truthteller

try-on (n., u.m.)

tryout (n., u.m.)

trysquare

tryworks

tube-eyed (u.m.)

tube-fed (u.m.)

tubeform

tubehead

tube-nosed (u.m.)

tubeworks

tuberculo (c.f., all one word)

tubo (c.f., all one word)

tubo-ovarian

tumbledown (n., u.m.)

tuneout (n., u.m.)

tuneup (n., u.m.)

tunnel-boring (u.m.)

tunnel-shaped (u.m.)

turbo (c.f., all one word)

turbo-ramjet (u.m.)

turf-built

turf-clad (u.m.)

turf-covered (u.m.)

turkeyback

turkey-red (u.m.)

turnabout (n., u.m.)

turnabout-face

turnagain (n., u.m.)

turnaround (n., u.m.)

turnback (n., u.m.)

turnbuckle

turncap

turncoat

turndown (n., u.m.)

turngate

turn-in (n., u.m.)

turnkey

turnoff (n., u.m.)

turnout (n., u.m.)

turnpike

turnpin

turnplate

turnscrew

turnsheet

turnsole

turnspit

turnstile

turnstitch

turntable

turn-to (n.)

turnunder (n., u.m.)

turnup (n., u.m.)

turned-back (u.m.)

turned-down (u.m.)

turned-in (u.m.)

turned-on (u.m.)

turned-out (u.m.)

turned-over (u.m.)

turner-off

turtleback

turtle-footed (u.m.)

turtleneck (u.m.)

twelvefold

twelvepenny

twelvescore

twice-born (u.m.)

twice-reviewed (u.m.)

twice-told (u.m.)

twin boat

twinborn

twin-engined

twinfold

twin-jet (u.m.)

twin-motor (u.m.)

twin-screw (u.m.)

two-a-day (u.m.)

two-along (n.)

two-decker

two-faced (u.m.)

twofold

two-handed (u.m.)

twopenny

two-piece (u.m.)

two-ply (u.m.)

twoscore

two-seater

twosome

two-spot

two-step (dance)

two-striper

two-suiter

two-thirder

two-up (n., u.m.)

two-way (u.m.)

two-wheeler

tympano (c.f., all one word)

typecase

typecast

typecutter

typeface

typefoundry

type-high (u.m.)

typescript

typeset

typewrite (v.)

typho (c.f., all one word)

typo (c.f., all one word)

tyro (c.f., all one word)

U

U-boat

U-cut

U-magnet

U-rail

U-shaped

U-tube

ultra (pref., all one word)

ultra-ambitious

ultra-atomic

ultra-English

ultrahigh frequency

ultra-high-speed (u.m.)

ultra valorem

un (pref., all one word)

un-American

uncalled-for (u.m.)

unheard-of (u.m.)

un-ionized (u.m.)

unself-conscious

unsent-for (u.m.)

unthought-of (u.m.)

under (pref., all one word)

underage (deficit)

underage (younger, n., u.m.)

under cultivation (tillage)

undercultivation (insufficient)

under secretary

under-secretaryship

uni (c.f., all one word)

uni-univalent

union-made (u.m.)

union shop

unit-set (u.m.)

up-anchor (u.m., v.)

up-and-coming (u.m.)

up and up

upbeat

upcoast

upcountry

updip

upend (v.)

upgrade

upgradient

upkeep

uplift

up-over (u.m.)

uprate

upriver

upstairs

upstate

upstream

upswing

uptake

uptight (n., u.m.)

up tight (v.)

up-to-date (u.m.)

up to date

uptown

uptrend

upturn

upwind

uppercase

upper class

upperclassman

uppercrust (n., u.m.)

uppercut

uppermost

urano (c.f., all one word)

uretero (c.f., all one word)

urethro (c.f., all one word)

uro (c.f., all one word)

used-car (u.m.)

utero (c.f., all one word)

V

V-connection

V-curve

V-engine

V-neck

V-shaped

V-type

vacant-eyed (u.m.)

vacant-looking (u.m.)

vacant-minded (u.m.)

vagino (c.f., all one word)

valve-grinding (u.m.)

valve-in-head (u.m.)

vandriver

vanguard

vanmost

vanpool

vapor-filled (u.m.)

vapor-heating (u.m.)

vase-shaped (u.m.)

vaso (c.f., all one word)

vegeto (c.f., all one word)

vein-mining (u.m.)

vein-streaked (u.m.)

vellum-bound (u.m.)

vellum-covered (u.m.)

velvet-crimson (u.m.)

velvet-draped (u.m.)

velvet-green (u.m.)

velvet-pile (u.m.)

venthole

ventri (c.f., all one word)

ventro (c.f., all one word)

vertebro (c.f., all one word)

vesico (c.f., all one word)

vibro (c.f., all one word)

vice admiral

vice-admiralty

vice consul

vice-consulate

vice governor

vice-governorship

vice minister

vice-ministry

vice-presidency

vice president

vice-president-elect

vice-presidential

vice rector

vice-rectorship

viceregal

vice-regency

vice regent

viceroyal

vice versa

vice warden

vice-wardenship

viewfinder

viewpoint

vile-natured (u.m.)

vine-clad (u.m.)

vine-covered (u.m.)

vinedresser

vinegrowing

vinestalk

vinegar-flavored (u.m.)

vinegar-hearted (u.m.)

vinegar-making (u.m.)

vinegar-tart (u.m.)

violet-blue (u.m.)

violet-colored (u.m.)

violet-eared (u.m.)

violet-rayed (u.m.)

violet water

violin-shaped (u.m.)

virtue-armed (u.m.)

viscero (c.f., all one word)

vitreo (c.f., all one word)

vitro (c.f., all one word)

vitro-clarain

vitro-di-trina

vivi (c.f., all one word)

volleyball

voltammeter

volt-ampere

volt-coulomb

voltmeter

voltohmmeter

volt-second

volta (c.f., all one word)

vote-casting (u.m.)

votegetter

vote-getting (u.m.)

vow-bound (u.m.)

vowbreaker

vow-pledged (u.m.)

vulvo (c.f., all one word)

W

W-engine

W-shaped

W-surface

W-type

wage-earning (u.m.)

waistband

waistbelt

waistcloth

waistcoat

waist-deep (u.m.)

waist-high (u.m.)

waiting room

walkaround (n., u.m.)

walkaway (n., u.m.)

walk-on (n., u.m.)

walkout (n., u.m.)

walkup (n., u.m.)

walkie-talkie

walleyed

wall-like

wall-painting (u.m.)

wallpaper

wallplate

wall-sided (u.m.)

walled-in (u.m.)

walled-up (u.m.)

war-disabled (u.m.)

war-famed (u.m.)

warfare

warhead

warhorse (nonliteral)

war-made (u.m.)

warpath

warship

war-swept (u.m.)

war time (clock)

wartime (duration)

wardheeler

wardrobe

wardship

warmblooded

warm-clad (u.m.)

warmup (n., u.m.)

warmed-over (u.m.)

warpsetter

washbasin

washbasket

washbowl

washcloth

washday

washdown (n., u.m.)

wash-in (n., u.m.)

washoff (n., u.m.)

washout (n., u.m.)

washpot

washrag

washstand

washtray

washtrough

washtub

washup (n., u.m.)

washed-out (u.m.)

washed-up (u.m.)

wastebasket

wasteleaf

wastepaper

wasteword

watchband

watchcase
watchdog
watch-free (u.m.)
watchglass
watchtower
watchword
waterbag
waterbank
waterbearer
water-bearing (u.m.)
water-beaten (u.m.)
water-bind (v.)
waterbloom
waterbuck
watercolor
water-colored (u.m.)
water-cool (v.)
water-cooled (u.m.)
watercourse
waterdog
water-drinking (u.m.)
waterdrop
waterfall
water-filled (u.m.)
waterfinder
waterflood
waterflow
waterfog
water-free (u.m.)
waterfront
watergate
waterhead
waterhole
waterhorse
water-inch
water-laden (u.m.)

waterlane
waterleaf
water-lined (u.m.)
waterlocked
waterlog
watermark
watermelon
watermeter
waterplant
waterpot
waterproofing
waterquake
water-rot (v.)
waterscape
watershed
watershoot
waterside
water-soak (v.)
water-soaked (u.m.)
water-soluble (u.m.)
waterspout
waterstain
waterwall
waterworks
waterworn
watt-hour
wattmeter
watt-second
wave-cut (u.m.)
waveform
waveguide
wave-lashed (u.m.)
wavelength
wavemark
wavemeter
wave-moist (u.m.)

wave-on (n., u.m.)

waveoff

wave-swept (u.m.)

wave-worn (u.m.)

wax-billed (u.m.)

waxchandler

waxcloth

wax-coated (u.m.)

wax-headed (u.m.)

wax stone

wax-yellow (u.m.)

wayback (n., u.m.)

waybeam

waydown (n., u.m.)

wayfarer

wayfellow

waygoing

waylaid

waylay

waymark

waypost

wayside

way-sore (u.m.)

way-up (n., u.m.)

wayworn

weak-backed (u.m.)

weak-eyed (u.m.)

weakhanded

weak-kneed (u.m.)

weakminded

weakmouthed

weatherbeaten

weatherblown

weather-borne (u.m.)

weatherbreak

weatherglass

weathergoing

weather-hardened (u.m.)

weather house

weather-marked (u.m.)

weathermost

weatherproofing

weather-stain (v.)

weatherstrip

weather-stripped (u.m.)

weatherworn

web-fingered (u.m.)

webfoot

web-footed (u.m.)

wedge-billed (u.m.)

wedge-shaped (u.m.)

weed-choked (u.m.)

weed-hidden (u.m.)

weedhook

weedkiller

weekday

weekend

week-ender

week-ending (u.m.)

weeklong (u.m.)

week-old (u.m.)

weighbridge

weigh-in (n., u.m.)

weighlock

weighout (n., u.m.)

weighshaft

well-being (n.)

well-beloved (u.m.)

well-born (u.m.)

well-bound (u.m.)

well-bred (u.m.)

well-clad (u.m.)

well-deserving (u.m.)

well-doer

well-doing (n., u.m.)

well-drained (u.m.)

well-drilling (u.m.)

well field

well-grown (u.m.)

wellhead

well-headed (u.m.)

wellhole

well-informed (u.m.)

well-known (u.m.)

well-looking (u.m.)

well-meaner

well-nigh (u.m.)

well-off (u.m.)

well-read (u.m.)

well-set-up (u.m.)

well-settled (u.m.)

wellside

well-spoken (u.m.)

wellspring

wellstead

well-thought-of (u.m.)

well-thought-out (u.m.)

well-to-do (u.m.)

well-wisher

well-wishing

well-worn (u.m.)

welterweight

werewolf

west-central (u.m.)

west-faced (u.m.)

westgoing

westmost

west-northwest

west-sider

wet-cheeked (u.m.)

wet-clean (v.)

wet-nurse (v.)

wetpack

wetwash

whaleback

whale-backed (u.m.)

whalebone

whale-built (u.m.)

whale-headed (u.m.)

whale-mouthed (u.m.)

whaleship

wharf boat

wharfhand

wharfhead

wharfside

whatever

what-is-it (n.)

whatnot (n.)

whatsoever

wheatcake

wheat-colored (u.m.)

wheatear

wheat-fed (u.m.)

wheat-rich (u.m.)

wheatstalk

wheelband

wheelbarrow

wheelbase

wheelchair

wheel-cut (u.m.)

wheelgoing

wheelhorse (nonliteral)

wheel load

wheel-made (u.m.)

wheelplate

wheelrace

wheelspin

wheelstitch

wheel-worn (u.m.)

wheelwright

whenever

when-issued (u.m.)

whensoever

whereabouts

whereafter

whereas

whereat

whereby

wherefor

wherefrom

wherein

whereinsoever

whereinto

whereof

whereon

wheresoever

whereto

whereunder

whereupon

wherewith

wherewithal

wherever

whichever

whichsoever

whiffletree

whipcord

whipcrack

whip-graft (v.)

whiplash

whip-marked (u.m.)

whippost

whipsaw

whip-shaped (u.m.)

whipsocket

whipstaff

whipstalk

whipstall

whipstick

whipstitch

whipstock

whip-tailed (u.m.)

whipper-in

whippersnapper

whirlabout (n., u.m.)

whirlblast

whirlpool

whirl-shaped (u.m.)

whirlwind

whiskbroom

whisk tail

whistlestop

whiteback

whitebeard (n.)

white book (diplomatic)

whitecap (n.)

whitecoat (n.)

white-collar (u.m.)

whitecomb (n.)

whitecorn

white-eared (u.m.)

white-eyed (u.m.)

whiteface

white-faced (u.m.)

whitefoot (n.)

white-footed (u.m.)

whitehanded

white-hard (u.m.)

whitehead

white-headed (u.m.)

white-hot (u.m.)

white line

whiteout (u.m., v.)

whitepot

white-tailed (u.m.)

white-throated (u.m.)

whitetop (n.)

whitewash

whoever

whosoever

whole-headed (u.m.)

whole-hogger

wholesale

wholesome

whomsoever

wicker-woven (u.m.)

wicketkeeper

wicketkeeping

wide-angle (u.m.)

wide-awake (u.m.)

wide-handed (u.m.)

widemouthed

wide-open (u.m.)

widespread

wide-spreading (u.m.)

widow bird

widowhood

wifebeater

wifehood

wifekiller

wigwag

wildcat (n.)

wild-eyed (u.m.)

wildfire

wild land

wildlife

wild man

wildwind

will-less

will-o'-the-wisp

wilt-resistant (u.m.)

windbag

windball

windblown

windbrace

windbreaker

windburn

windcatcher

wind-chapped (u.m.)

windchill

winddown (n., u.m.)

windfall

windfast

wind-fertilized (u.m.)

windfirm

windflow

windgall

wind-galled (u.m.)

windhole

wind-hungry (u.m.)

windjammer

windpipe

wind-pollinated (u.m.)

wind-rode (u.m.)

windrow

windscreen

wind-shaken (u.m.)

wind-shear (u.m.)

windshield

windshock

windside

windsleeve

windsock

windspeed

windstop

windstorm

windstream

windswept

windup (n., u.m.)

windworn

windowbreaker

window-breaking (u.m.)

window-cleaning (u.m.)

window-dressing (u.m.)

windowpane

window-shop (v.)

window-shopping (u.m.)

windowsill

window work

winebag

wine-black (u.m.)

wine-drinking (u.m.)

wineglass

wine-red (u.m.)

wineseller

winetaster

winetester

winevat

wingband

wingbar

wingbeat

wingbolt

wingbone

wingbow

wingcut

wing-footed (u.m.)

winghanded

wing-heavy (u.m.)

wing-loading (u.m.)

wing-loose (u.m.)

wingnut

wing-shaped (u.m.)

wing-shot (u.m.)

wingspan

wing-swift (u.m.)

wingtip

wingtop

wingwalker

wingwall

wing-weary (u.m.)

winter-beaten (u.m.)

winter-clad (u.m.)

winter-fallow (v.)

winter-fed (u.m.)

winterfeed

winter green (color)

wintergreen (plant)

winter-hardy (u.m.)

winterkill

winter-made (u.m.)

winter-sown (u.m.)

wintertide

winter-worn (u.m.)

wirebar

wire-caged (u.m.)

wire-cut (u.m.)

wirecutter

wiredancer

wiredraw (v.)

wire-edged (u.m.)

wirehair

wire-haired (u.m.)

wireless

wire line

wirephoto

wirepuller

wirespun

wirestitch

wire-stitched (u.m.)

wire-tailed (u.m.)

wiretap

wirewalker

wireworks

wire-wound (u.m.)

wiseacre

wisecrack

wisehead (n.)

wise-headed (u.m.)

wise-spoken (u.m.)

wishbone

witch-hunting (u.m.)

withdraw

withhold

within

without

withstand

within-bound (u.m.)

within-named (u.m.)

woebegone

woeworn

wolf-eyed (u.m.)

wolf fish

wolfhound

wolfpack

womanfolk

womanhood

womankind

womenfolk

wonderstrong

wonder-struck (u.m.)

woodbark

woodbin

woodbined

woodblock

wood-built (u.m.)

wood-cased (u.m.)

woodchipper

woodchopper

woodchuck

woodcut

woodgrub

woodhole

woodhorse

woodhung (u.m.)

wood-lined (u.m.)

woodlot

wood-paneled (u.m.)

woodpile

wood-planing (u.m.)

woodprint

woodpulp

woodranger

woodrock

woodshed

woodside

woodstock

woodturner

wood-turning (u.m.)

wood-walled (u.m.)

woodwind

woodenhead (n.)

wooden-hulled (u.m.)

wooden-weary (u.m.)

woolfell

woolgatherer

woolgrader

woolgrowing

woolhead

wool-laden (u.m.)

wool-lined (u.m.)

woolpack

woolpress

woolshearer

woolshed

woolsorter

woolstock

woolwasher

woolwheel

wool-white (u.m.)

woolwinder

woolly-coated (u.m.)

woolly-headed (u.m.)

woolly-looking (u.m.)

woolly-white (u.m.)

word-blind (u.m.)

wordbuilder

wordcatcher

word-clad (u.m.)

word-deaf (u.m.)

wordjobber

wordlist

word-perfect (u.m.)

wordplay

wordseller

wordslinger

workaday (n., u.m.)

work-and-turn (u.m.)

workaway (n., u.m.)

workbag

workbasket

workbench

workcard

workday

work-driven (u.m.)

workflow

workfolk

workhand

work-hardened (u.m.)

workhorse

work-hour (u.m.)

workhoused

worklife

workmanship

workout (n., u.m.)

workpan

workpaper

workpeople

workplace

worksaving

worksheet

workshoe

work-shy (n., u.m.)

work-shyness (n., u.m.)

workslip

workspace

work-stained (u.m.)

workstand

workstream

worktable

workup (n., u.m.)

workways

work-weary (u.m.)

workweek

workworn

working load

working room
worldbeater
world-conscious (u.m.)
world consciousness
world line
world power
world-self
world-weary (u.m.)
worm-eaten (u.m.)
worm-eating (u.m.)
wormhole
worm-riddled (u.m.)
worm-ripe (u.m.)
wormseed
wormshaft
worndown (u.m.)
wornout (u.m.)
worrywart
worthwhile (u.m.)
wraparound (n., u.m.)
wrap-up (n., u.m.)
wreath-crowned (u.m.)
wreck-free (u.m.)
wringbolt
wringstaff
wristband
wristbone
wristdrop
wristfall
wristlock
wristpin
wristplate
wristwatch
writeback (n., u.m.)
write-in (n., u.m.)
writeoff (n., u.m.)

writeup (n., u.m.)
writing room
wrongdoer
wrong-ended (u.m.)
wrong-minded (u.m.)
wrong-thinking (u.m.)
wrought-up
wrybill
wry-billed (u.m.)
wry-faced (u.m.)
wry-looking (u.m.)
wry-mouthed (u.m.)
wryneck
wry-set (u.m.)

X

X-body
X-disease
X-virus
X-shaped
x ray (n.)
x-ray (u.m.)
xantho (c.f., all one word)
xeno (c.f., all one word)
xero (c.f., all one word)
xylo (c.f., all one word)

Y

Y-chromosome
Y-joint
Y-level
Y-potential
Y-shaped
Y-track
Y-tube

Yankee-Doodle
yardarm
yard-deep (u.m.)
yard-long (u.m.)
yardstick
yard-wide (u.m.)
yawmeter
yaw-sighted (u.m.)
yearday
yearend
year-hour (u.m.)
yearlong (u.m.)
year-old (u.m.)
year-round (u.m.)
yellowback
yellow-backed (u.m.)
yellow-bellied (u.m.)
yellowbelly
yellow-billed (u.m.)
yellow-headed (u.m.)
yellow-tailed (u.m.)
yellow-throated (u.m.)
yellowtop
yes-man
yes-no
yesterday
yesteryear
yokefellow

yokemating
yoke-toed (u.m.)
youngeyed (u.m.)
young-headed (u.m.)
young-ladylike
young-looking (u.m.)
young-manlike (u.m.)
young-old
young-womanhood
youthtide
yuletide

Z

Z-bar
Z-chromosome
zeroaxial
zero-dimensional (u.m.)
zerogravity
zigzag
zinc-coated (u.m.)
zinc-white (u.m.)
zoo (c.f., all one word)
zoologico (c.f., all one word)
zygo (c.f., all one word)
zygomatico (c.f., all one word)
zygomatico-orbital
zymo (c.f., all one word)

Index

A

A/an, 86
Abbreviations. *See also* Acronyms
    apostrophes with, 86
    articles before, 86
    defining in text, 85
    discussion, 84-85
    in figure labels, 138
    numerals with, 87
    periods with, 86
    plurals, 69, 85-86
    proofreading, 112
    in tables, 142
Accept/except, 28-29
Accessible/assessable, 29
Acronyms
    definition, 84
    plural form, 69
Active voice, 21-22
Adjectives. *See also* Modifiers
    commas with series of, 64
    compound, 75
    hyphens with, 75
    suspended compound, 75-76
Adverbs, 57-58, 75
Adverse/averse, 29
Affect/effect, 29-30
Agreement between subject and verb,
    45-46
All-caps text legibility, 120
Alphabetical order, 163
Ambiguity of pronoun antecedents, 53-54
Among/between, 30
And
    at beginning of sentence, 38-39
    in a list, 89

Apostrophes, 66-69
    abbreviations with, 86
    contractions with, 52-53, 67, 68-69
    inserting when proofreading, 108
    plurals of letters and numbers with, 69
    possessives with, 51-52, 67-68
Appositives with commas, 63-64, 66
Appraise/apprise, 30
Apprise/appraise, 30
Art works. *See* Titles of works
Articles, definite and indefinite. *See A/an*
Assembly line approach to making
    revisions, 154
Assessable/accessible, 29
Assure/ensure, 30
Audience, 3-6
Averse/adverse, 29

B

Bar charts, 130, 132-133
Bernstein, Theodore, 37
Between/among, 30
Bias-free language, 23-28
    the bias test, 26
    list of biased terms and alternatives,
        27-28
Bimonthly/semimonthly, 31
Block quotations, 72
Bluelines, 165-166
"Boilerplate" trap, 4-5
Boldface, 114
Book titles. *See* Titles of works
Brackets, 80, 102, 163
Bullets, 89, 141
Business graphics, 128-137
But at beginning of sentence, 38-39